Images of America
San Jose Prohibition

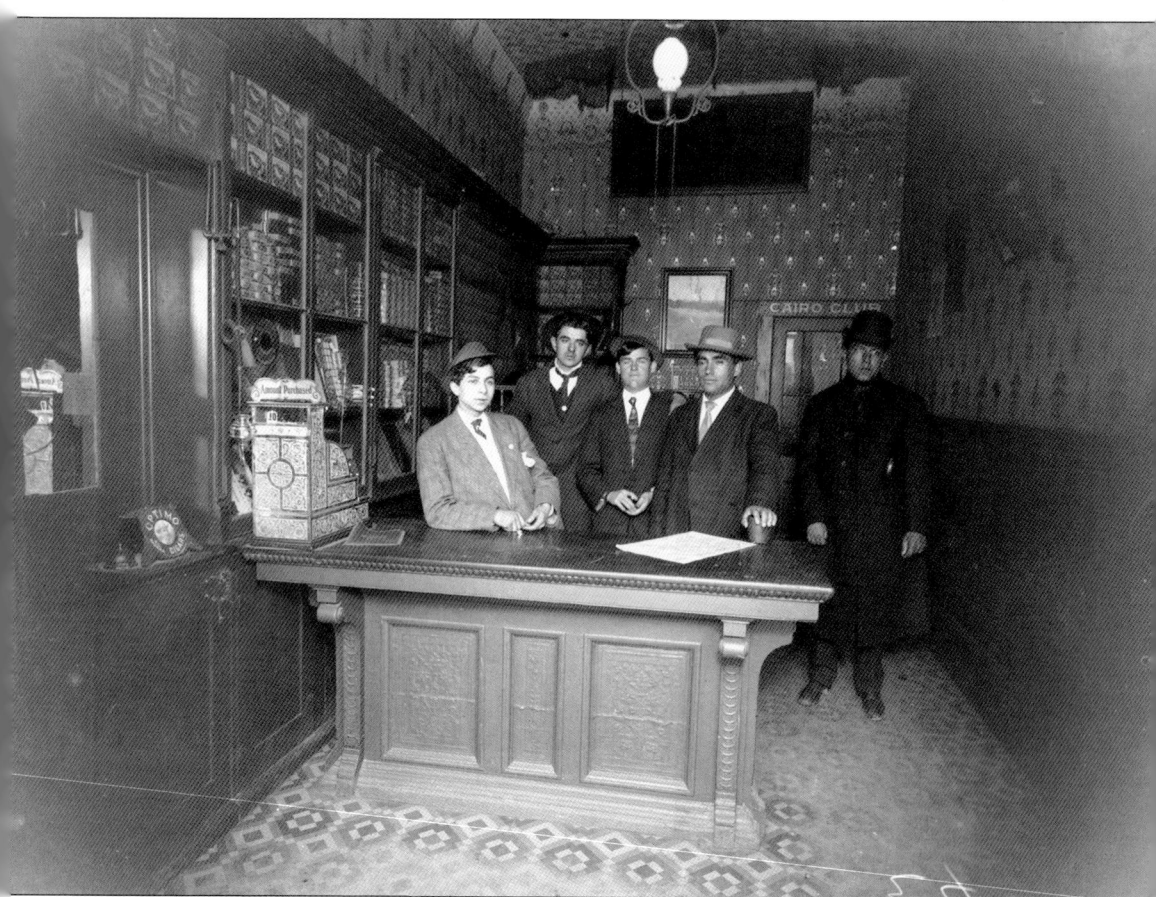

This unknown cigar shop in downtown San Jose exemplifies how speakeasies often operated behind the facade of legitimate businesses during Prohibition. In this picture, the cigar shop serves as the front for a speakeasy known as the Cairo Club, which operated in the back. The large, intimidating gentleman standing in front of the door is the security, ensuring only trusted patrons could enter the hidden establishment. (Courtesy of History San Jose.)

ON THE COVER: Sheriff George Lyle (right) stands with two of his deputies in front of a display of confiscated illegal alcohol stored in barrels, jugs, and bottles. Sheriff Lyle would often showcase the seized alcohol in front of the courthouse and the sheriff's office before publicly destroying it for the community to witness. (Courtesy of the Sourisseau Academy.)

Images of America
SAN JOSE PROHIBITION

Ted Ramos

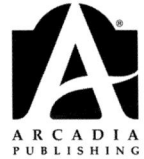

Copyright © 2025 by Ted Ramos
ISBN 9781-4671-6205-0

Published by Arcadia Publishing
Charleston, South Carolina

Printed in the United States of America

Library of Congress Control Number: 2024952731

For all general information, please contact Arcadia Publishing:
Telephone 843-853-2070
Fax 843-853-0044
E-mail sales@arcadiapublishing.com

Visit us on the Internet at www.arcadiapublishing.com

Contents

Acknowledgments		6
Introduction		7
1.	Pre-Prohibition	9
2.	Speakeasies and Roadhouses	17
3.	Raids	35
4.	Cops and Bootleggers	57
5.	A Violent Business	73
6.	Little Tijuana	81
7.	The Locurtos	89
8.	Post-Prohibition	97
9.	Remaining Relics of Prohibition	113

ACKNOWLEDGMENTS

When researching the topic of Prohibition, many photographs and articles were easy to find but only on a national level involving the nation's largest cities and bootleggers. Information on Prohibition in San Jose was not so easy to find. So coming up with information was a strenuous effort requiring a lot of my information and photographs coming from family members of San Jose's Prohibition past. Although some photographs in this book are from my personal collection, most were contributed by the following people and organizations, to whom I want to give thanks: Mark Cozzalio; Norm Koepernik; Tony Gairnese; Craig LoCurto; Jeanne Rene Watson; Darlene Bursch; Laura Ravizza Winter; Dave and Christina Anaya; Charles Ciraulo; Gwyneth Hancock-Hanson; Linda Hancock; Tom Loproto; Jeff Mazzone; Catherine Mills and staff at History San Jose; Leilani Marshall of the San Jose State University collection and Sourisseau collection; the California Room at the San Jose State Library; the San Jose Public Library; Santa Clara County Historical Archives; the San Jose Police History Collection; and the California State Archives.

I want to give out a special thanks to my sons, Tyler and Tanner, for not only making me a better person and role model but for also assisting me with their ideas and with gathering photographs of today. It's things like this that make me proud to be their dad. I hope that this book inspires them to follow their dreams and work hard. To my parents, Richard and Kathy, thank you for helping me to be the person I am today and teaching me that good things happen to those who work hard.

Finally, a very special thanks to my wife, Teri Ramos, who supported me during the creation of my second book. She continues to help me make my vision a reality by providing me with assistance in writing and promoting this book as well as lending me her technology skills. She was always available to assist me when I needed it. For that, I am forever grateful.

Introduction

On January 17, 1920, the 18th Amendment was enacted, marking the first time an amendment took away a right from the people rather than guaranteeing individual rights, as previous amendments had. This amendment, also known as the Volstead Act, prohibited the manufacture, sale, or transportation of intoxicating liquors. It was intended to rid society of the effects of alcohol but instead turned millions of law-abiding citizens into lawbreakers. San Jose was already aware of alcohol-related problems, possibly due to having large popular breweries like Eagle Brewery and Fredericksburg Brewery, wineries such as Mirassou, Almaden, and Paul Mason, and 78 bars and saloons, generating 58 percent of the city's revenue from liquor taxes. In 1918, the city passed the Tompkins Ordinance, prohibiting saloons but allowing licensed restaurants to serve alcohol with meals at specific times and residents to keep liquor at home. Without this license, businesses faced a $100 fine and license revocation, resulting in the closure of all 78 bars and saloons. Only 13 hotels and restaurants were licensed to serve alcohol, with many former saloons transforming into soda shops, ice cream parlors, cigar shops, and candy stores. However, a wink and a nod could still get you a drink, leading to the birth of San Jose's speakeasies.

Unlike the glamorous speakeasies depicted in movies, most of San Jose's were operated out of homes, soda shops, hotels, barbershops, candy stores, pool halls, and cigar shops. Numerous stills operated throughout the large valley orchards outside the city limits. San Jose's bootleggers had two years to perfect their underground liquor business before the Volstead Act was nationally enforced in 1920. By then, they were already selling and manufacturing illegal alcohol. Many speakeasies and storage warehouses were in downtown areas, with places like Maggiore's Place and Finley's Inn on Post Street, Casino Grill, Zaro's Grill, and Sokalares Restaurant on Market Street. Roadhouses and manufacturing stills were scattered across unincorporated areas such as Monterey Road, Willow Glen, Evergreen, the Burbank District, Alviso, and Coyote, operated by notable bootleggers like Clarence "Chick" Leddy, Peter Maggiore, and Dave Holt.

San Jose's Prohibition era had its share of violence, though not as extensive as in larger cities like New York or Chicago. Most of the alcohol manufacturing and selling was done by respectable family men who turned to bootlegging for extra money, growing their small businesses into large illegal industries. John Locurto, for instance, started as a rancher and automobile salesman before becoming San Jose's biggest bootlegger, operating the lavish Locurto's Gardens speakeasy off Almaden Road. After Prohibition, it became the popular Hawaiian Gardens supper club. Other bootleggers included a 16-year-old who made whiskey in his dad's garage and an out-of-town bootlegger who killed a Santa Clara County sheriff deputy.

By 1921, a year after national Prohibition began, alcohol-related crimes had significantly increased, with public intoxication and vagrancy rates doubling. The public accused the police and sheriff's offices of lax enforcement. San Jose police chief John Newton Black conducted many raids but lacked enough officers and needed help from state and federal agencies, which were focused on larger cities like San Francisco. Sheriff George Lyle complained about the lack of federal cooperation, citing insufficient county funds for enforcing a federal law. Consequently, Santa Clara County had the most stills in Northern California. A high-profile murder in a county roadhouse in 1928 led to a grand jury investigation, revealing the ease of obtaining alcohol and other illicit activities at these establishments. The report suggested the sheriff's office handle all illegal alcohol enforcement, recommended warrantless raids, and called for the district attorney to keep detailed records of prior convictions.

After Prohibition was lifted in 1933 and alcohol became legal again, many speakeasy operators transitioned to running legitimate licensed bars, which became popular neighborhood watering holes and clubs. These included Sam's Cavern, the San Carlos Club, Frank's Place, and Locurto's Hawaiian Gardens. However, some continued their illegal activities, such as manufacturing untaxed liquor and running gambling establishments and brothels.

Today, most of these bars are closed, and their operators have passed away. Many buildings have been torn down, but a few remain, passed daily by hundreds who are unaware of their history. Some buildings are designated as historic, while others are endangered. Hopefully, this history will help shine a light on the importance of preserving these buildings.

One
PRE-PROHIBITION

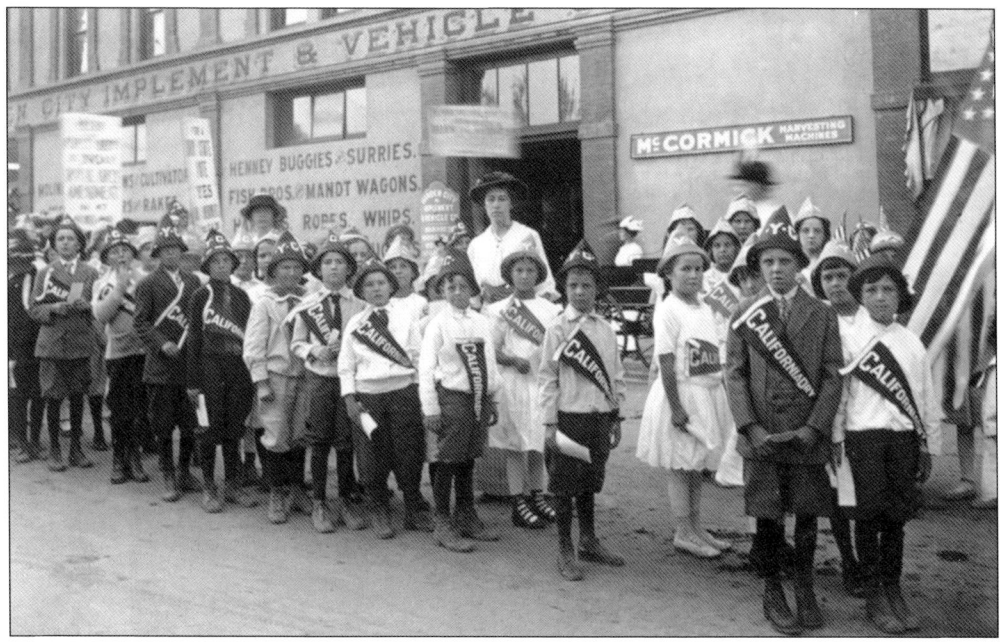

Before Prohibition became a national law, San Jose enacted its own prohibition by outlawing saloons, issuing licenses to serve alcohol only to restaurants and hotels, and allowing possession of alcohol for personal use at home. During the Prohibition era, groups known as "the Crusades" were formed. These groups, mostly consisting of women and children, would gather in front of saloons to pray and protest alcohol consumption. (Courtesy of the Sourisseau Academy.)

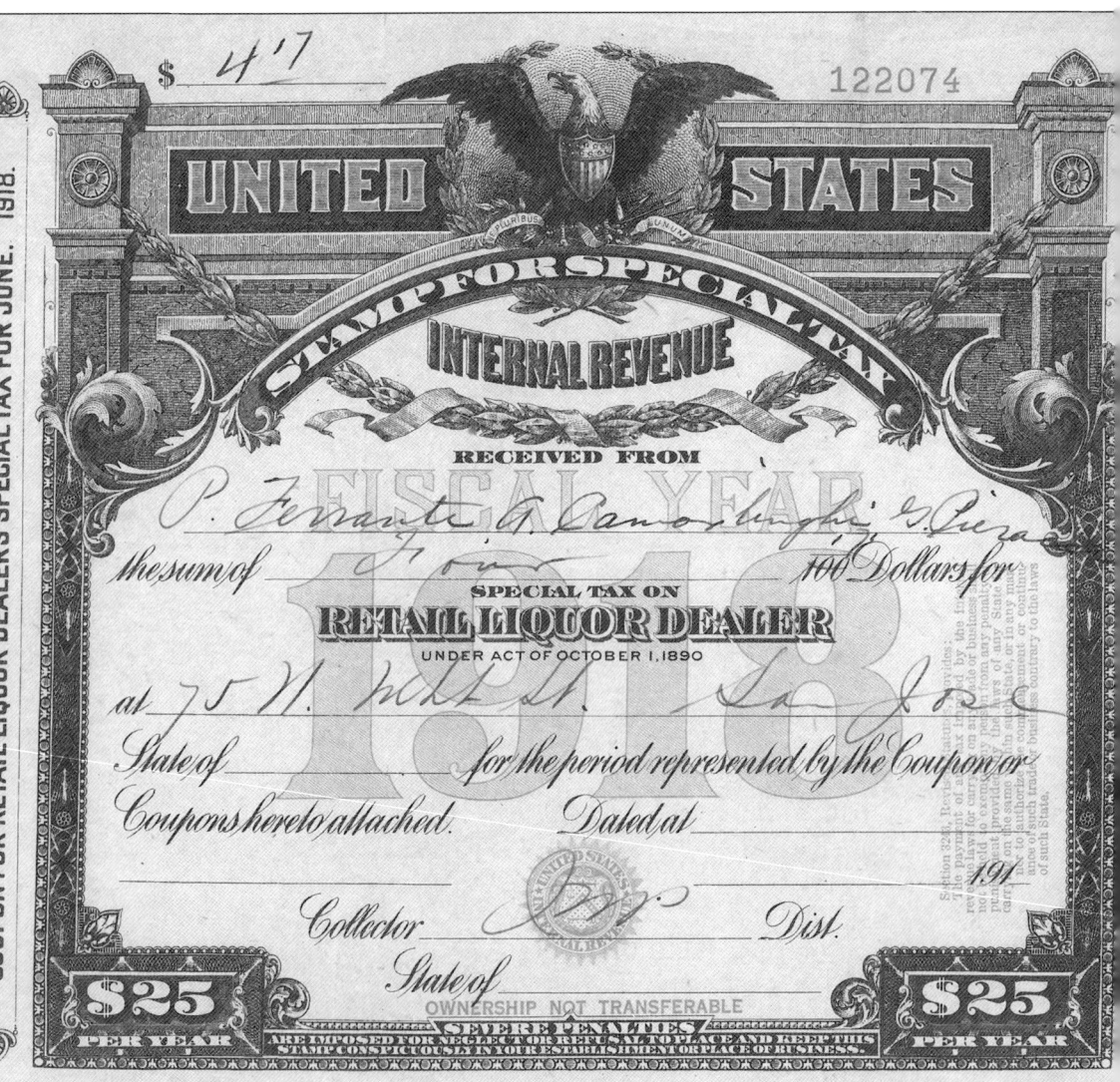

In 1918, the Tompkins Ordinance was enacted by the electors of San Jose, aiming to prohibit saloons. This ordinance granted the city council the authority to issue liquor licenses to a limited number of restaurants, allowing them to sell alcohol with meals during specific hours. Additionally, residents were permitted to keep liquor in their private homes for personal use. Out of the numerous establishments in the city, only 13 restaurants and hotels were issued such licenses. One notable example is the Genova Hotel, located at 73 North Market Street. The liquor license issued to the proprietors G. Pieracci, P. Ferrante, and A. Camorlinghi in 1918 is pictured here. This document represents a significant piece of San Jose's history during the Prohibition era, highlighting the limited and controlled way alcohol was legally permitted. (Courtesy of History San Jose.)

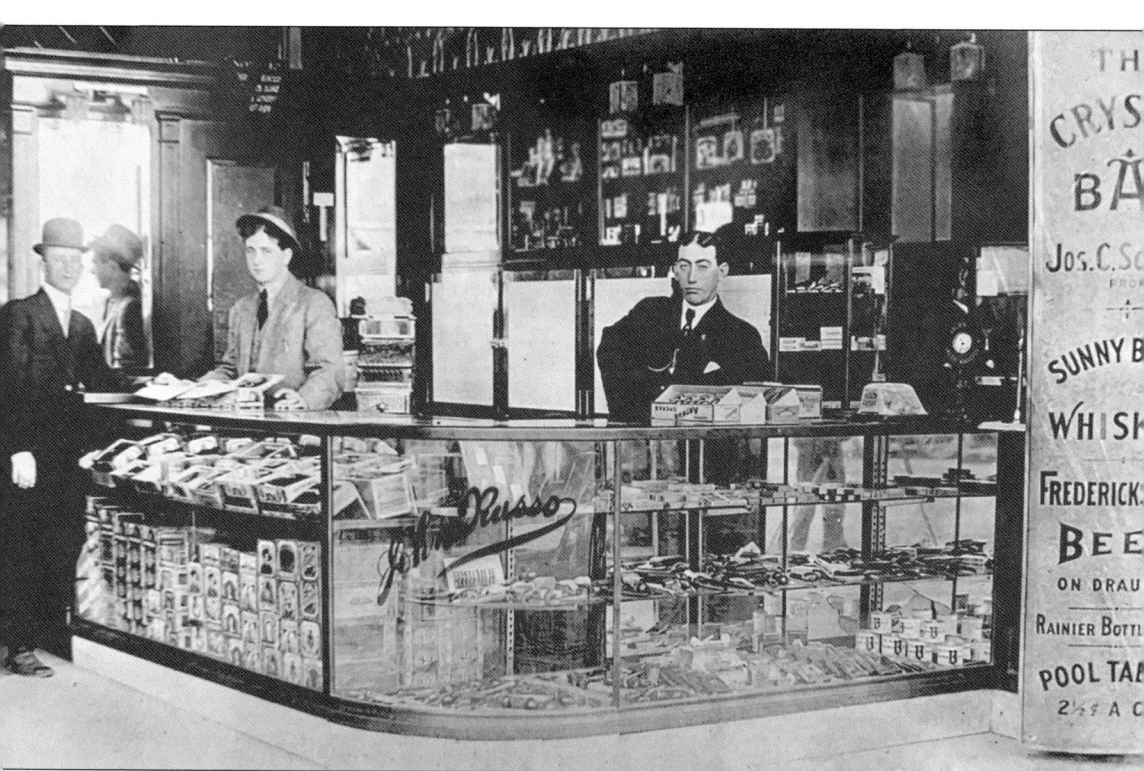

Located at 43 West San Fernando Street, the Crystal Bar was one of the many downtown saloons in San Jose before Prohibition. When Prohibition was enforced, the Crystal Bar transformed into the Crystal Café and billiard parlor, ostensibly serving soft drinks. However, the venue continued to be a hub of illegal activities, including liquor sales, gambling, and bookmaking. Pictured here is John Russo's cigar stand, which was positioned in front of the Crystal Bar's entrance. The cigar stand remained operational during Prohibition, serving as a front for the covert activities inside the Crystal Café. John Russo, seen behind the counter on the right wearing a dark coat, managed the cigar stand, maintaining a facade of legitimate business while the illegal operations thrived within the café. (Courtesy of the Anaya family.)

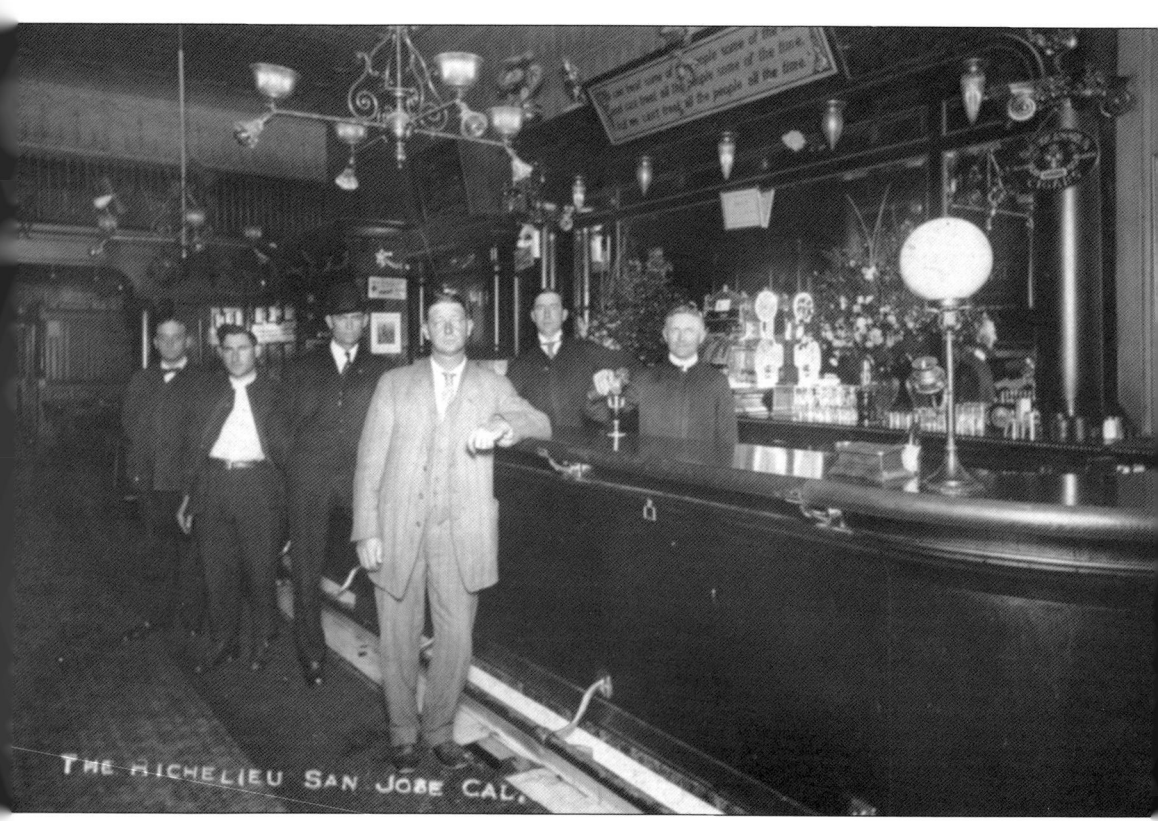

The Richelieu Saloon, located at 20 North First Street, was one of San Jose's most popular saloons before Prohibition. When San Jose enacted its own prohibition laws in 1918, the Richelieu Saloon transitioned into a soft drink establishment known as Bud Brown's Emporium. On February 15, 1918, acting on information that several soft drink establishments in the city were harboring alcohol, police chief John Newton Black conducted a raid on Bud Brown's Emporium. During the raid, officers discovered 32 bottles of beer and a jug of whiskey. Bud Brown claimed that the alcohol was for his personal use and not for sale. However, this defense did not prevent the city from revoking the Emporium's soft drink license. (Courtesy of the Sourisseau Academy.)

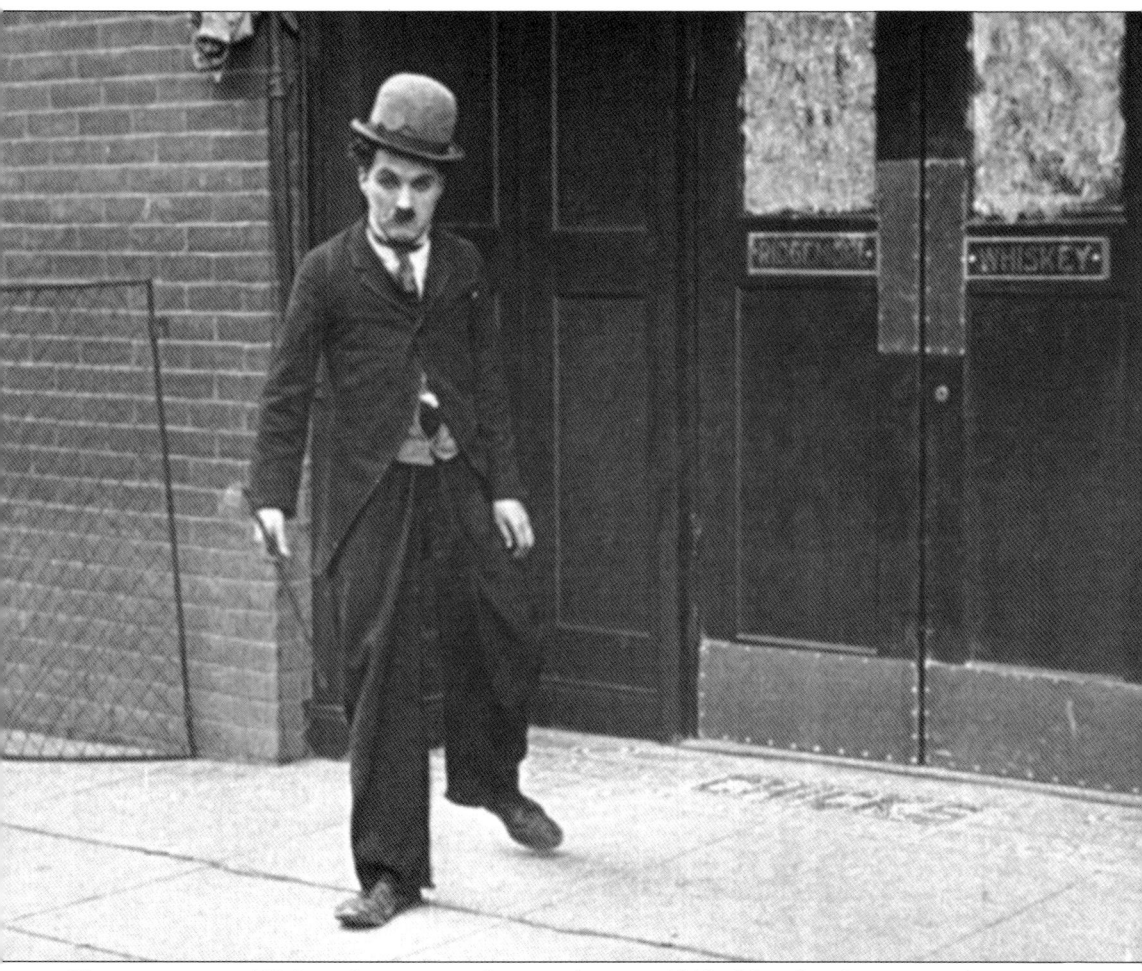

The property at 107 Post Street opened as a saloon in 1909. After San Jose enacted its own liquor laws prior to national Prohibition, the saloon became the Ark Café, owned by Clarence "Chick" Leddy. The Ark Café operated under a soft drink license but had its license revoked in February 1928 by the city council for serving beer and spirits. The city council hearing regarding this matter lasted three hours, reflecting the contentious nature of enforcing Prohibition laws. The photograph accompanying this story shows Charlie Chaplin in front of Leddy's Saloon, as captured in the 1915 movie *A Night Out*. The image is notable not only for featuring Chaplin but also for the engraving of Clarence Leddy's nickname "Chick" on the ground below the front doors, highlighting the personal touch Leddy brought to his establishment. (Courtesy of History San Jose.)

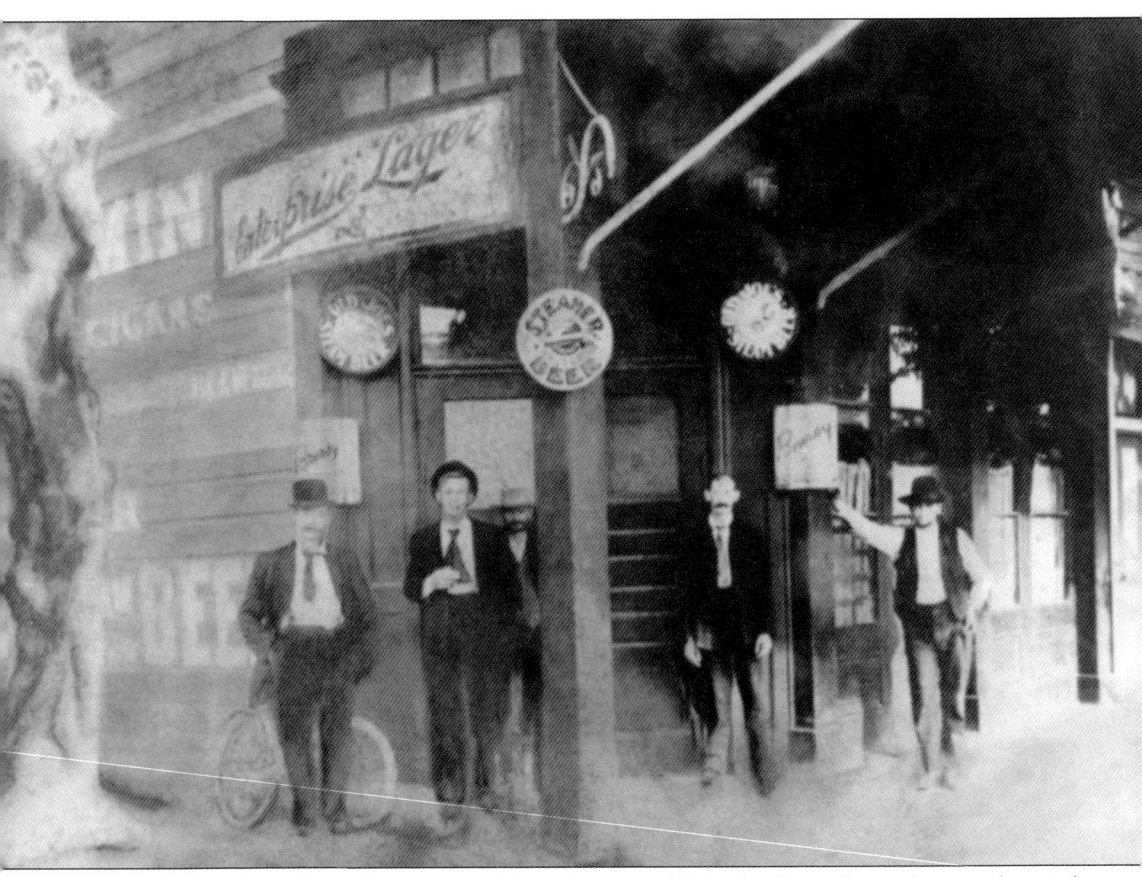

The building located on the corner of First Street and Martha Street has a long and varied history. Initially recorded as a saloon and grocery store, it changed hands multiple times before the Prohibition era. The last owners before its closure due to San Jose's Tompkins Ordinance in 1918 were the Benjamin brothers: Joseph, Peter, and Nuncy. In response to the ordinance, which prohibited the operation of saloons, the establishment rebranded itself as a soft drink stand. Despite the official front, alcohol continued to be sold in the back, maintaining its legacy as a covert speakeasy during the Prohibition era. (Courtesy of History San Jose.)

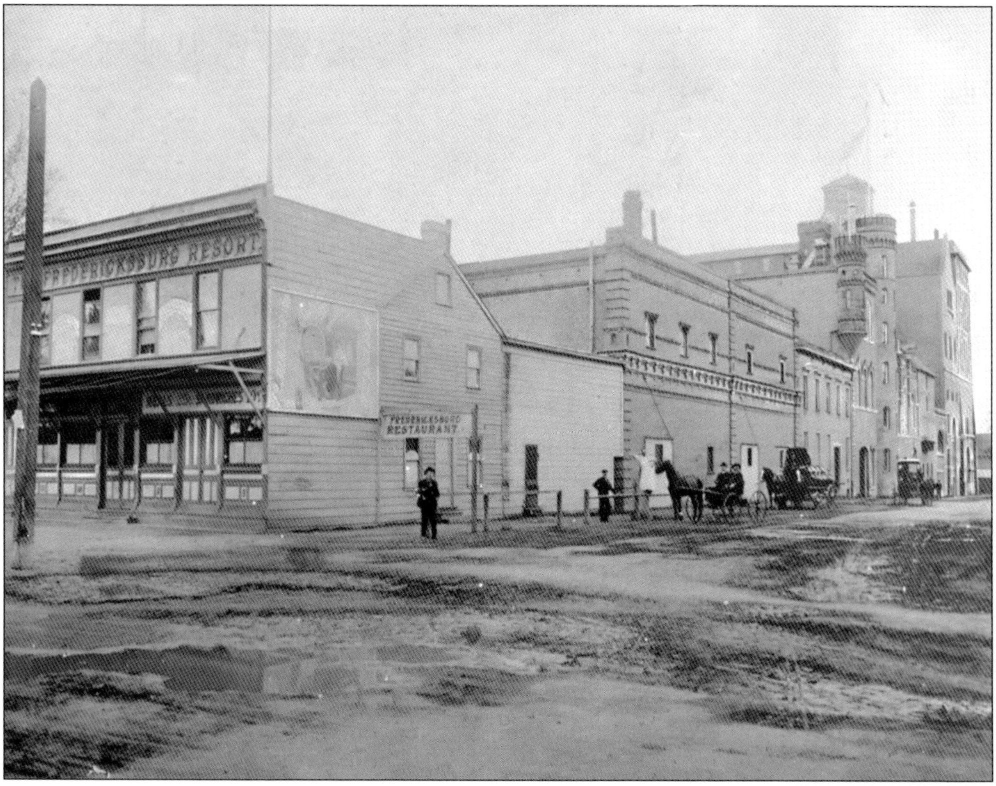

The Fredericksburg Brewery, located near the Alameda and Cinnabar Street, was a significant landmark in San Jose's brewing history. Established in 1867, it operated until 1973. Prior to suspending operations in 1918 due to San Jose's early prohibition act, the brewery was one of the largest and best in California, producing over 10,000 barrels of beer annually and distributing it across the Bay Area and the Pacific coast. After Prohibition was lifted in 1933, the brewery resumed operations, continuing its legacy as a major player in the state's brewing industry. (Above, courtesy of Tony Gairnese; right, courtesy of History San Jose.)

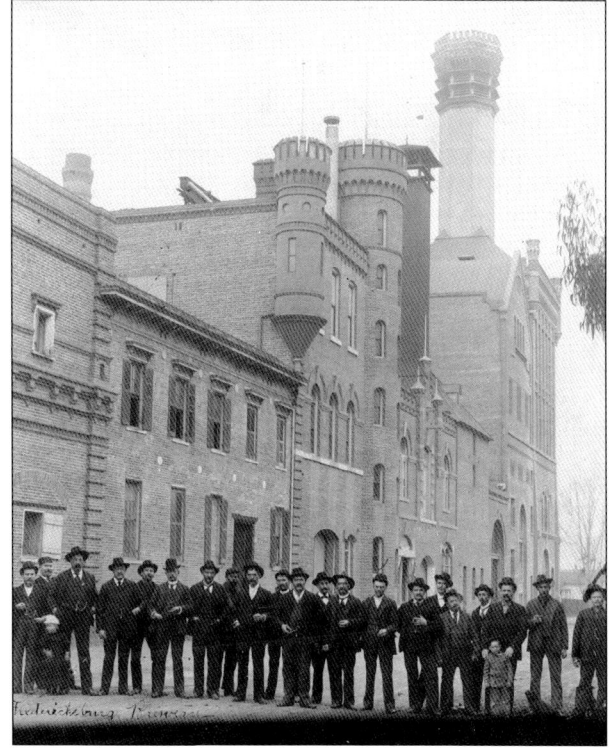

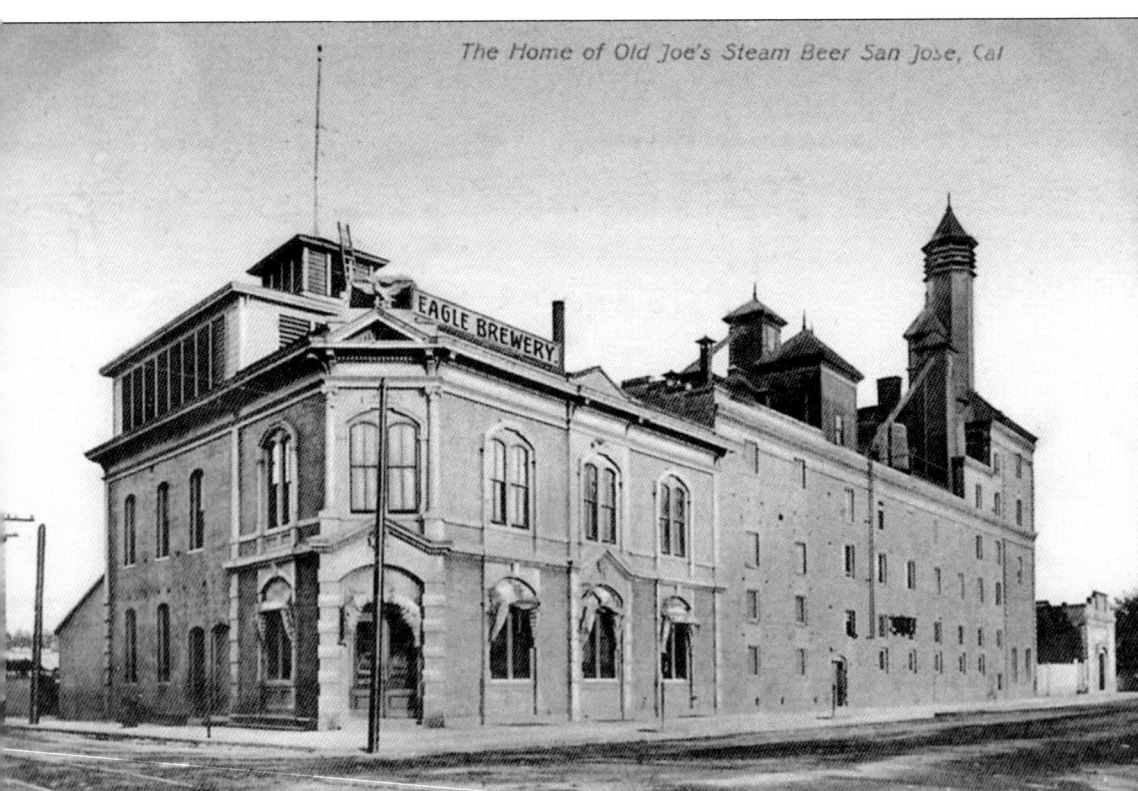

The Eagle Brewery, situated on the corner of San Carlos and Market Streets, occupied the space where the Sainte Claire Hotel now stands. Established in 1853 by J. Hartmann and later operated by G. Scherrer, the Eagle Brewery was one of San Jose's prominent brewing establishments. Renowned for its flagship brand, Old Joe's Steam Ale, it held a significant place in the city's brewing landscape. However, the onset of Prohibition in 1920 forced its closure, and the brewery building was demolished in 1926, marking the end of an era for this historic establishment. (Courtesy of History San Jose.)

Two

SPEAKEASIES AND ROADHOUSES

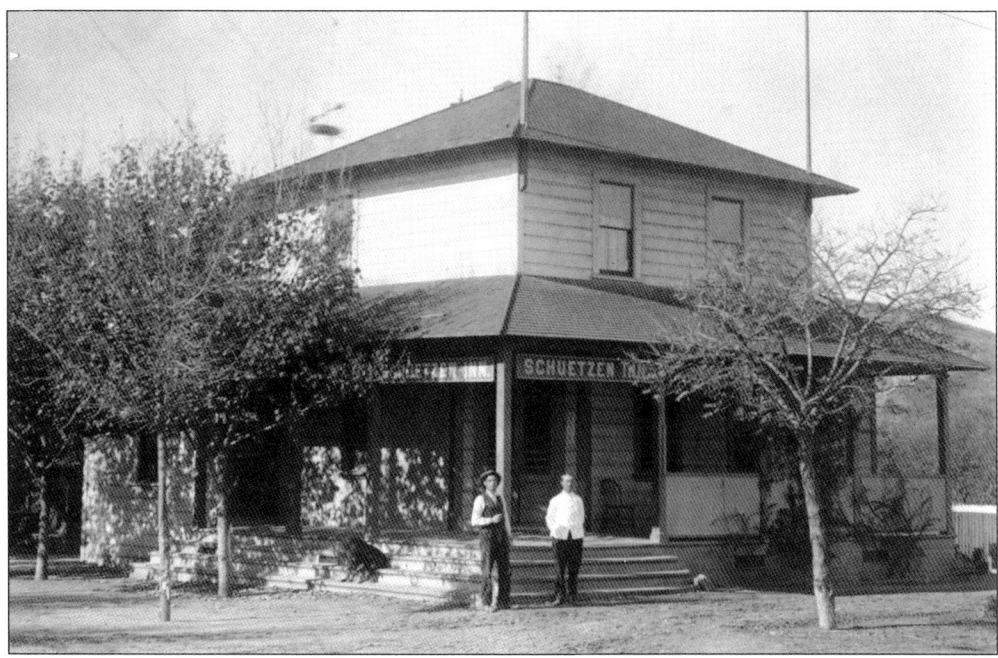

Speakeasies in San Jose were in basements of residences, back rooms of pool halls, soda shops, and hotels. One of these resorts was Dave Holt's Palm Inn, also referred to as Dave Holt's Place and the 4 Mile House, which stood along Monterey Road near Schuetzen Park and the Santa Clara County Fairgrounds. Renowned as one of the area's most popular speakeasies, it was no stranger to raids and arrests. (Courtesy of History San Jose.)

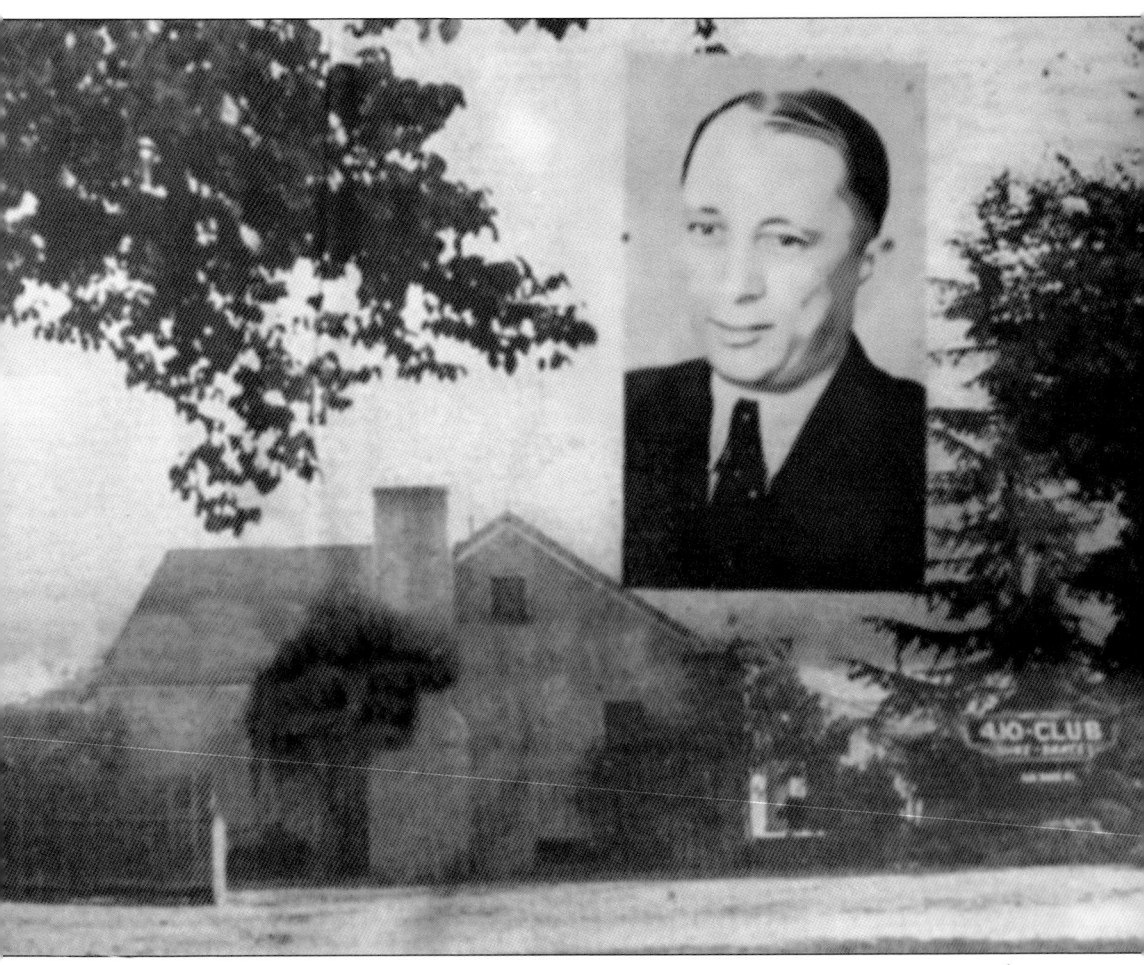

The 410 Club, nestled in the basement of a residence at 410 Race Street, was a notorious hotspot owned by Frank Gairnese (pictured) and operated by John Locurto. Both Gairnese and Locurto were well-known bootleggers with a history of operating illegal alcohol stills and other speakeasies. In 1928, the club faced a significant setback when Locurto was arrested after undercover federal Prohibition agents infiltrated the establishment. Their observations of alcohol sales and slot machine gambling led to charges against Locurto, who denied them and contested them in court. Despite his efforts, Locurto was eventually convicted. However, with the repeal of Prohibition, the 410 Club transitioned into a legitimate establishment serving licensed alcohol. Yet its troubles persisted, as it continued to face issues with after-hours alcohol service and gambling. (Courtesy of Tony Gairnese.)

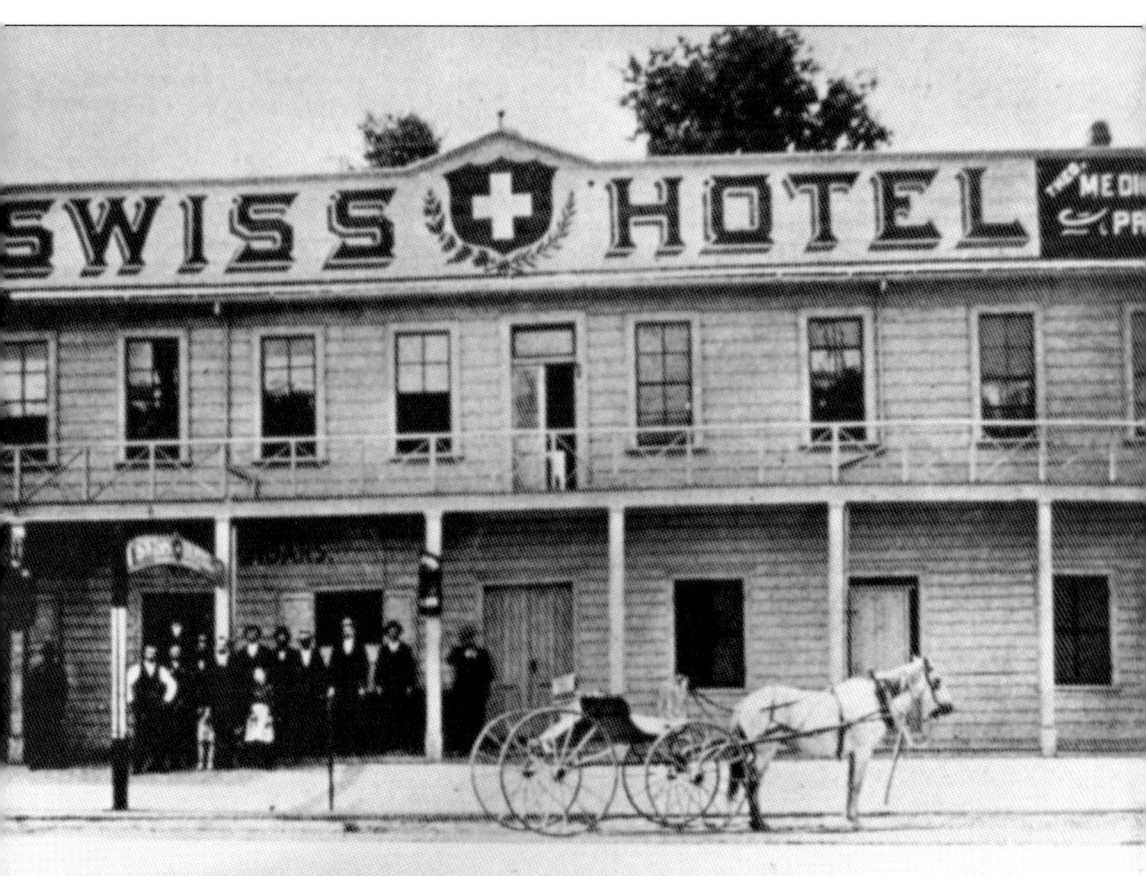

Swiss Hotel, Established in 1855, N. Market St.

235

The Swiss Hotel was located at 85 North Market Street. The hotel was raided five times during the Prohibition years. One of the raids happened in March 1920, when 16 gallons of red wine were found in the dishwashers' sleeping quarters in the hotel. The investigation showed that both the hotel proprietor and the dishwasher carried keys to the room. A table with a wine-stained paper cloth and numerous glasses containing wine were taken as evidence. During the raid, two men walked inside the hotel wanting a drink until they noticed the raiding officers and made a quick exit. (Courtesy of History San Jose.)

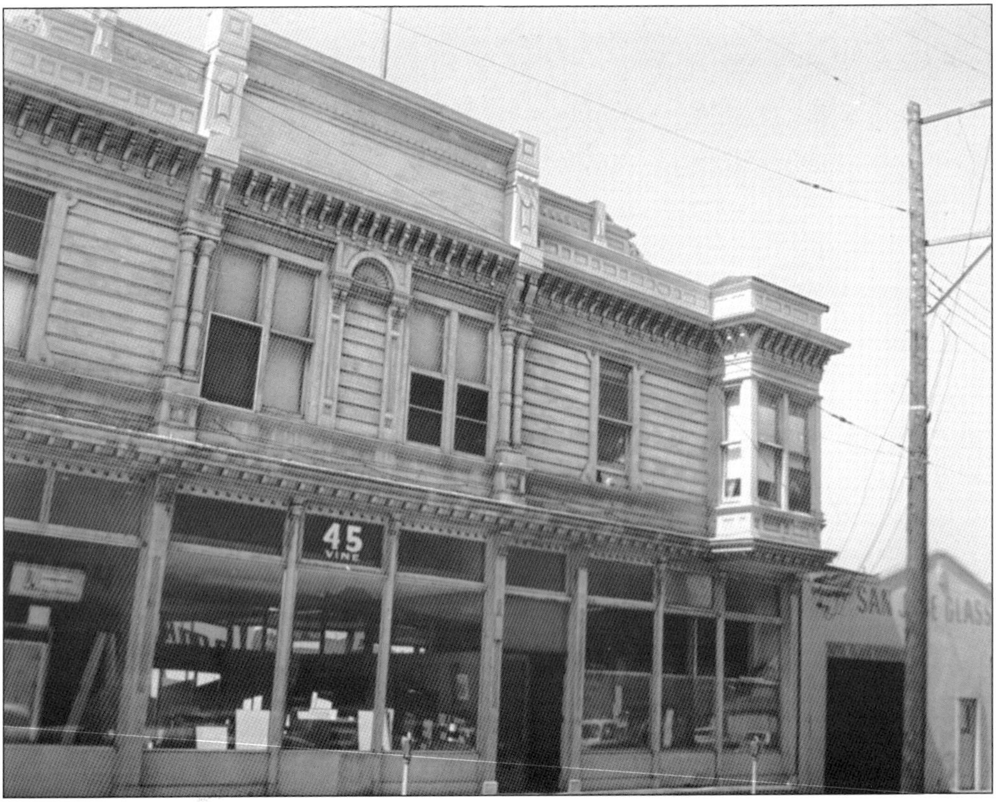

Clarence Leddy and Q.D. Maggiori's saloon at 41 Vine Street was a discreet establishment hidden behind three locked doors within the building. However, their efforts to maintain secrecy were thwarted in April 1924 when they were arrested and fined $500 for operating the saloon. Evidence collected by an operative from the Anti-Saloon League organization led to their apprehension. In compliance with the orders of the superior court, Sheriff Lyle acted by placing locks on the doors and shutting down the saloon for a period of one year due to violation of the Wright Act, a California statute governing alcohol regulation. This incident marked a significant setback for Leddy and Maggiori, underscoring the challenges faced by saloon operators during the Prohibition era. (Both, courtesy of History San Jose.)

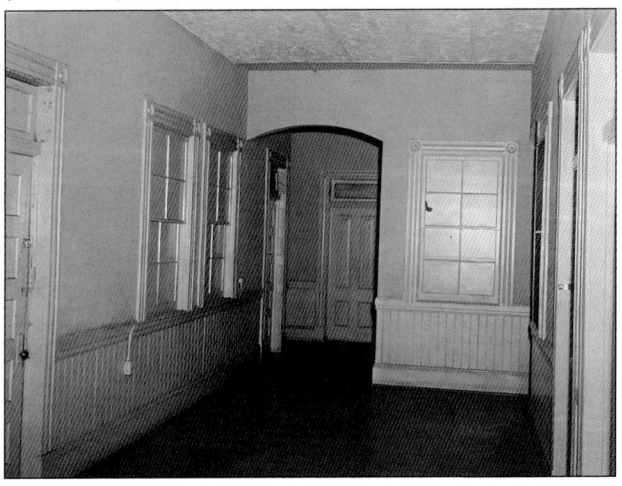

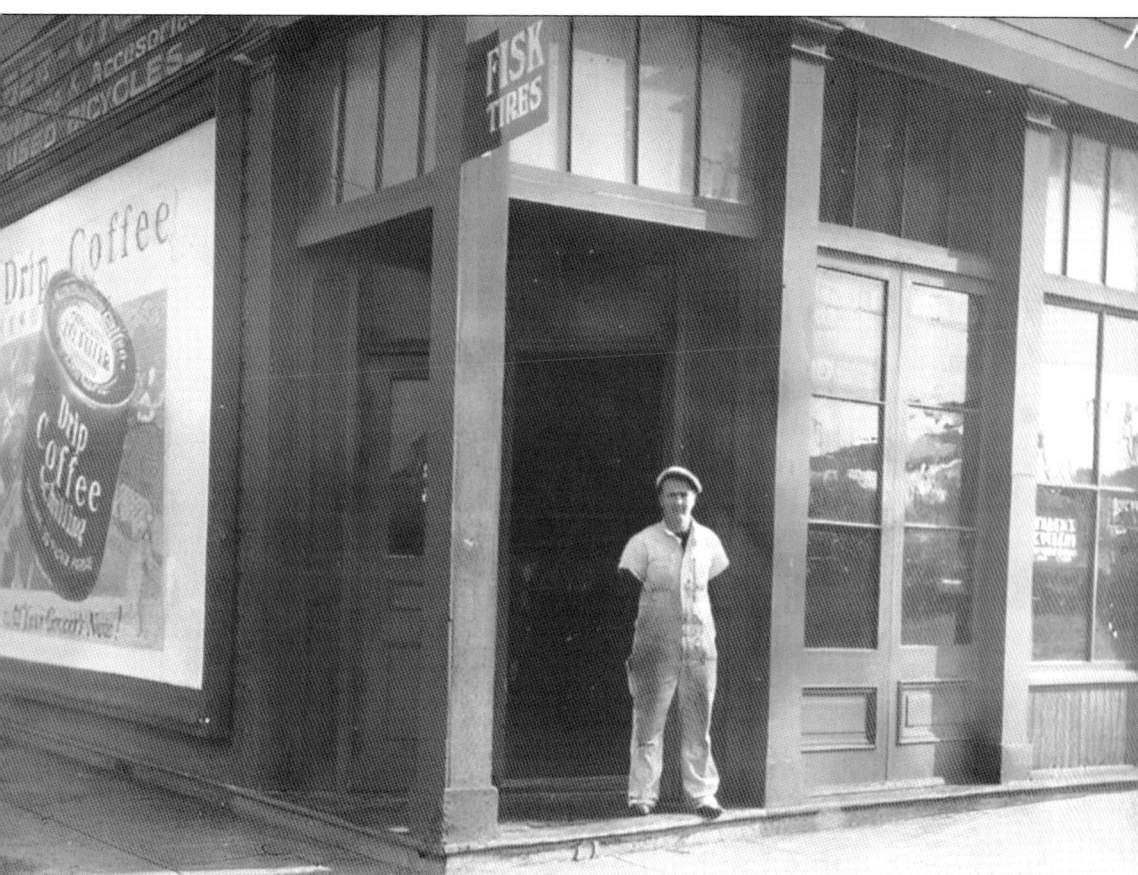

Before transforming into Faber's Cyclery in 1921, the building located at 702 South First Street had a colorful past. On March 18, 1920, it found itself at the center of a raid conducted by federal agents. Led by federal revenue officer E.J. Aplustill, the agents entered the upstairs area of the saloon housed within the building. In a frantic attempt to dispose of the evidence, proprietor G. Rotanzi tried to pour the wine down the sink. However, fate intervened, as the sink became clogged, leading to the collection of ample incriminating evidence. Rotanzi's efforts to conceal illegal activities were in vain, resulting in his subsequent arrest. (Courtesy of History San Jose.)

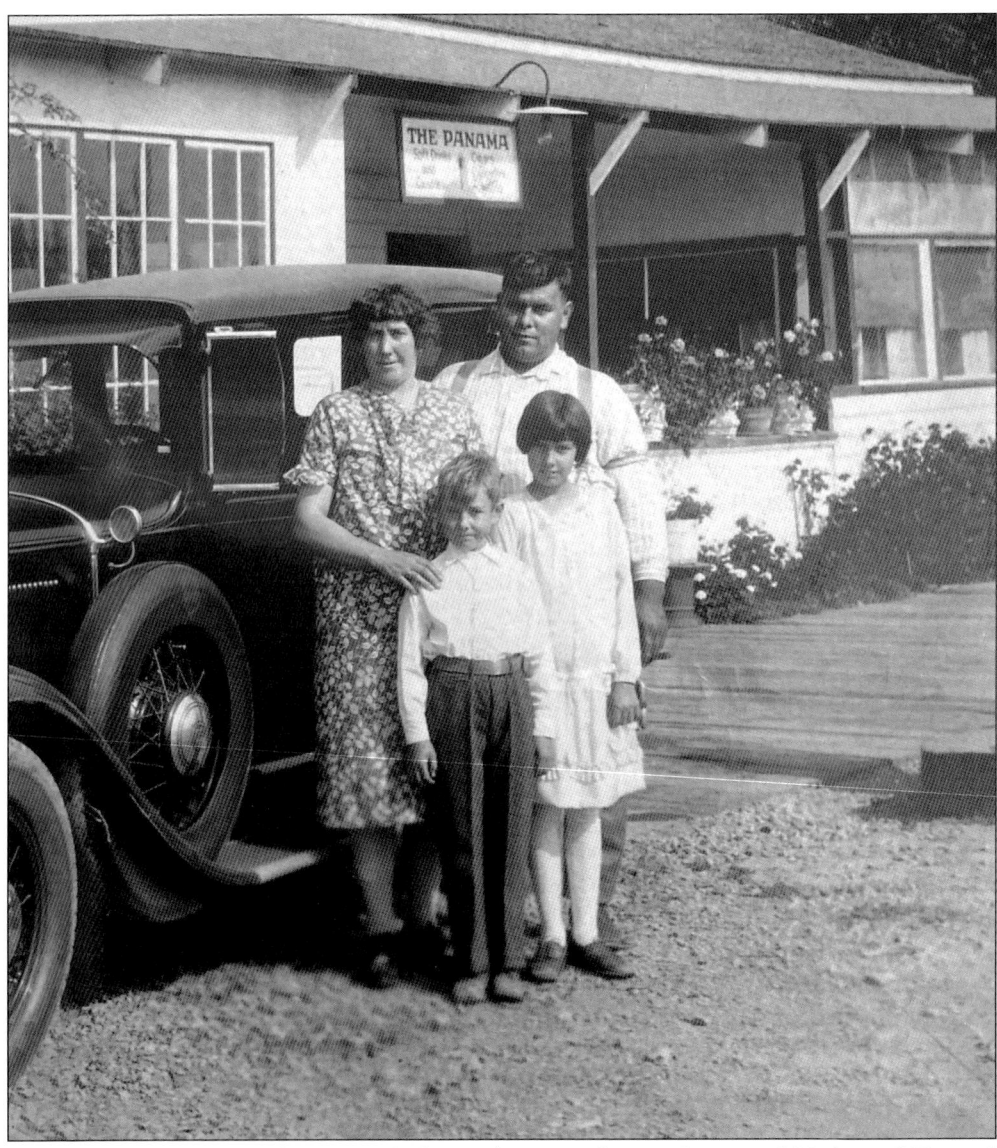

The Panama Inn was in the town of Alviso where North First Street and Highway 237 stand today. Operated by George Smock, in August 1920, the Panama Inn was raided by US deputy marshal Butler and Prohibition enforcement officer A. Schurtliff of San Francisco. Employees E.J. Oliver and E.J. Hirt were arrested during the raid for selling alcohol. In 1929, new owner Joe Sutter Sr. was arrested by Prohibition officers at the Panama Inn for selling beer. The charges were later dismissed when the beer, which was offered as evidence against him, was found not to exceed the legal alcohol content. Pictured here in front of the Panama Inn are Elizabeth Sutter and Joseph Sutter Sr. with their children Joseph Sutter Jr. and Agnes Sutter. (Courtesy of Charlene Sutter Arvizu.)

The Zaro Grill was originally located in the early 1920s at 65 West Santa Clara Street, owned and operated by Steve Zaro. The Zaro Grill had been raided a few times during its legitimate restaurant operation, including in 1921 and 1922. In 1921, Prohibition officers raided the Zaro Grill, and several bottles of liquor were found and confiscated. Steve Zaro and his employee Louis Dosse were arrested. In 1923, the Zaro Grill moved to the corner of Post Street and Lightstone Alley, where it remained in business for almost 30 years. Pictured here, the Good Fellows Grill is where the Zaro Grill was located on Santa Clara Street before moving to Post Street. This coin was issued to customers and was worth 5¢ in trade or credit to the Zaro Grill. (Right, courtesy of History San Jose; below, courtesy of Ted Ramos.)

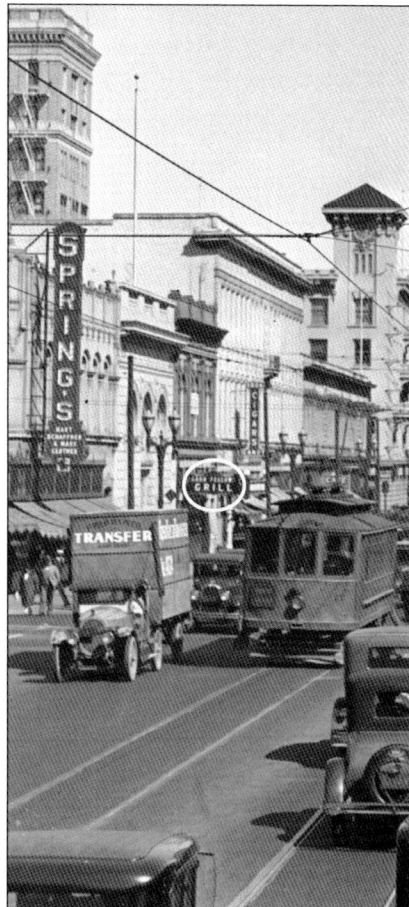

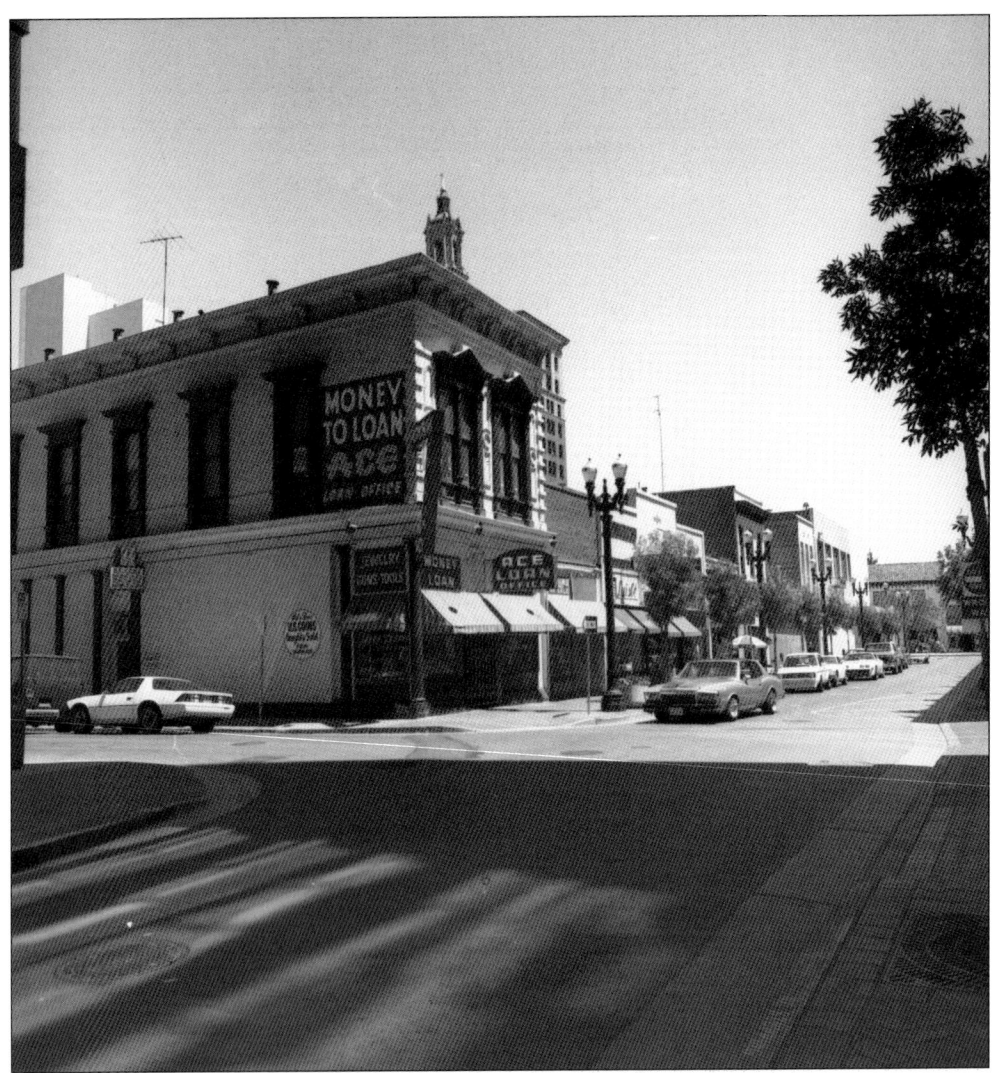

Finley's Inn, situated at 65 Post Street, was owned and operated by William Fenerin, better known as "Billy Finley," during the Prohibition era. Despite the risks, Finley's establishment was subject to approximately eight raids throughout this period. To conceal his illicit activities, Finley ingeniously operated a small barbershop as a speakeasy. Within this covert setup, he implemented a signaling system: a push button installed on the floor. This allowed him to discreetly notify his associates next door when law enforcement was approaching. Liquor was stored upstairs, protected by a double set of doors. Only individuals with proper credentials, screened by Finley himself, were granted access. (Courtesy of History San Jose.)

Circled in this photograph is Maggiore's Place. Located at 42 Post Street, it was owned in 1921 by Q.D. Maggiore, who also owned and operated many speakeasies and liquor manufacturing stills in the San Jose area. This location would later change ownership to Louis Albertini and became known as Albertini's Place. Operated as a cigar and soft drink stand, Albertini's was raided frequently as one of the three speakeasies on Post Street that initiated the blockade of Post Street that police chief Black had started. Chief Black also convinced the city council to revoke Albertini's soft drink and tobacco license in 1927. (Courtesy of History San Jose.)

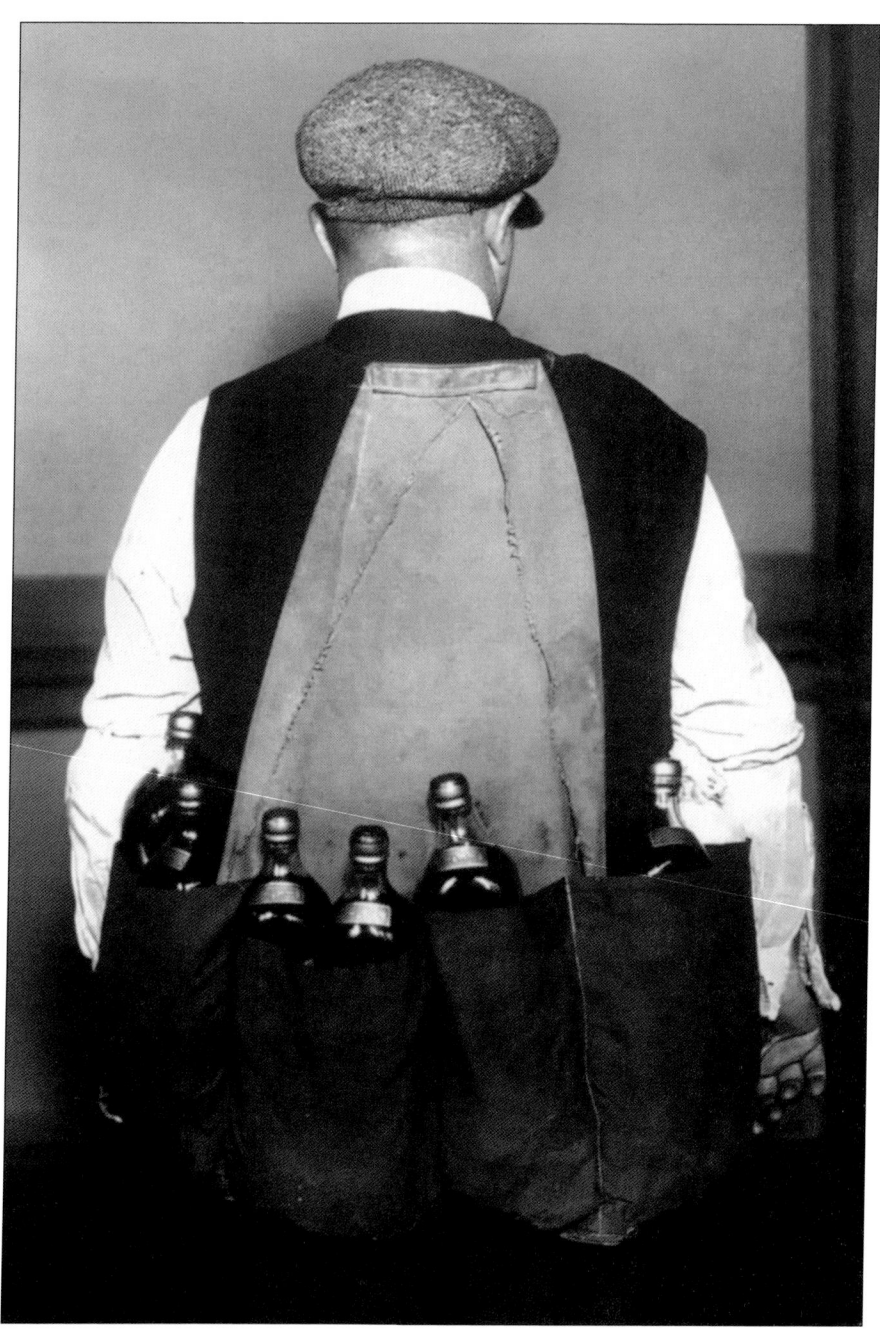

In October 1920, police chief Black initiated a 24-hour blockade on Post Street bootleg joints. Uniformed officers were posted on Post Street, and anyone attempting to enter any of the three suspected bootleg joints (Finley's at 65 Post Street, Pastime Club at 37 Post Street, and Albertini's at 42 Post Street) was to be stopped, questioned, and searched. If a bottle or more of booze was found on them, they would be immediately arrested. These establishments were run with a very small supply of liquor on site. Runners (like the one pictured here) would get more liquor from a storage supply location as fast as needed and smuggled it past the blockade. (Courtesy of Ted Ramos.)

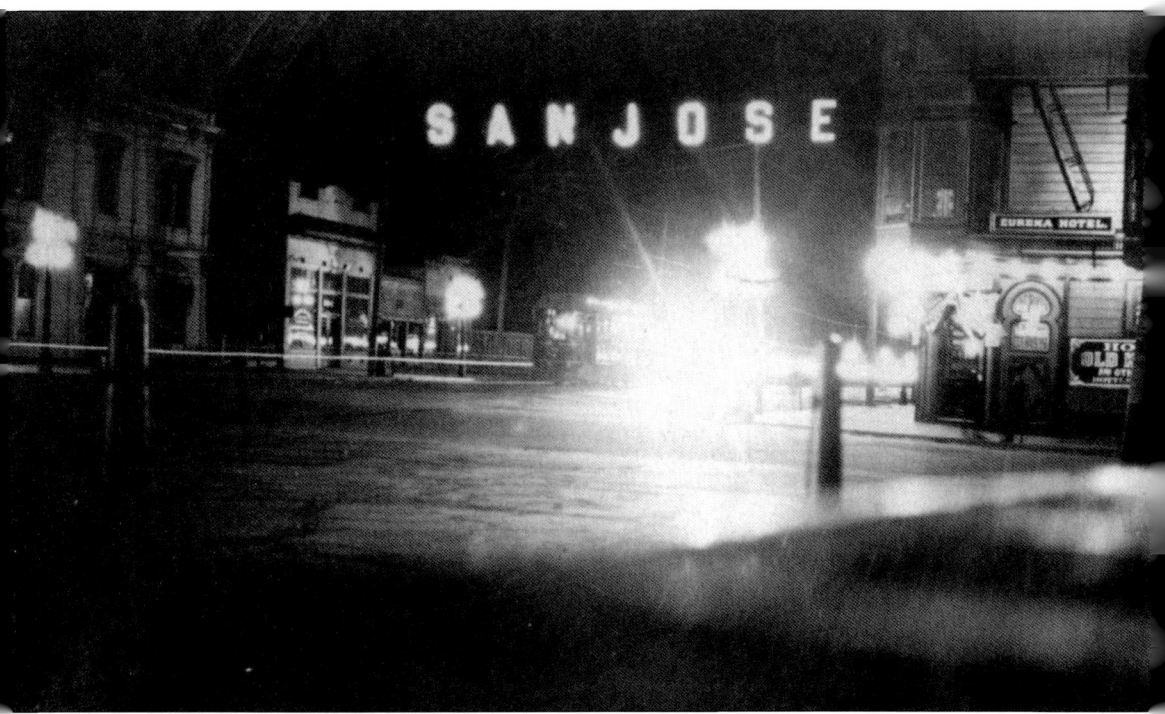

The Eureka Hotel, positioned at 369 North Market Street (at the corner of Market and Basset Streets) held a prime location near the train station, making it a bustling spot. However, its allure also attracted the attention of federal Prohibition officers. In July 1922, the hotel was subjected to a raid by these officers, leading to the discovery and confiscation of approximately $30,000 worth of rare whiskey, wine, and other liquors. Eugene Pazolia, the proprietor of the hotel, faced arrest in connection with this illicit stash. (Courtesy of the Sourisseau Academy.)

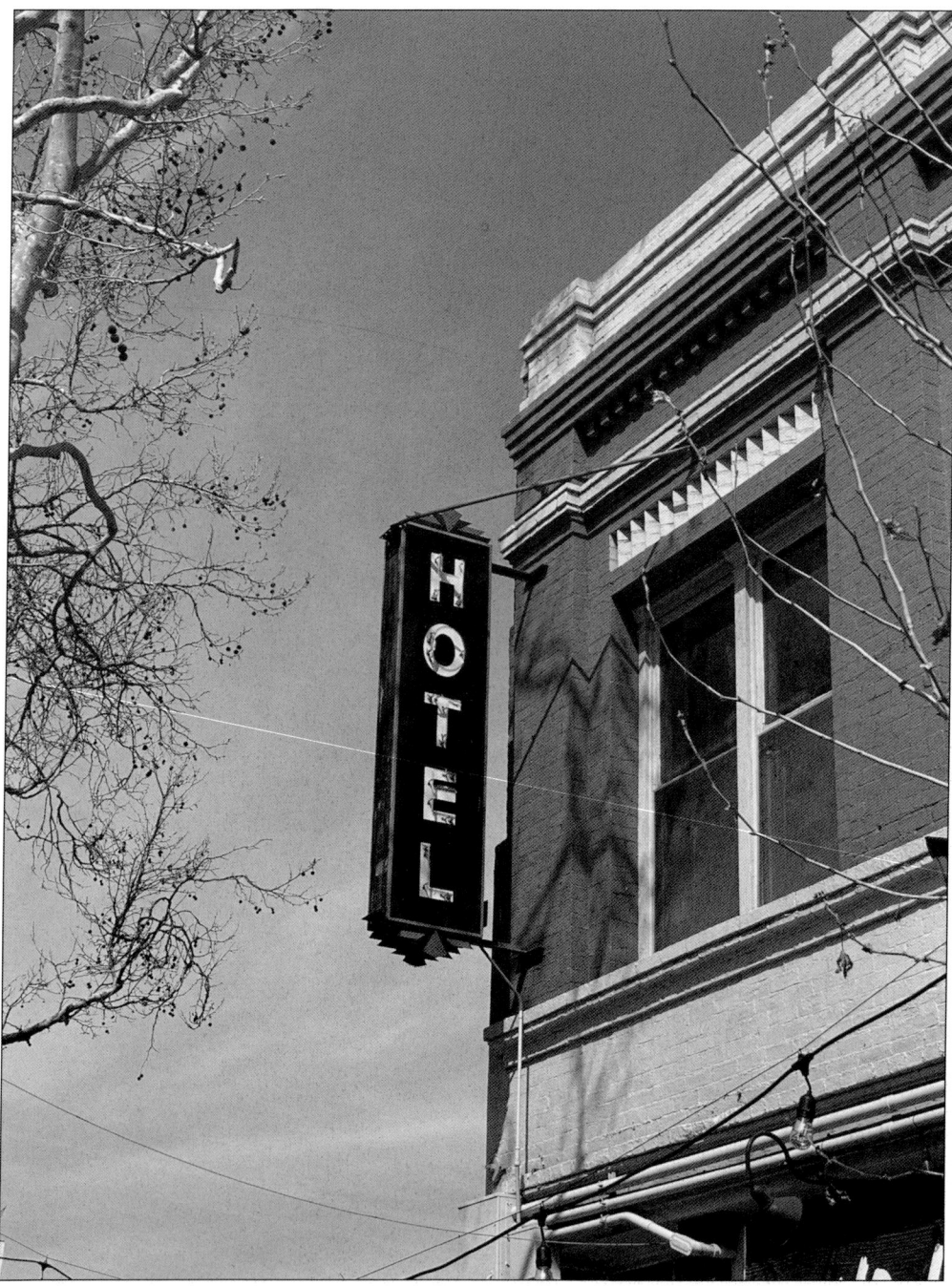

The Argonaut Hotel was located at 86 North Market Street. In September 1929, a police foot patrolman was confronted by a man who said he had been robbed at the Argonaut Hotel. The patrolman contacted two police detectives, and the three of them went into the hotel to investigate. The investigation resulted in the arrest of the hotel proprietor, A.M. Codahengo, after a 26-gallon keg of wine and several bottles of alcohol were found in the hotel icebox. As for the alleged robbery, the victim had disappeared when officers tried to settle the robbery allegation. Police believed the robbery allegation was to get the police to discover the alcohol. (Courtesy of History San Jose.)

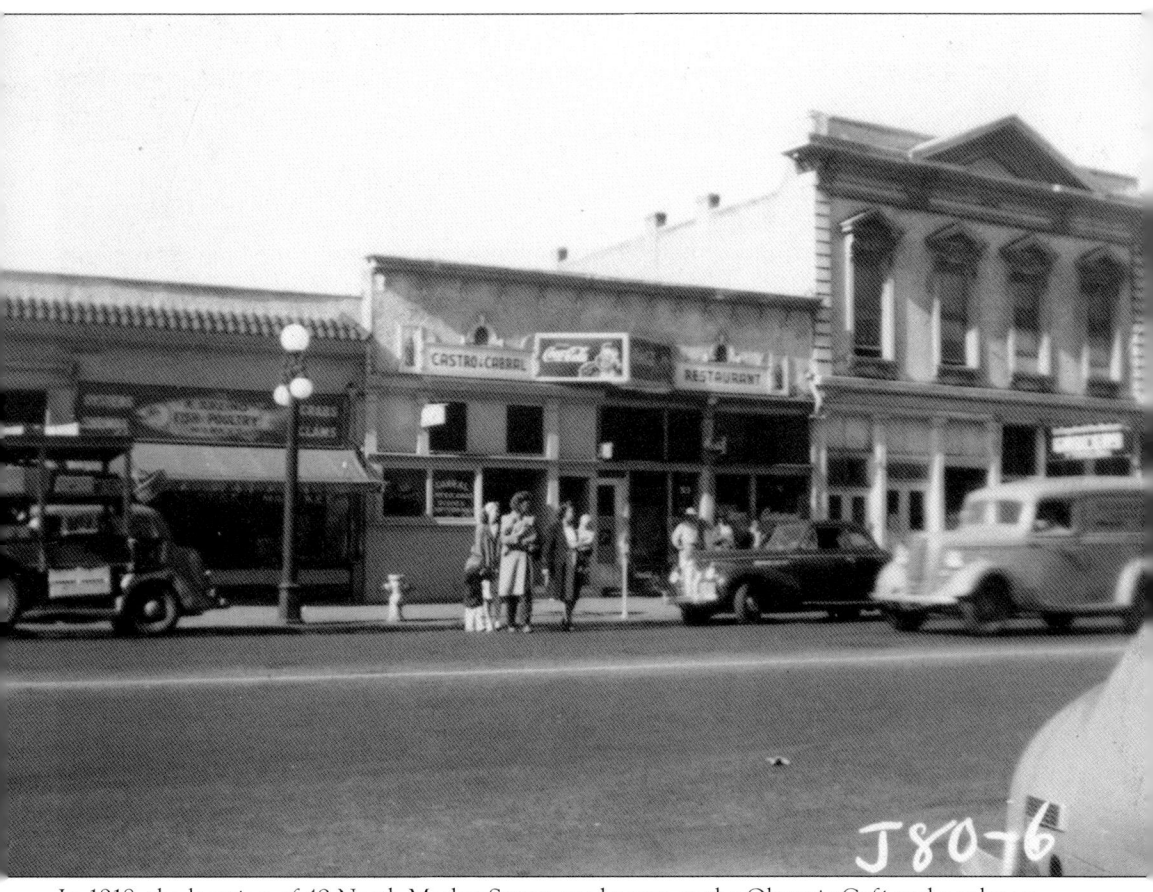

In 1918, the location of 49 North Market Street was known as the Olympic Café and poolroom. The Olympic Café was first raided during the city's campaign against the illegal selling of liquor in violation of the Tompkins Ordinance. Multiple gallons of whiskey were confiscated. Undercover officers observed that in the rear of the café were a bar and pool tables. Liquor was being served at the bar, and café proprietor Chris Delio was carrying a flask, going around to his customers at the pool tables, and selling the liquor. Delio was arrested. The Olympic Café was also raided in 1921 and 1922 during nationwide Prohibition. (Courtesy of History San Jose.)

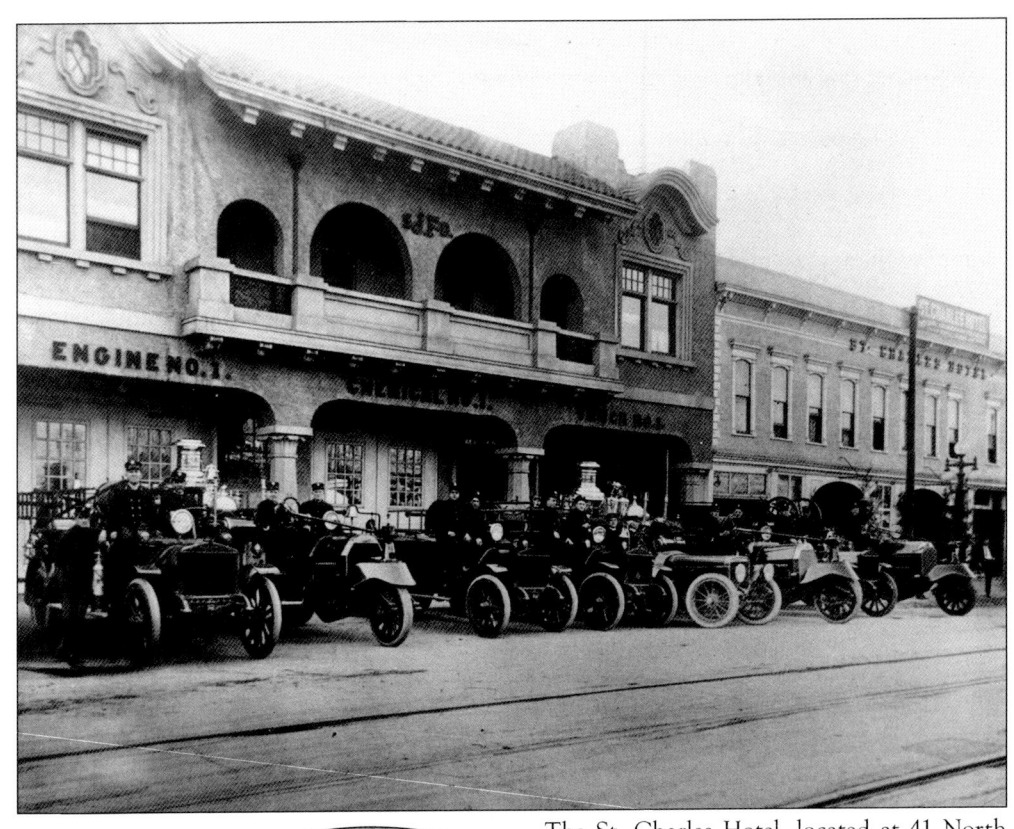

The St. Charles Hotel, located at 41 North Market Street, was raided multiple times between 1921 and 1922. In July 1921, hotel owner G. Falauchi was arrested for selling alcohol. In December 1921, the St. Charles Hotel had become one of the leading bootleg places in San Jose when Falauchi and his bartender were arrested again during a raid for selling alcoholic drinks. Two more raids occurred in 1922, and abatement proceedings started, shutting down the hotel for a year. Seen here are the St. Charles Hotel in an image taken in the early 1900s and a coin given to hotel customers for 5¢ in trade or credit. (Above, courtesy of History San Jose; left, courtesy of Ted Ramos.)

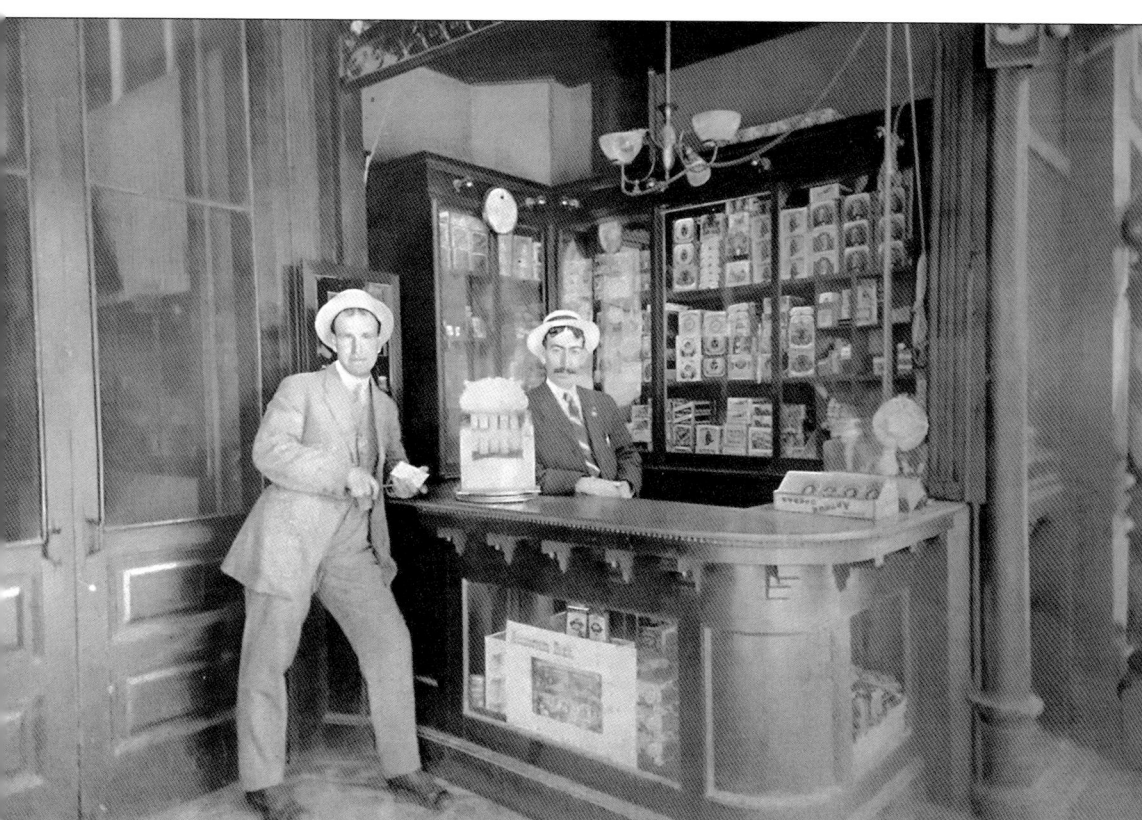

Even after Prohibition came into effect, John Russo's cigar stand continued to operate, serving as a front for the Crystal Bar's transformation into the Crystal Café and Billiard Parlor. However, behind the facade of the café, illegal activities persisted, including the sale of alcohol and illicit bookmaking. In March 1922, law enforcement authorities raided the Crystal Café. During the raid, café proprietor L. Sullins was apprehended for possession and sale of alcohol, marking yet another instance of enforcement action against the establishment. In the photograph, John Russo can be seen behind the cigar counter, presumably overseeing operations within the establishment. (Courtesy of Dave and Christina Anaya.)

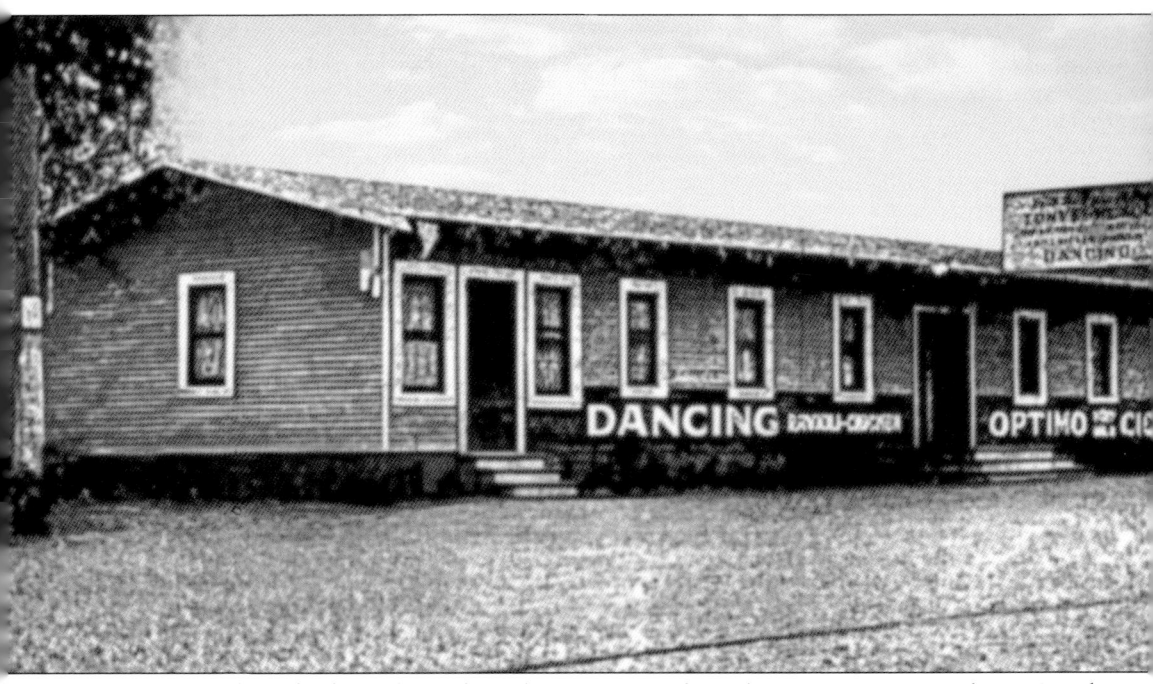

Tony's Chicken Shack was located north of San Jose along the San Francisco Highway. In July 1928, federal Prohibition agents and deputized civilians working independently of the sheriff's office and the police department raided Tony's Chicken Shack. Agents found liquor concealed inside a storage area under a trapdoor beneath a bed in the back bedroom. Owner Tony Dillio was arrested and charged with possession of intoxicating liquor. (Courtesy of the San Jose Public Library.)

In August 1928, after weeks of investigation by police chief Black, a raid was conducted at the Knox building. Chief Black and federal Prohibition agents arrested R.F. Tarney, a chemist and patent medicine manufacturer, for unlawful sales and possession of liquor after a whiskey manufacturing plant was found in a suite of rooms inside the Knox building. (Courtesy of History San Jose.)

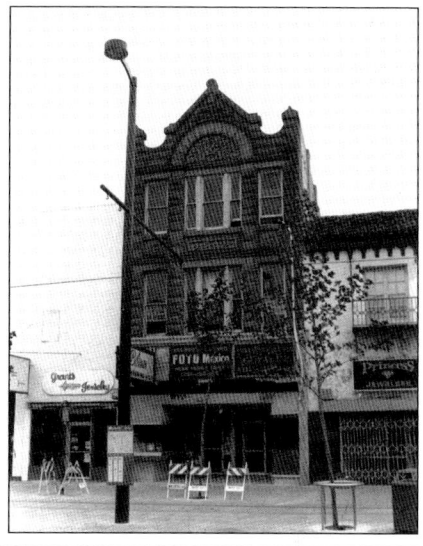

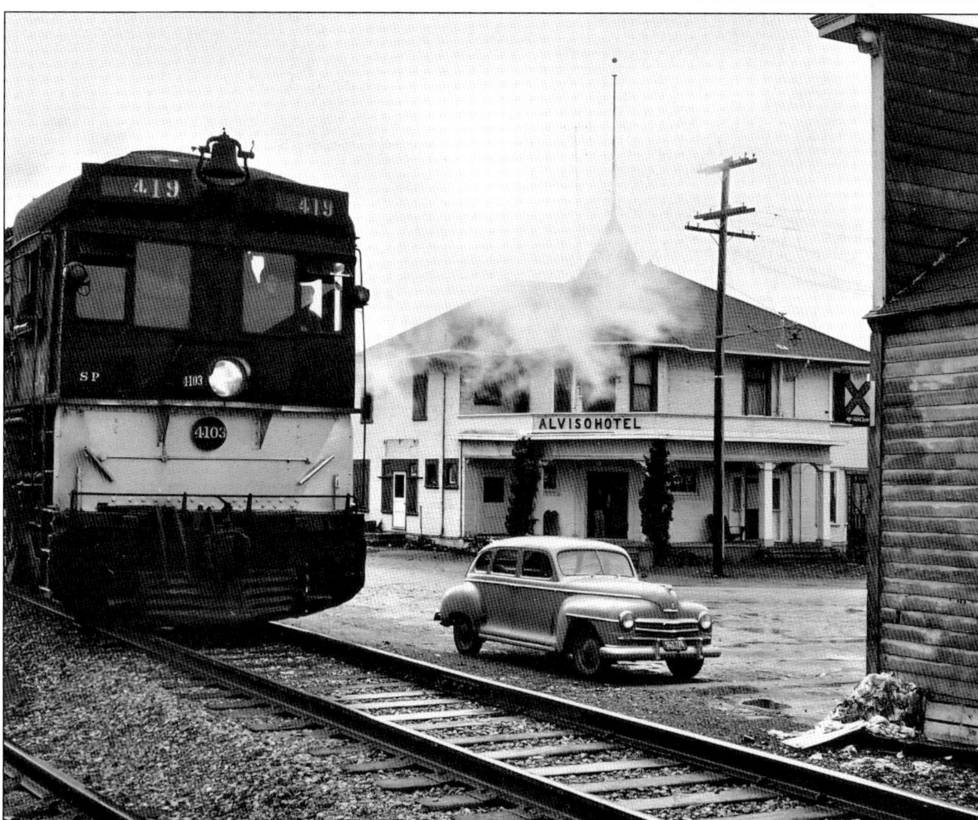

The Alviso Hotel is located at 995 Elizabeth Street. In February 1932, sheriff's deputies and federal Prohibition agents raided the Alviso Hotel and arrested bartender Oddy Renner. The hotel had been raided many times and had been abated by the sheriff three different times. The hotel was managed by Alviso councilman John Ackerman. While undercover agents were purchasing alcohol as evidence for their case, Alviso police chief William Perkins was at the hotel bar drinking alcohol. (Courtesy of History San Jose.)

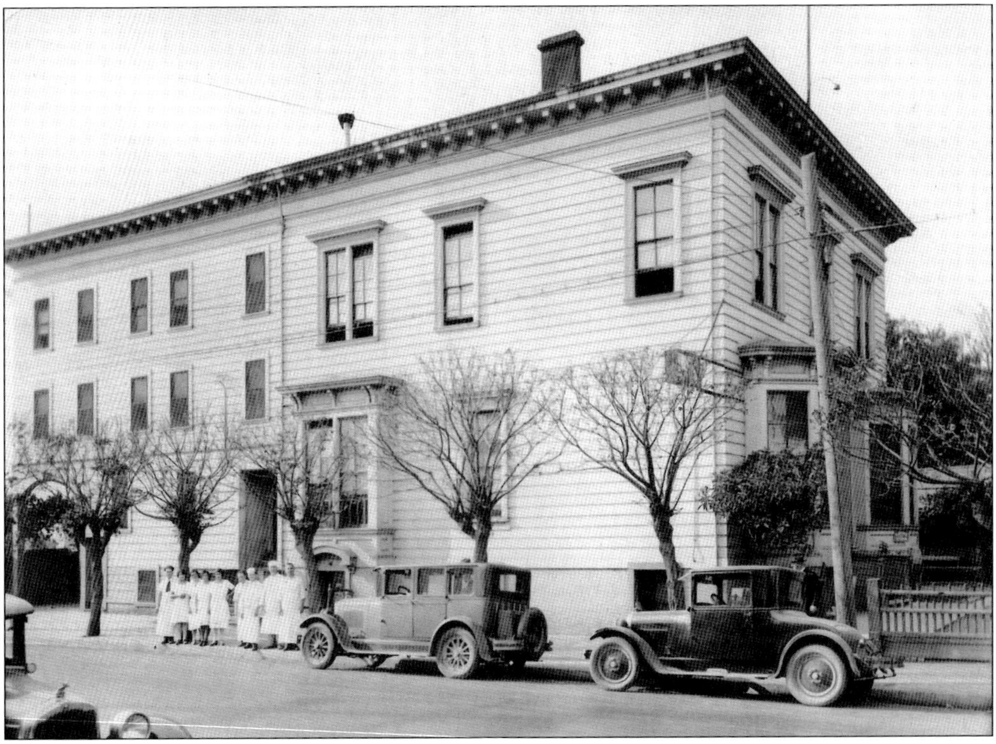

The Italian Hotel, also known as the Italia Hotel, was situated within the Thomas Falon building, constructed in 1846 and located at 109 East San Augustine Street. This establishment, primarily serving as a hotel catering to male boarders, faced law enforcement action on multiple occasions during the Prohibition era. In August 1920, local police conducted a raid on the Italian Hotel, resulting in the arrest of proprietor A. Vogliazzo. The raid yielded the discovery and confiscation of wine and whiskey, implicating the establishment in illegal alcohol-related activities. Subsequently, in 1923, a squad of federal Prohibition officers conducted another raid on the Italian Hotel. During this operation, a small quantity of liquor was seized, and employee Peter Baua was arrested. It is worth noting that at the time of this raid, the Italian Hotel was undergoing the abatement process, indicating ongoing efforts to address its involvement in illegal activities related to alcohol. (Both, courtesy of History San Jose.)

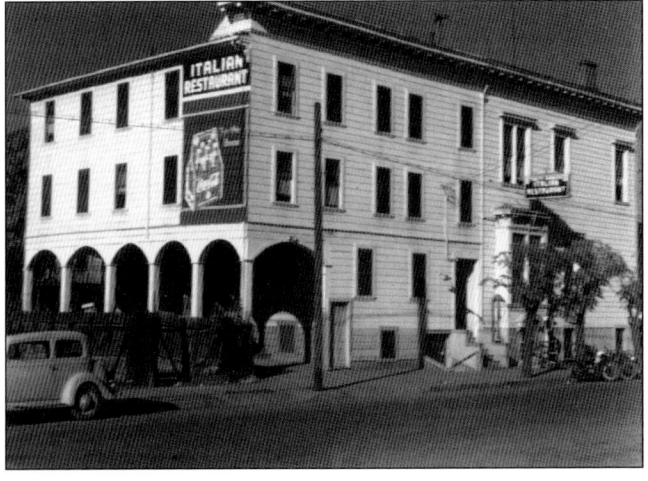

Three

RAIDS

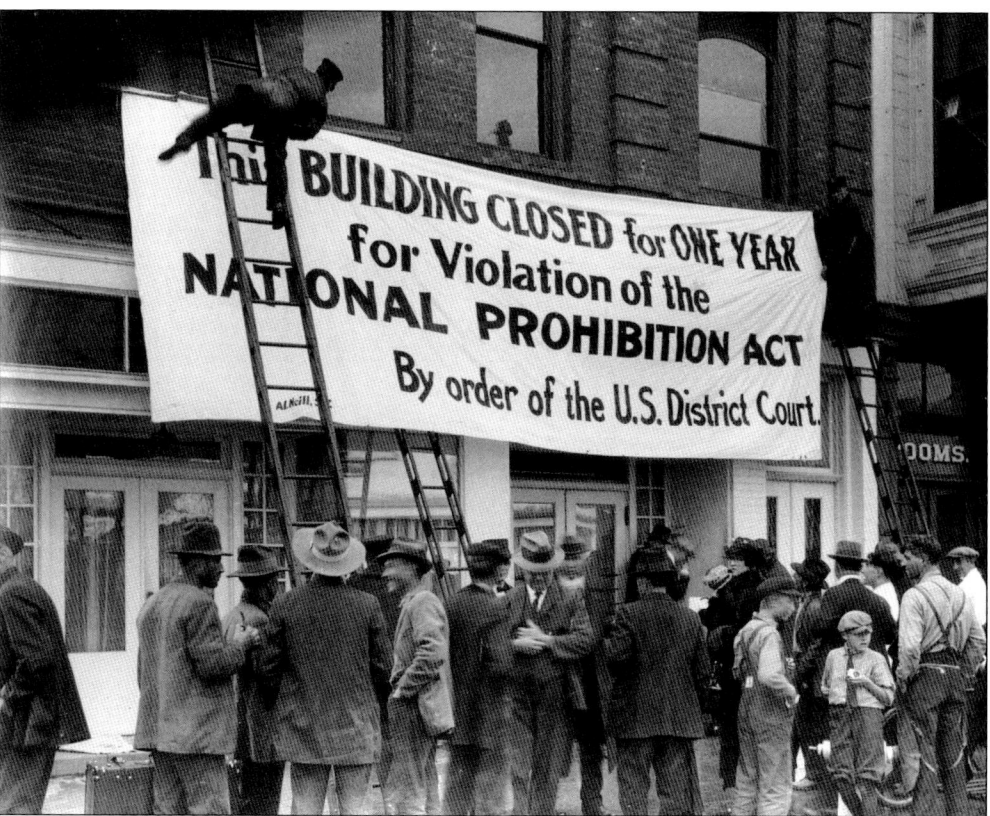

Raids on speakeasies and distillery plants were conducted by the San Jose Police Department, the Santa Clara County Sheriff's Department, federal Prohibition agents from the San Francisco office, deputized citizens, and private temperance groups. Raids were conducted after evidence was collected by undercover operators. The closing of the Milano Hotel at 101 North Market Street due to alcohol and slot machines found during a raid was dramatically carried out before a crowd of several hundred people to serve as an example. (Courtesy of the Sourisseau Academy.)

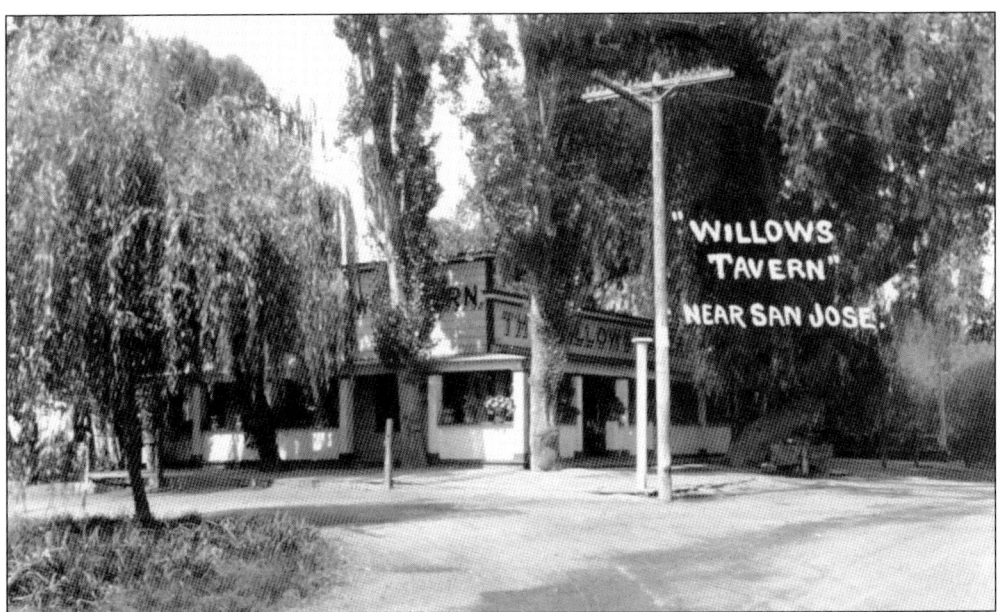

On January 31, 1923, Santa Clara County sheriff Lyle and two of his deputies visited the Willow Tavern, located near the corner of North First Street and Montague Expressway, after receiving multiple complaints from the public that alcohol was being sold. After observing several transactions, Lyle and his deputies confiscated all the liquor and serving glasses as evidence. The Willow Tavern proprietor, Gordon Jones, was arrested for possession and sale of intoxicating liquor. Three other patrons were arrested, including a 16-year-old girl. This was the first of multiple raids at the Willow Tavern that found liquor on-site resulting in arrests. (Above, courtesy of History San Jose; below, courtesy of the San Jose Public Library.)

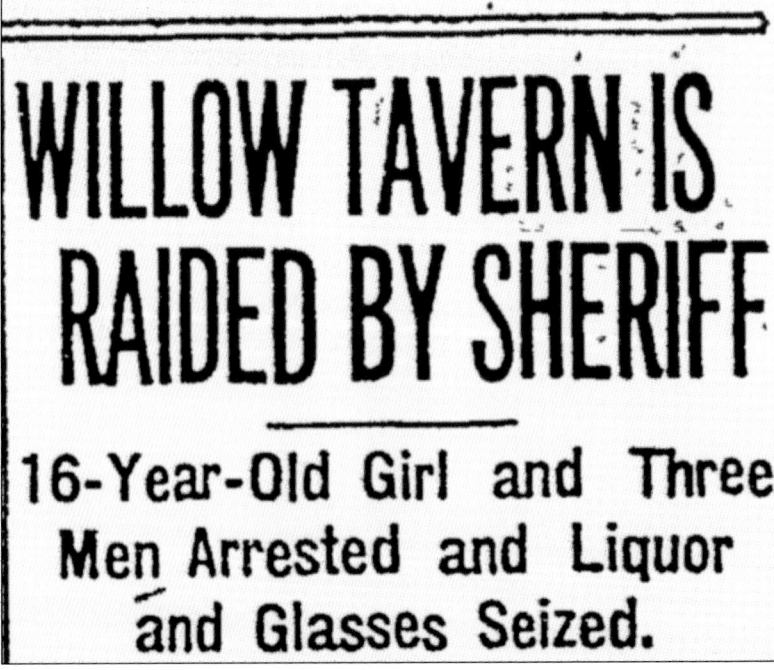

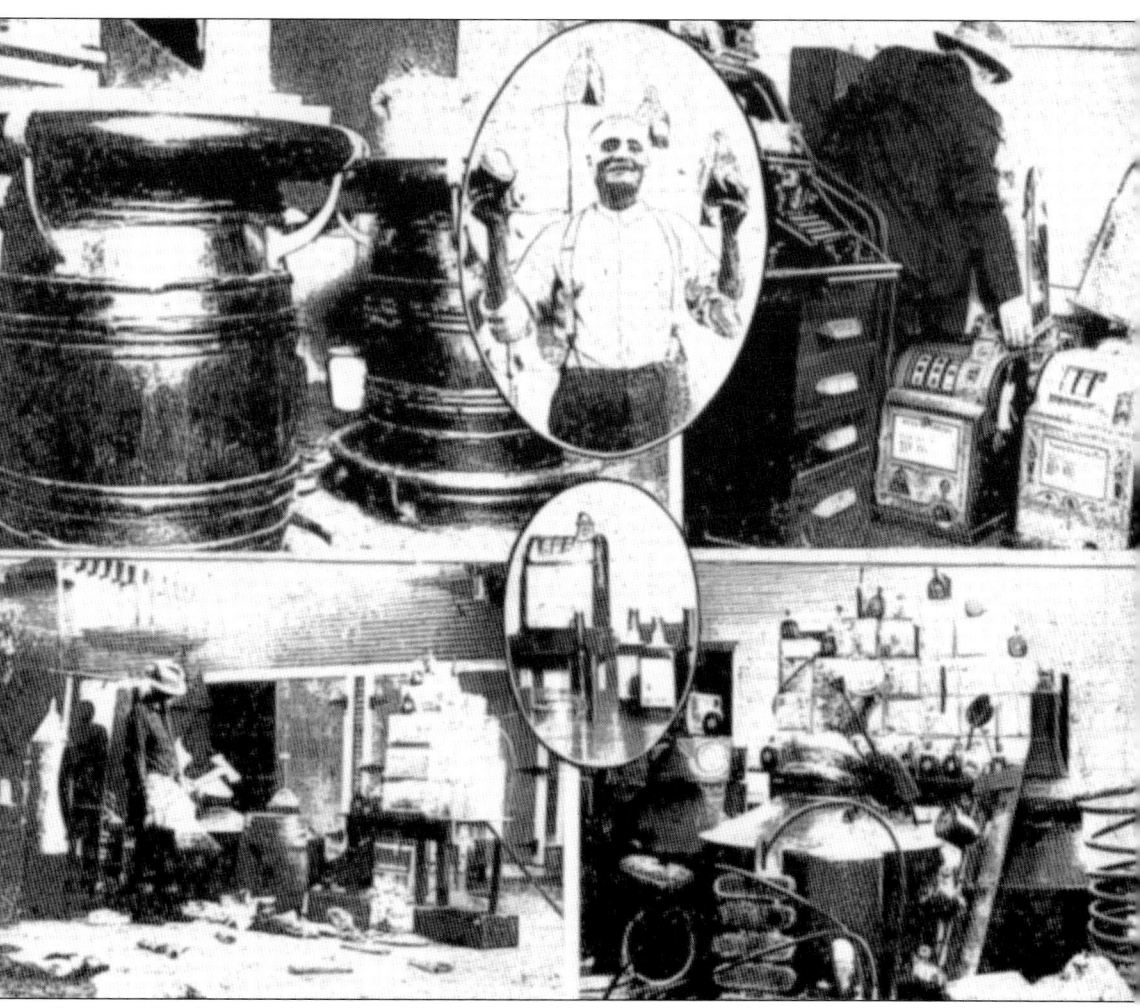

Jack and Jane's Place, located on Monterey Road, was owned and operated by John and Jane Lindville. In July 1928, they were arrested during a raid for possession and sale of alcohol. The sheriff's deputies went through the place and reported that no liquor was found, and no arrests were made. Two hours later, federal officers, with Prohibition administrator E.B. Bohner, broke through the rear door and window, finding a barroom, a large quantity of whiskey, glasses, carbonated water, 15 bottles of labeled "Old Taylor" whiskey, and a couple dozen unlabeled bottles containing beer of high alcoholic content. Three slot machines were also found. Pictured here were the items confiscated at Jack and Jane's Place. (Courtesy of the San Jose Public Library.)

SAN JOSE "WETTEST" CAL. CITY

This the Declaration of Federal Officer, Who Conducts "Raids" on Hotels.

At the end of 1920, federal revenue officer E.J. Aplustill declared San Jose the "wettest" town in the state of California after a series of raids on hotels and speakeasies. Aplustill worked under W.A. Kelly of San Francisco, who was the federal Prohibition supervisor with jurisdiction over California, Nevada, Oregon, Washington, and Arizona. (Courtesy of the San Jose Public Library.)

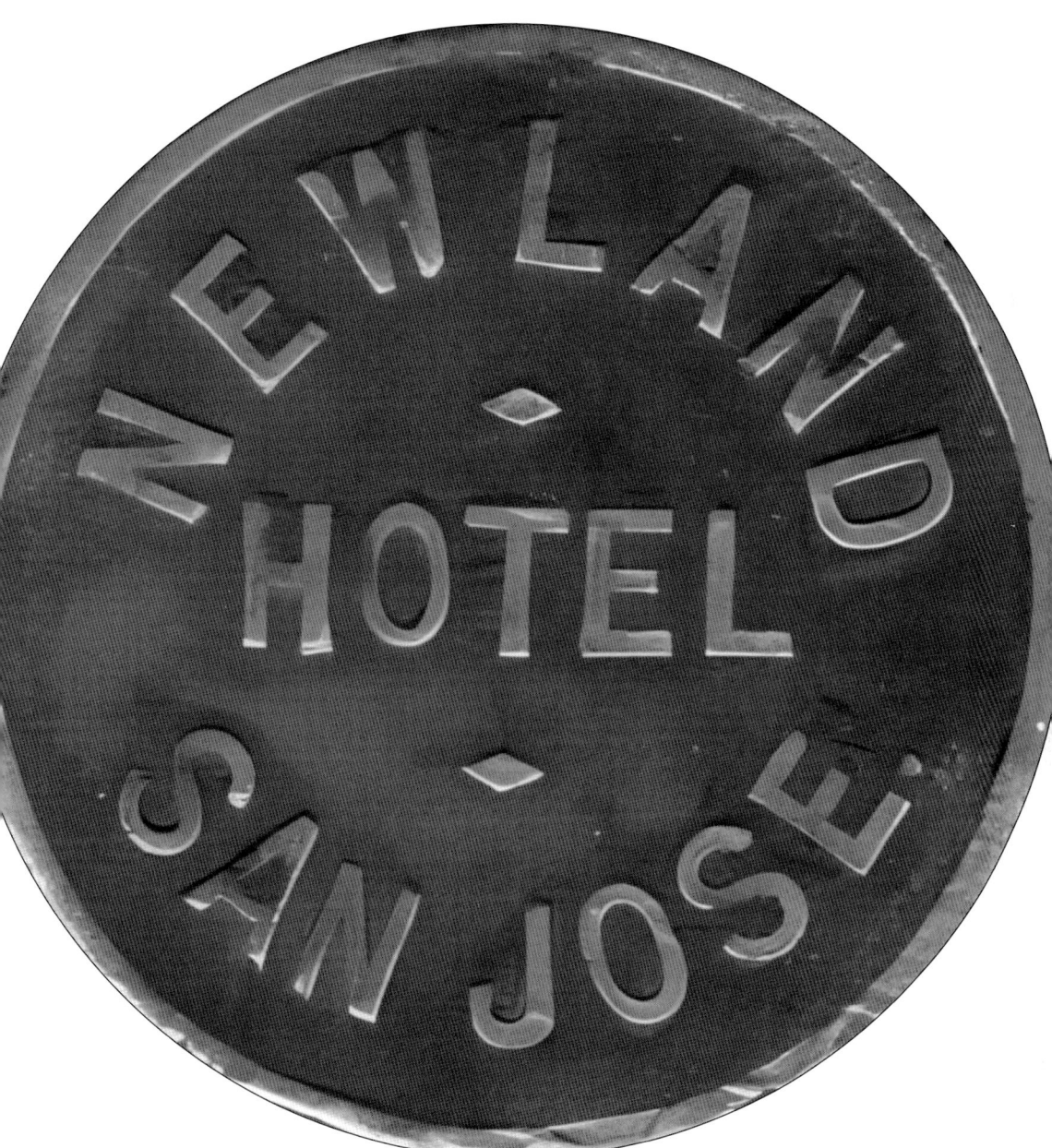

The Newland Hotel, situated alongside another hotel at the intersection of Market and Basset Streets, was subject to multiple raids during the Prohibition era. In one such incident on January 20, 1924, federal Prohibition agents from San Francisco conducted a raid on the Newland Hotel. During the operation, liquor intended for sale was discovered on the premises, leading to the arrest of employee M. Martinelli. Subsequently, on August 9, 1924, the Newland Hotel was raided once again, this time by police chief Black and his detectives. During this operation, proprietor James Henry was arrested for possession of alcohol. (Courtesy of Ted Ramos.)

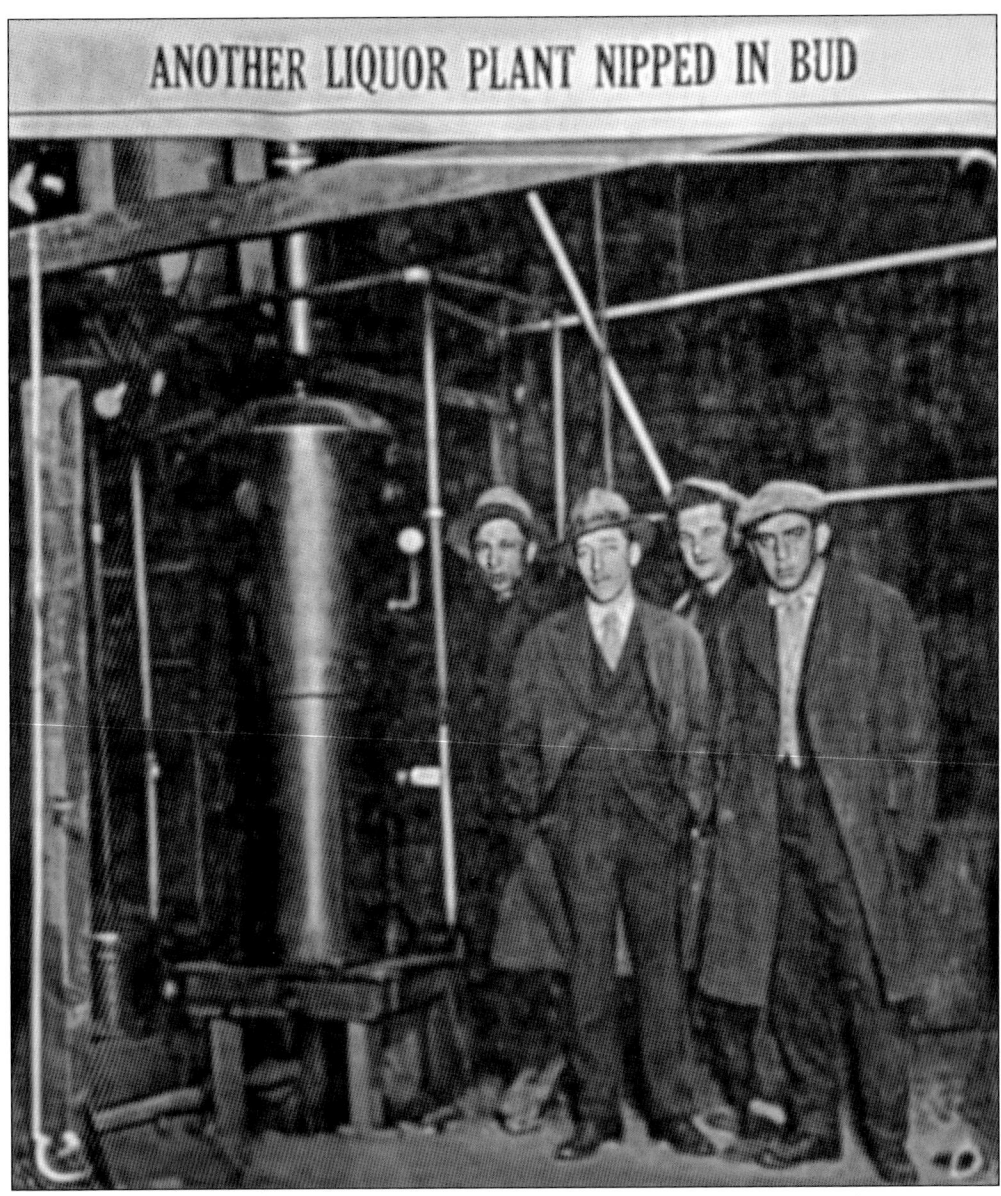

ANOTHER LIQUOR PLANT NIPPED IN BUD

In March 1927, sheriff's deputies and federal Prohibition agents raided a ranch belonging to Joe Yentimiglia, located about one mile from the intersection of Almaden Road and Lincoln Avenue. They found a distilling plant consisting of a 300-gallon still, 75 sacks of sugar, 300 gallons of 190-proof alcohol, a steam boiler, and 10,000 gallons of mash ready for distillation. The four men pictured here, standing in front of the still, were arrested. They are, from left to right, Frank Gairnese, Sam Rieck, Vincent Armentia, and Fino Carcello. (Courtesy of Tony Gairnese.)

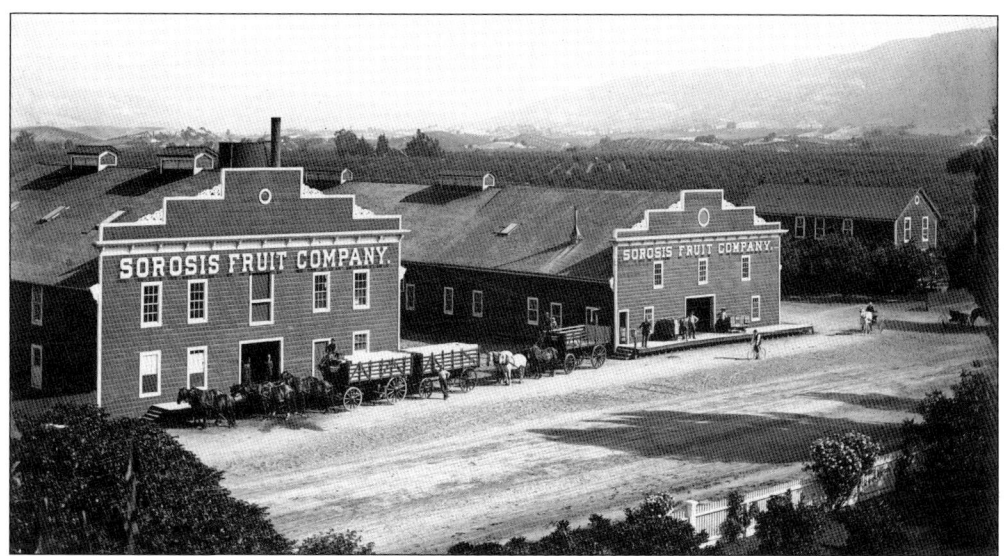

On February 1, 1924, law enforcement authorities made a significant discovery at the Sorosis Ranch, located on Saratoga Road. This operation unearthed the largest and most sophisticated bootlegging outfit found thus far. The raid on the Sorosis Ranch revealed the presence of two 150-gallon stills, a sizable steam boiler, condensers, and seven large vats containing a total of 15,000 gallons of mash. Additionally, authorities found 50 gallons of 192-proof alcohol, a ton of sugar, 100 new 5-gallon cans, and various other items essential for operating a still. The entire operation was situated in an old dairy barn half a mile from the ranch house. Those directly involved in the operation were swiftly apprehended. Operators M. Romero and Paul Valle, who had leased the building from ranch owner A. Teresi, were among those arrested. Alfred Mosane and R. Belli, who were involved in transporting liquor, were also taken into custody. Mosane was additionally linked to the Milano Hotel. Seen here is an aerial view of the Sorosis Ranch, along with sheriff's deputies standing next to the confiscated stills. (Above, courtesy of History San Jose; below, courtesy of the Sourisseau Academy.)

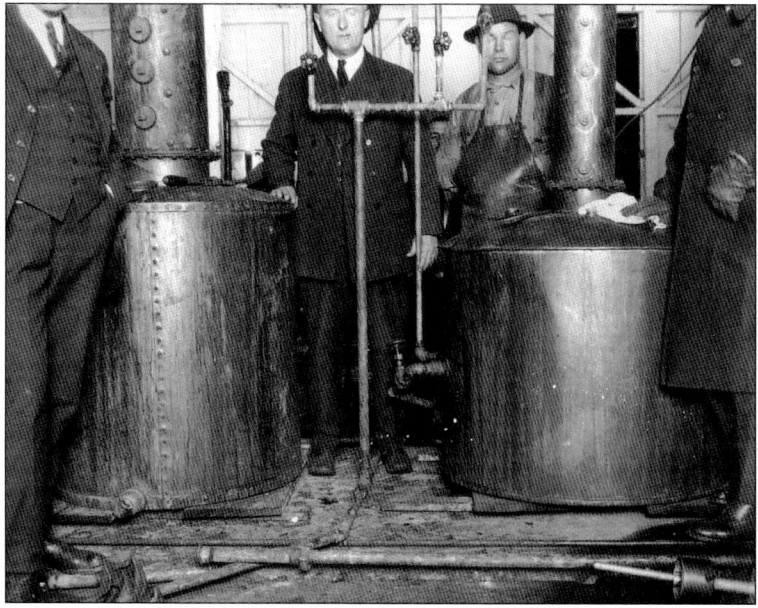

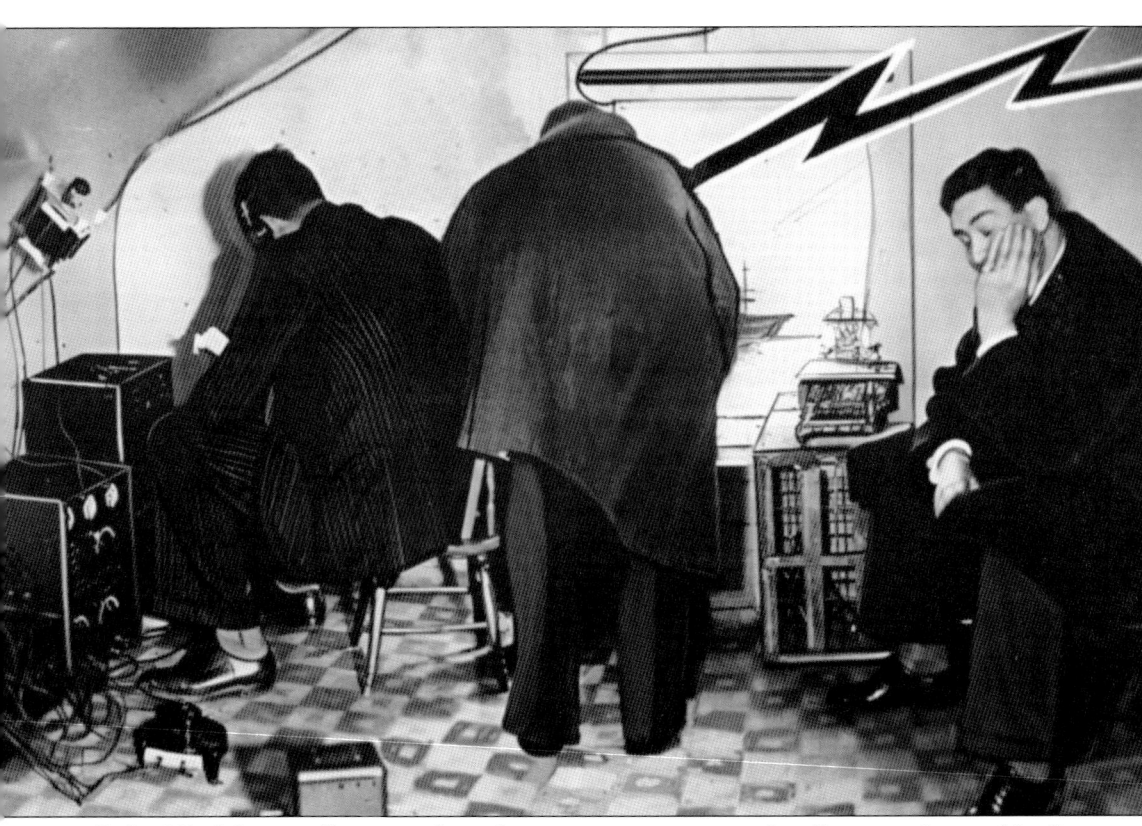

Federal Prohibition officers seized a radio station transmitter in San Francisco financed by San Jose bootlegger and West Coast rumrunner Peter Maggiore. This was one of three radio stations owned by Maggiore. These stations were used to notify rumrunners and mother ships off the West Coast of locations of Coast Guard cutters and of other conditions that would aid the alcohol smuggling operations. The San Jose radio station was found in a house owned by Harry Maggiore (Peter's brother) on Meridian Avenue. (Courtesy of Ted Ramos.)

'Chick" Leddy's Resort In San Jose Padlocked

SAN JOSE, March 29.—Clarence "Chick" Leddy's place on Almaden avenue, notorious bootleg and vice resort, today had a federal padlock on its door, which must remain closed for one year.

Clarence "Chick" Leddy was a prominent figure in the bootlegging scene in San Jose, known for operating several illicit resorts throughout the city. Among his establishments, the largest and most renowned was situated at 150 Almaden Street. In March 1927, after a series of raids targeting Leddy's resort, deputy sheriffs took decisive action by closing the establishment for a year. This action was undertaken pursuant to orders from district attorney Fred L. Thomas following substantial evidence compiled against the resort. County detective William J. Dreischmeyer played a pivotal role in gathering evidence that ultimately led to the resort's closure. As a result, legal proceedings were initiated against the individuals involved in the operation. W.A. Bradford, identified as the owner, along with Clarence Leddy and Clifford Snow, who were identified as operators, were subjected to the abatement process. (Courtesy of the San Jose Public Library.)

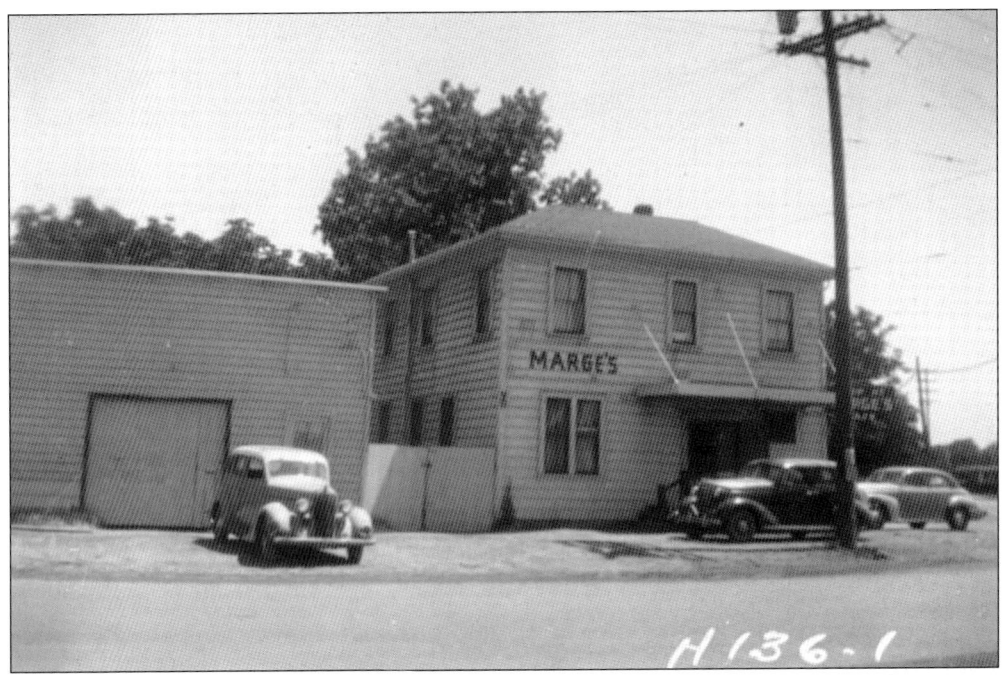

The Cottage Grove, at 220 Alma Street, was operated by persistent liquor law violator Steve Mignosi. In November 1931, Sheriff William Emig arrested Mignosi. As the deputies entered, Deputy Ed Lowell had to run and stop Mignosi as he was about to dump a half-gallon of whiskey into the sink. Lowell had to cover the drain with his hand to prevent losing the evidence. Mignosi was arrested and fined $500 or served 50 days in jail. (Courtesy of History San Jose.)

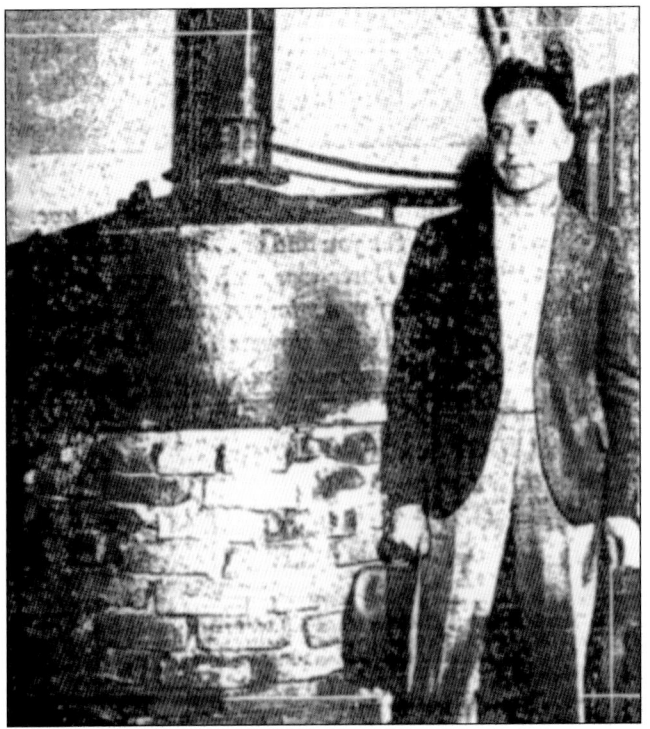

In May 1931, a 150-gallon still containing alcohol was located during a raid at 423 Josefa Street by the San Jose Police. Police chief Black and two of his detectives, W.C. Brown and Roy Farley, found the still in full operation, neatly arranged in the basement of the residence. Pictured here standing next to the seized still is the owner and operator, John Monte. (Courtesy of the San Jose Public Library.)

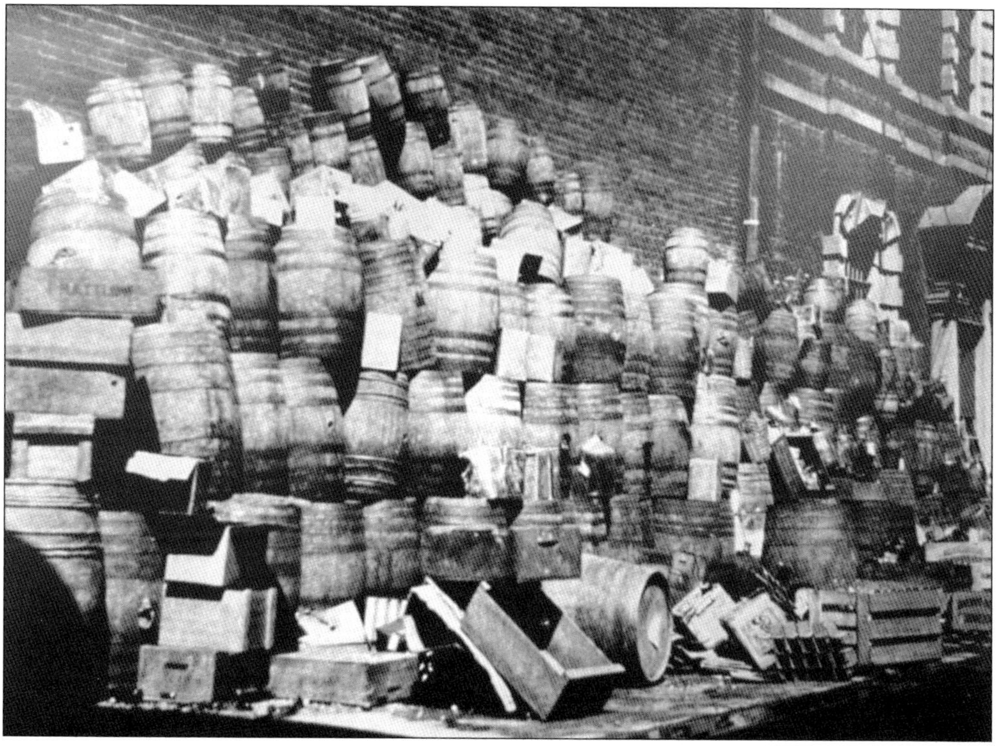

On March 25, 1929, Sheriff Lyle orchestrated a dramatic display of enforcement against bootlegging activities in San Jose. Over the course of two years, Sheriff Lyle and his deputies had conducted numerous raids, seizing a significant quantity of assorted liquors valued at $250,000 in the underground economy. In a public demonstration of his commitment to combating bootlegging, Sheriff Lyle ordered the dumping of 50,000 gallons of the confiscated liquor. This spectacle was intended to be a visible manifestation of law enforcement action against the illegal alcohol trade. By publicly disposing of the seized liquor, Sheriff Lyle aimed to address concerns raised by the public and the press regarding the effectiveness of his enforcement efforts. The dramatic act underscored the authorities' determination to crack down on bootlegging. (Above, courtesy of the Santa Clara County Archives; below, courtesy of the San Jose Police Historical Archives.)

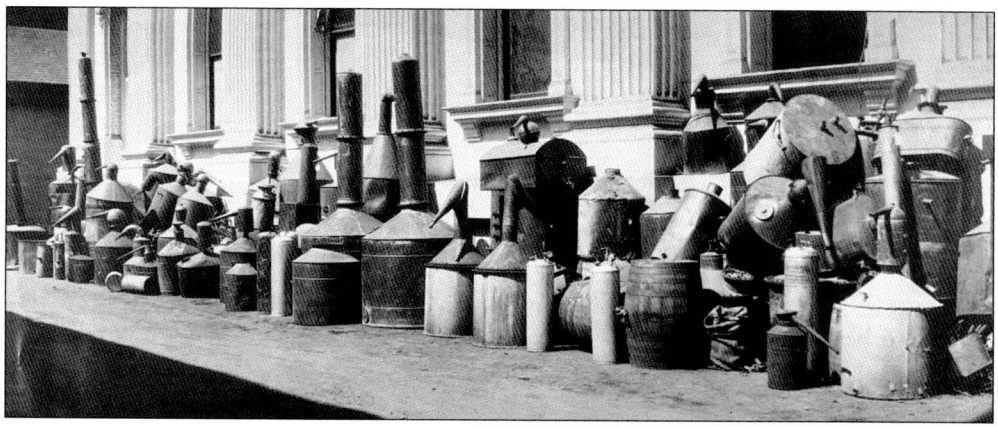

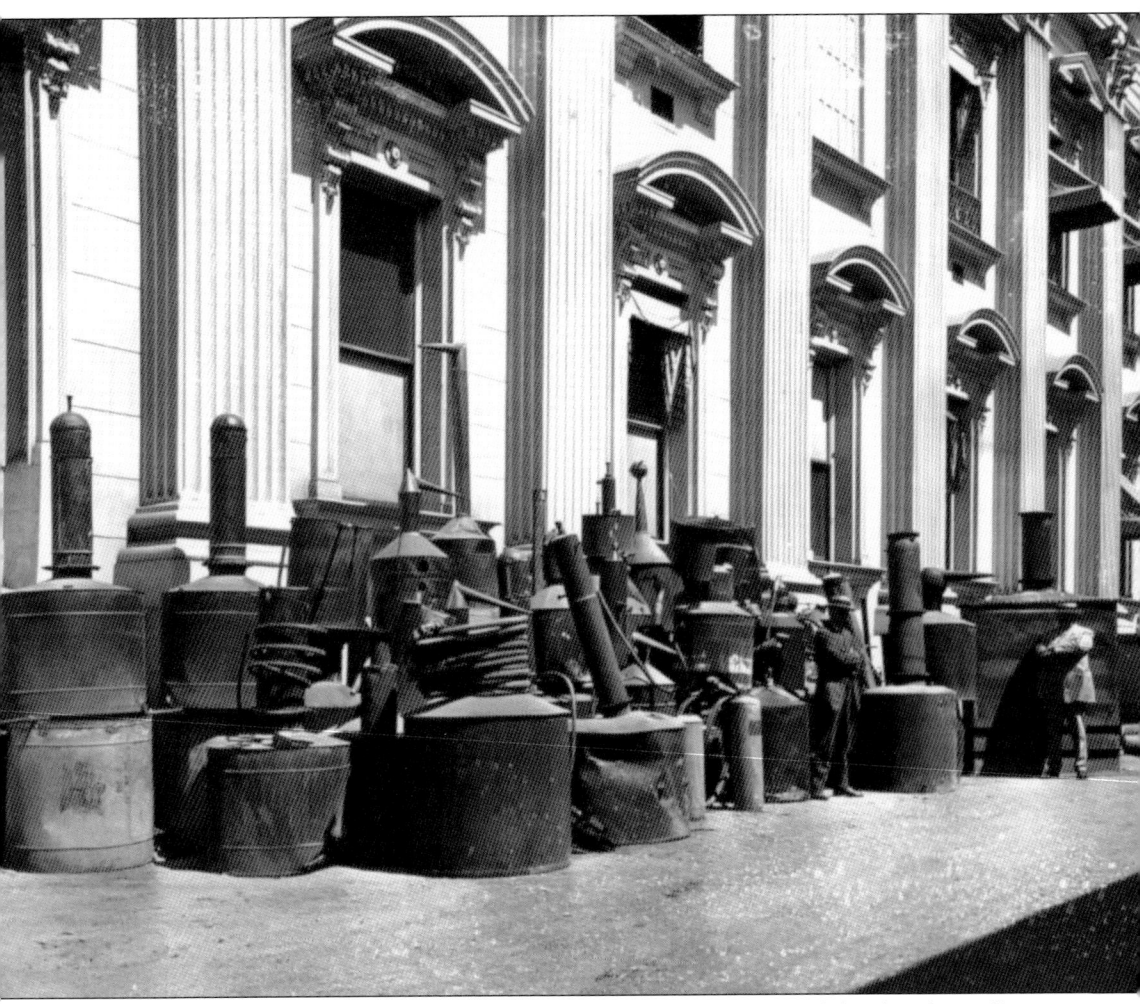

In a coordinated raid involving 40 volunteer citizens, deputies, and local police officers, a significant quantity of illegal stills and liquor was discovered and seized. The operation led to the arrest of 15 individuals involved in bootlegging activities. Sheriff Lyle, accompanied by one of his deputies, stood amidst the courtyard of the sheriff's office behind the courthouse, surrounded by the confiscated stills of various sizes, types, and descriptions. Following the raid, thousands of gallons of alcohol and mash were destroyed, symbolizing a decisive blow against the illicit alcohol trade in the region. The next day's newspaper headline read, "Once Bubbled Merrily, Now Still." (Courtesy of the Santa Clara County Archives.)

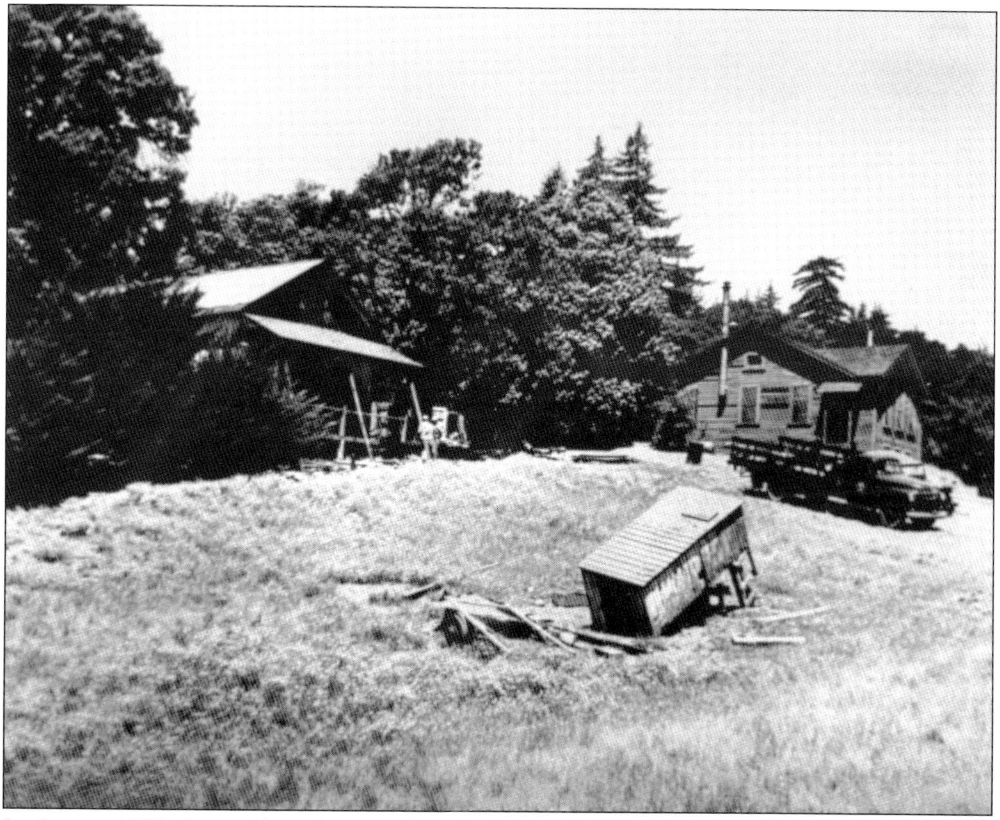

In August 1927, Santa Clara County sheriff's deputies raided the M.J. Terra ranch on Murphy Avenue. A still and other equipment were found. Valued at $10,000, seven large containers of about 2,000-gallon capacity were located in the building. Six of the containers were filled to the top with mash ready for distillation, and the seventh was used to hold the liquid for the mash before it was distilled. Three suspects were taken by surprise and arrested without any resistance. Pictured here is the Terra ranch and a picture of Deputy John Gibbes dismantling the still made with the most modern equipment at that time. (Both, courtesy of History San Jose.)

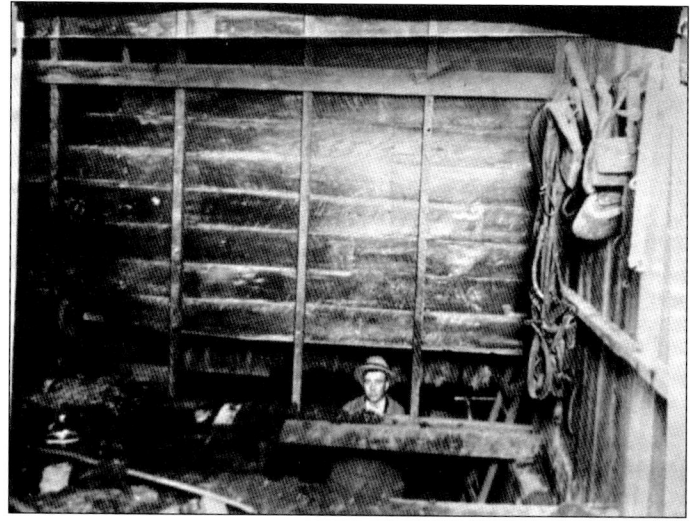

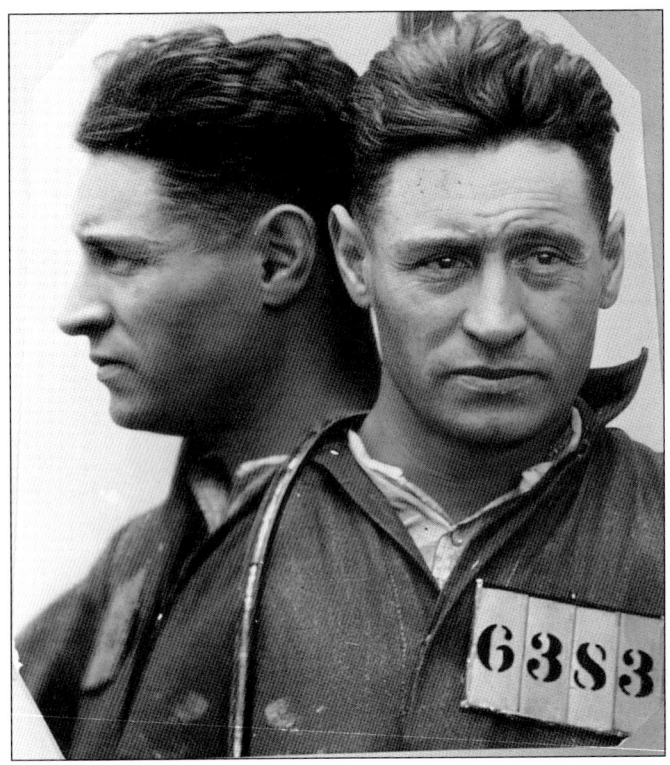

One of the three men arrested at the Terra ranch raid was John Kern (pictured here). A welder by trade, he used his craft to help assemble the stills. He was one of the first arrests in the county under the Jones Act, a new state law which made making or operating a still a felony with a mandatory prison sentence of one to five years. (Courtesy of the Santa Clara County Archives.)

The second of the three arrests was Louis Pietra, a boilermaker by trade who was working the still at the time of the raid at the Terra ranch. He was also convicted under the new Jones Act and was sentenced to serve two-and-a-half years at San Quentin Prison. (Courtesy of the Santa Clara County Archives.)

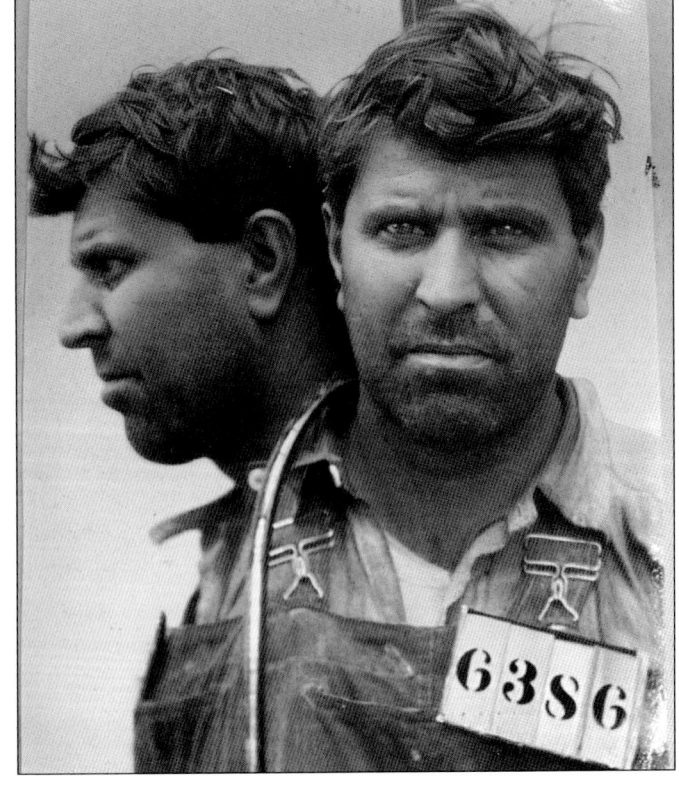

The third person arrested at the Terra ranch was Basil Peiccini, an auto mechanic from San Francisco. Peiccini, Pietra, and Kern were arrested together under the new Jones Act, which was only passed a couple of months prior to their arrest. (Courtesy of the Santa Clara County Archives.)

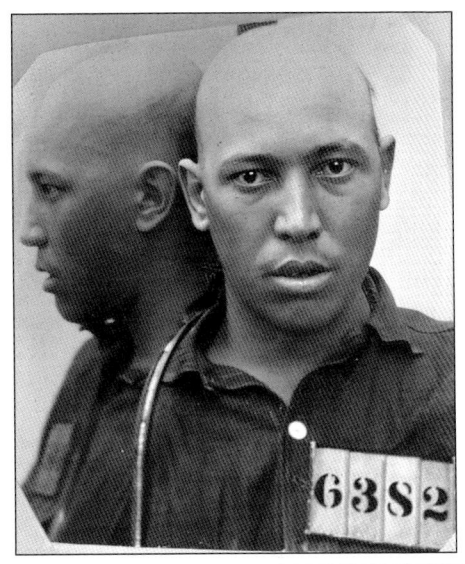

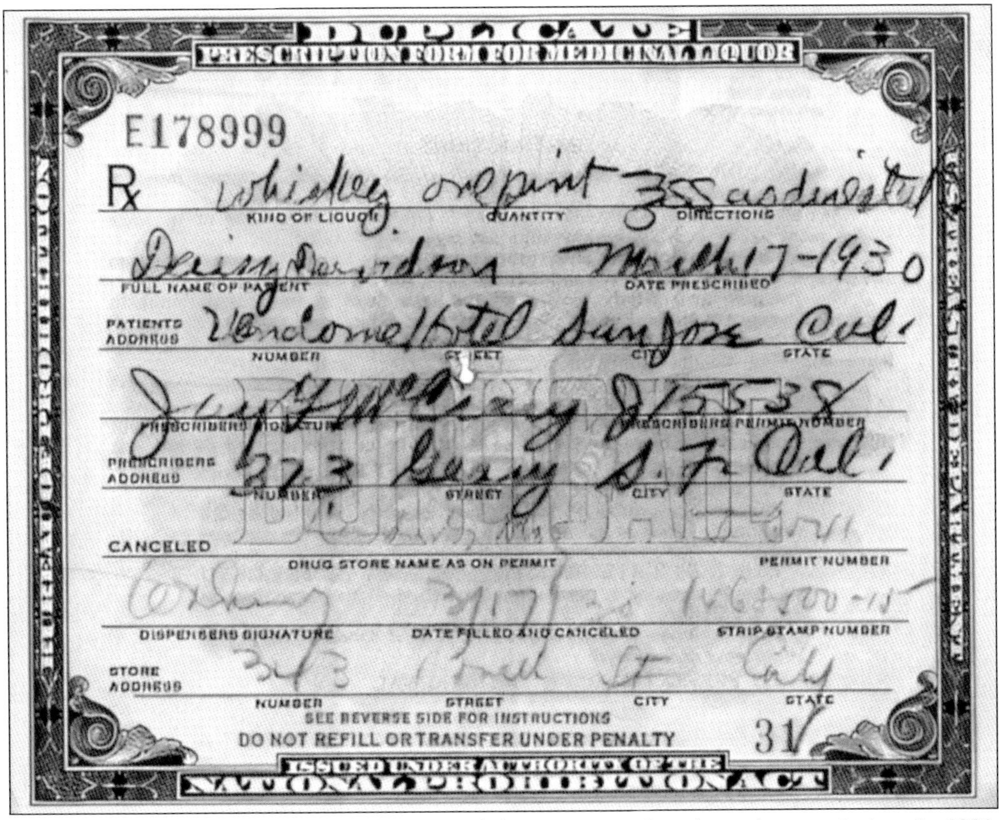

One way to obtain alcohol legally during Prohibition was with a doctor's prescription. In 1921, San Jose was exhausting its supply of medicinal whiskey. A new Prohibition enforcement officer was hired to check up on past prescription records before releasing any more prescribed whiskey. This prescription for medicinal whiskey was written for a San Jose resident by a doctor in San Francisco—probably to avoid San Jose's new Prohibition enforcement officer. (Courtesy of History San Jose.)

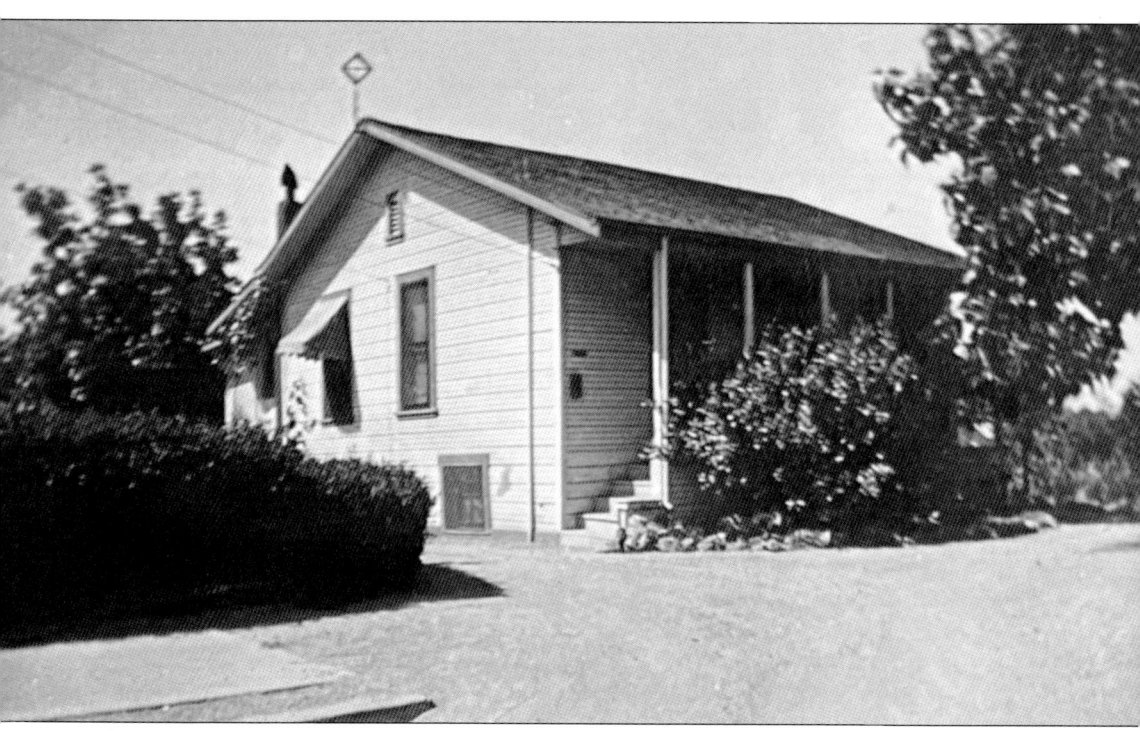

The house at 317 Lenzen Avenue, owned by the Celli family, was not uncovered through a planned raid but rather by accident. In 1929, a still explosion in the garage led to a fire, prompting an investigation by officers. As they searched the premises to determine the cause of the explosion and fire, they stumbled upon evidence of illicit alcohol production. Among the findings were the remnants of a small still, indicating the presence of illegal distillation activities. Additionally, officers discovered several hundred gallons of mash and wine stored in the basement of the house. (Courtesy of Dave and Christina Anaya.)

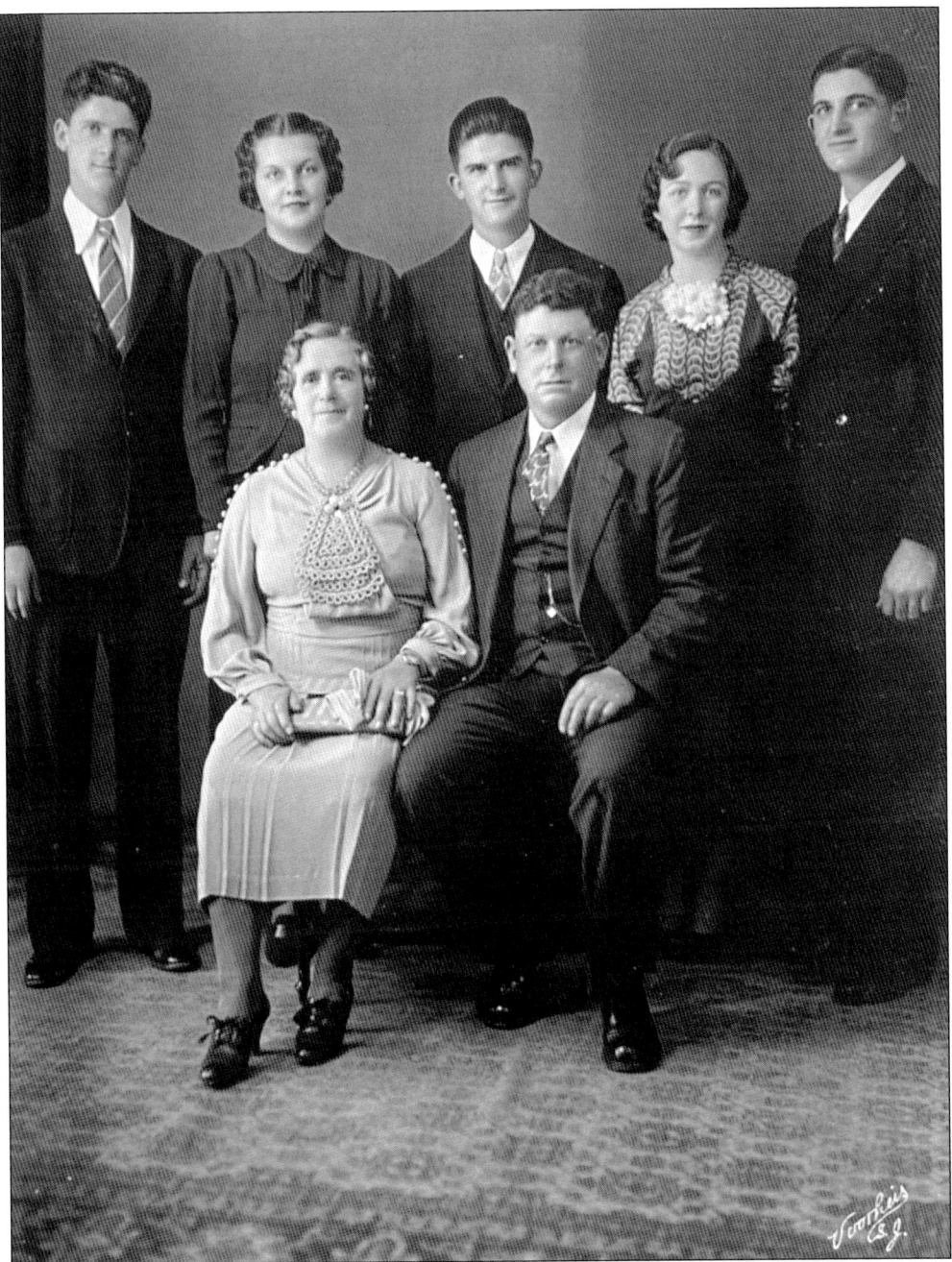

The person responsible for the stills, mash, and wine was Dante Celli. Dante was found to be San Jose's youngest bootlegger at the age of 16. Dante was 18 years old at the time of the explosion. Dante's father, Virgilio Celli, claimed responsibility and took the rap for his son. Virgilio was arrested and taken to the police department, where he was interviewed by police chief Black. Dante is pictured here (standing, far left) with the rest of the Celli family, including Virgilio Celli (seated). (Courtesy of Dave and Christina Anaya.)

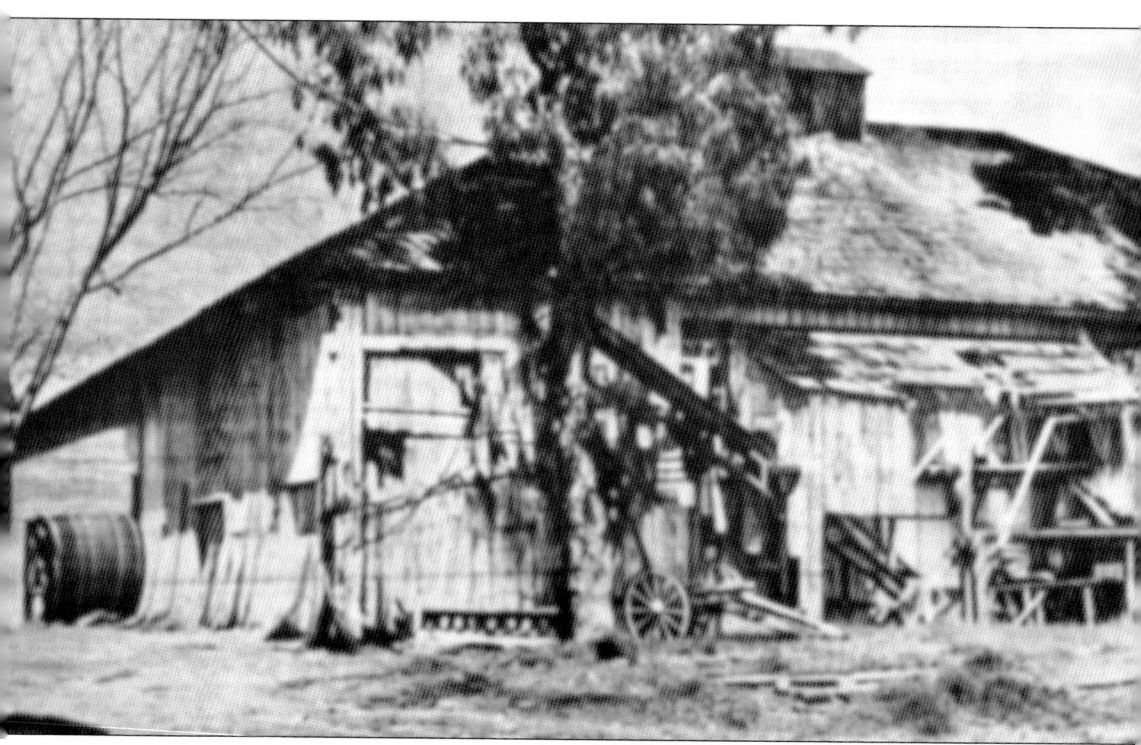

In March 1932, this large barn in the Robertsville District on Dent Avenue west of Almaden Road was raided by sheriff's deputies and federal Prohibition agents. During the raid, the still operators attempted to run away through the orchards. They stopped running after officers shot their guns above the fleeing still operators' heads. The barn had a four-story-high column running up from the still and was one of the largest ever seized at the time in Santa Clara County. The still was in a subcellar beneath the barn. The still was running full blast at the time of the raid and could produce about 1,000 gallons of alcohol per day. (Courtesy of Tony Gairnese.)

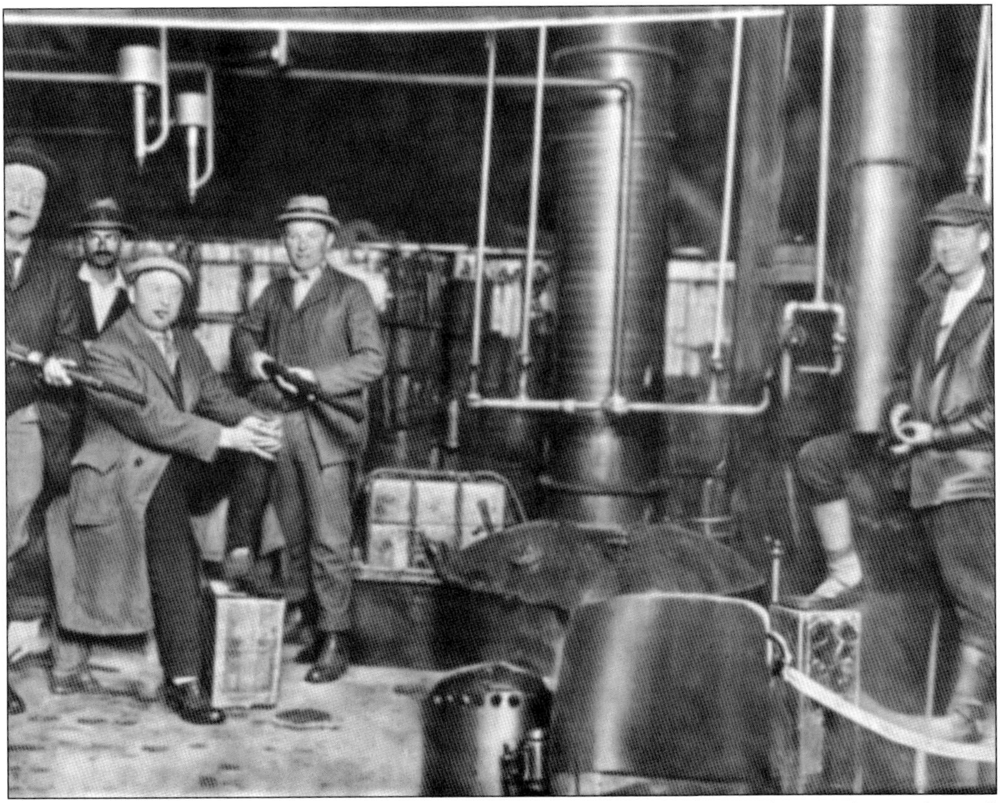

Santa Clara sheriff's deputies pose with portion of stills seized from a liquor plant. The still occupied both stories of a two-story barn in the hills just outside of San Jose. The federal inspector pronounced it the largest still seized in California at the time. In this picture are, from left to right, Special Deputy Sidney Minns, Deputy Sheriff George Pyne, Deputy Sheriff Ben Torres, Special Deputy C.B. Weast, and unidentified. (Courtesy of the Santa Clara County Archives.)

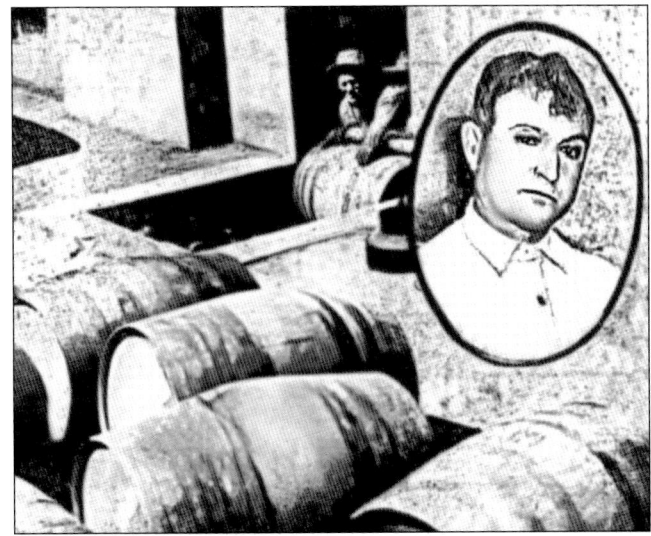

Rocco Mazzone operated a bootleg resort at a ranch on Hamilton Avenue. In July 1938, following a tip suggesting the establishment was serving as a wholesale supply storehouse, Sheriff Lyle dispatched agents to investigate. Agents raided the ranch and seized 2,000 gallons of whiskey and wine from the premises. Rocco Mazzone was arrested and booked into the county jail, marking a bust in the efforts to combat bootlegging operations. (Courtesy of the San Jose Public Library.)

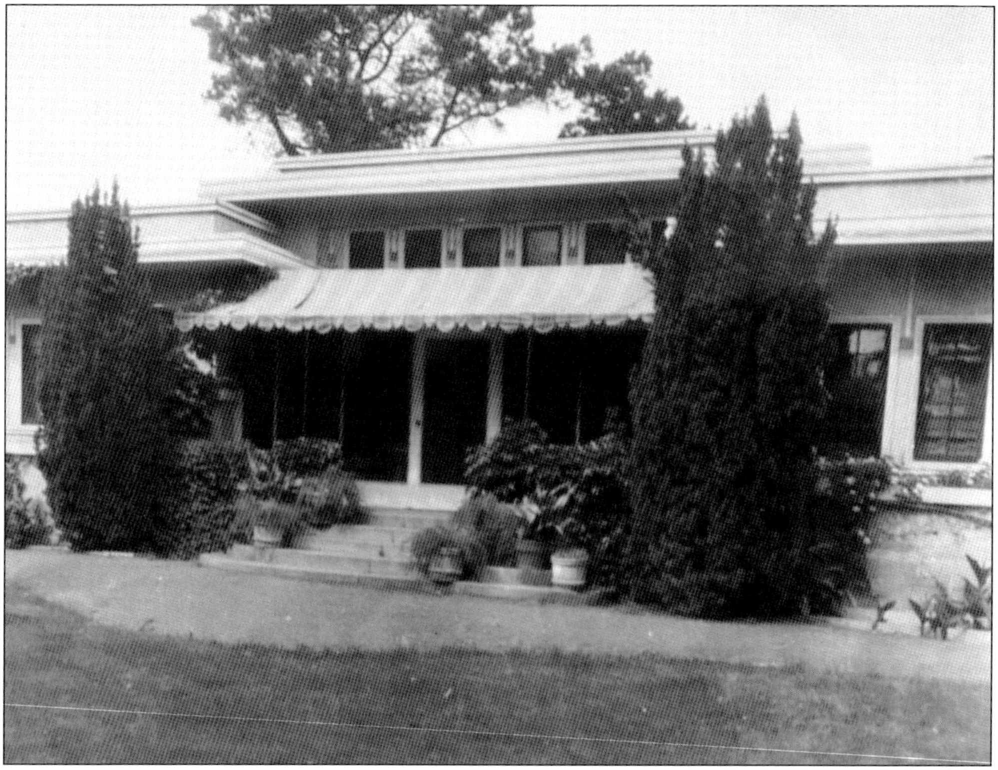

In 1932, Prohibition agents raided the ranch behind bootlegger and resort owner Dave Holt's residence. They located a still that was not in operation, dismantled and stored in several buildings. Also found was an outfit for making gin with counterfeit labels, numerous five-gallon cans of alcohol, and one hundred gallons of whiskey with an electrical aging device. A hundred gallons of sherry were found in the basement. Dave Holt and an employee of his, Peter Fox, were arrested. (Courtesy of Linda Hancock.)

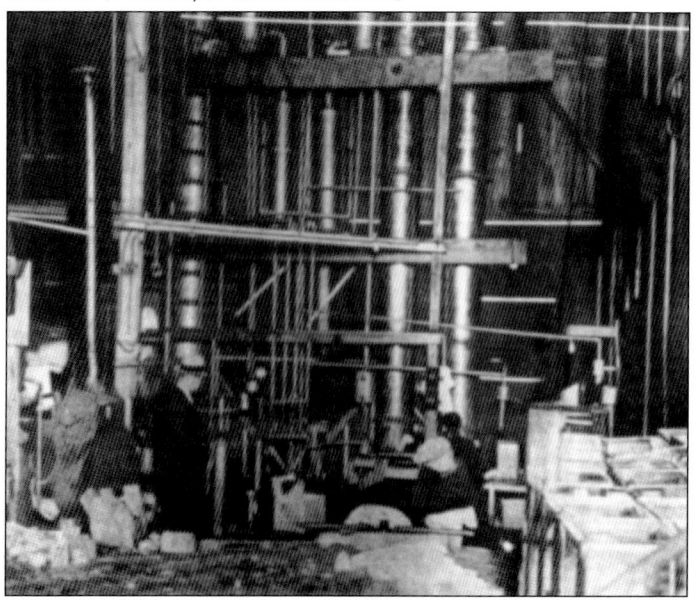

This liquor distillery was raided by federal Prohibition officers in February 1932 at the Thomas Porten ranch. The distillery consisted of a 750-gallon still with a boiler and a three-column condensing system. Three hundred gallons of alcohol were ready to ship along the Pacific coast. Raiding officers stated that it was one of the finest-constructed stills they had ever seen and declared that the alcohol found was the purest commercial variety. (Courtesy of Tony Gairnese.)

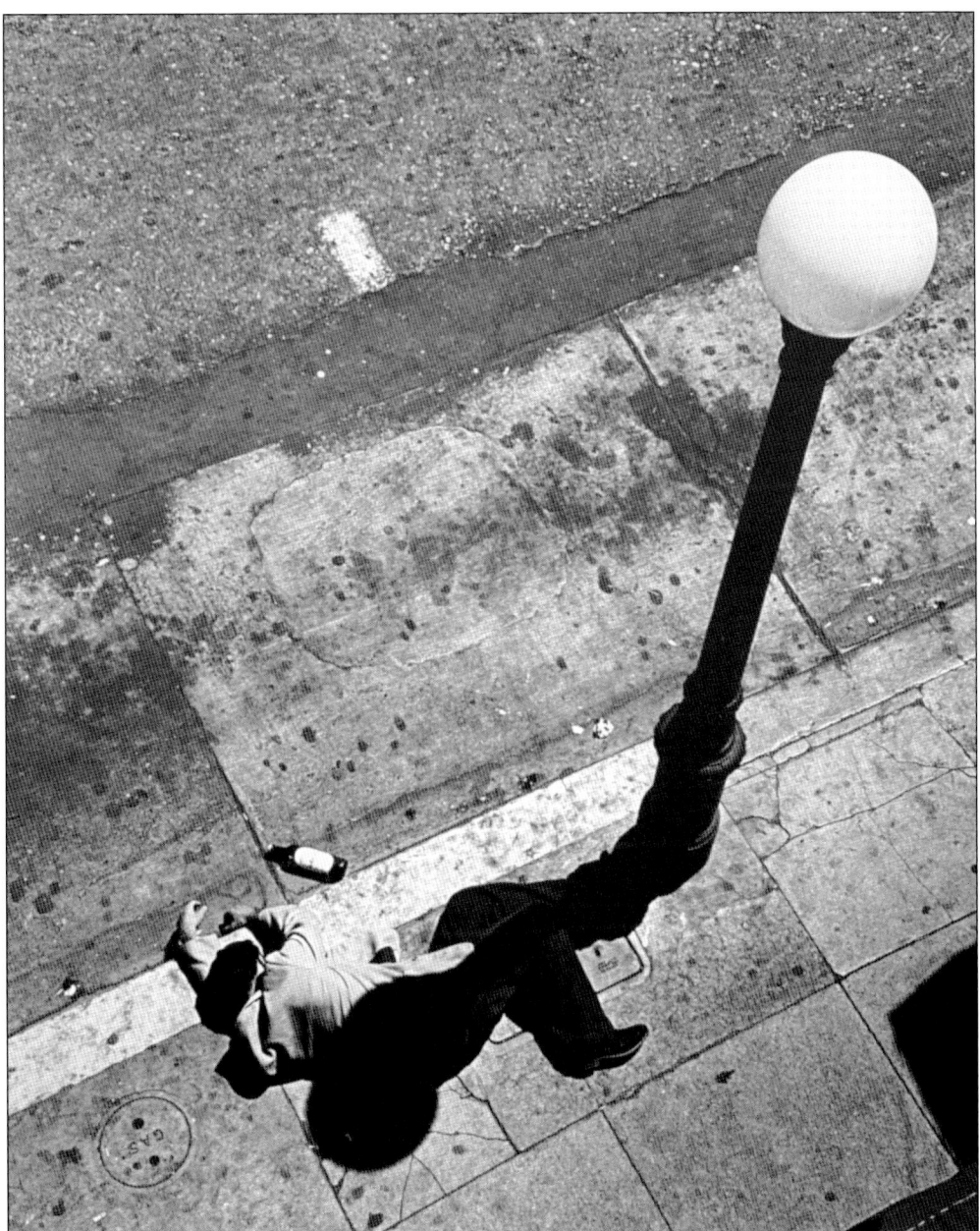

Even with all the raids, after a year into Prohibition, the effects of alcohol got worse than before Prohibition. The number of public drunkenness cases increased, with a 100 percent increase in drunkenness and vagrancy in 1921. According to the statistics, 305 drunks were arrested in 1921, as opposed to 147 in 1920. For vagrancy, there were 375 arrests in 1921, as opposed to 177 in 1920. Pictured here is a passed-out drunkard on Post Street in downtown San Jose. Post Street was historically known and had a reputation for its alcohol and vice crimes. (Courtesy of the Santa Clara County Archives.)

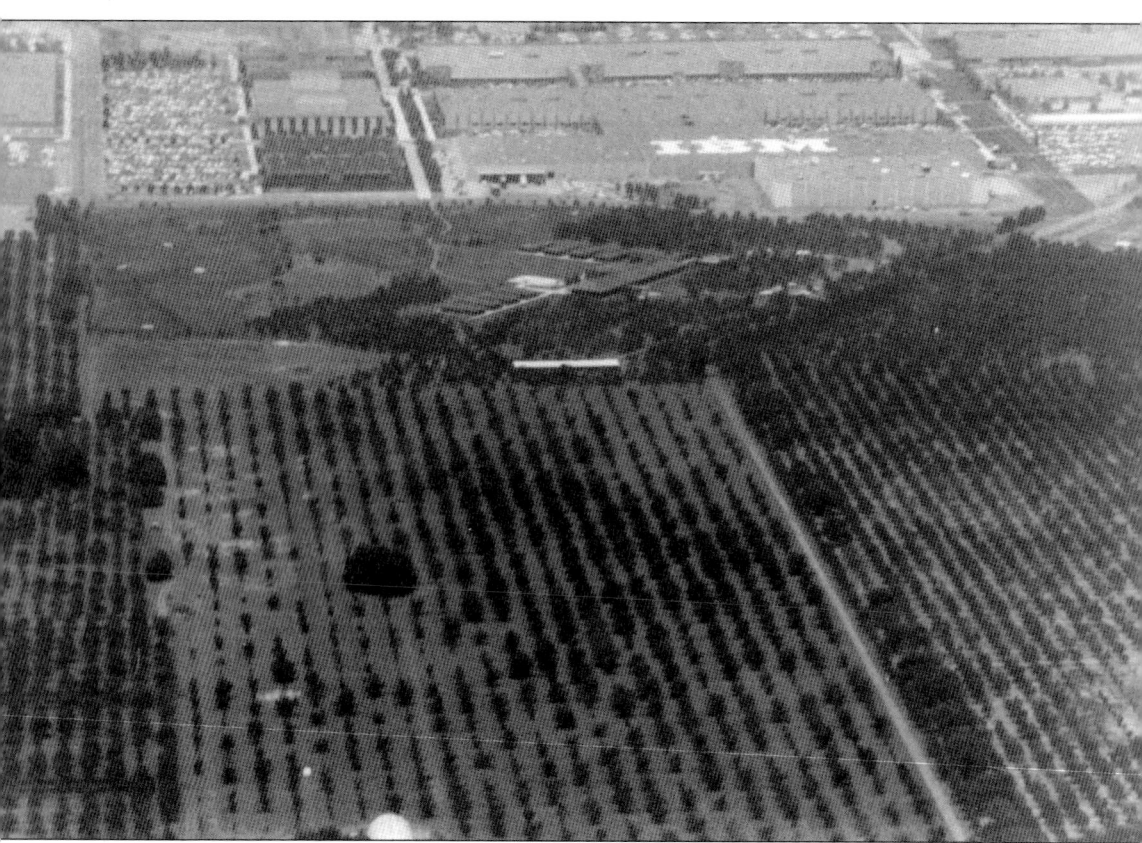

In 1924, Prohibition agents discovered an old-fashioned Kentucky-style moonshine still on a ranch on Cottle Road. Internal Revenue agents who inspected the still found it to be identical to the type of stills found in Kentucky and Tennessee. Ranch owner John Wurtsbaugh was accused of making the same type of corn whiskey and supplying most of the bootleggers in San Jose and Gilroy. (Courtesy of History San Jose.)

Four

Cops and Bootleggers

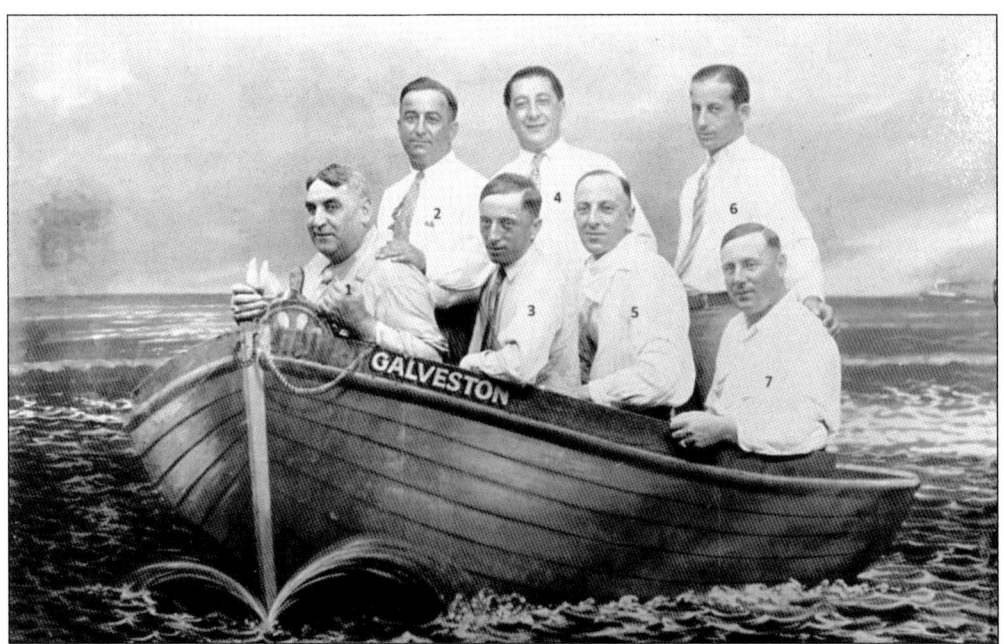

San Jose had its share of bootleggers and speakeasy operators during Prohibition, ranging from small-scale operations to larger enterprises involved in various illicit activities such as gambling, prostitution, and large-scale distribution of illegal alcohol. One notable family in San Jose not only ran speakeasies and stills but also operated the largest rum-running operation, transporting Canadian whiskey along the entire West Coast. In this photograph, some of San Jose's prominent speakeasy and still operators are depicted, including 1. Clarence "Chick" Leddy, 2. Peter Locurto, 3. Frank Gairnese, 5. Joe Locurto, and 7. John Locurto. Also present are 6. Tony Locurto (John Locurto's son) and 4. an unidentified individual. (Courtesy of Darlene Bursch.)

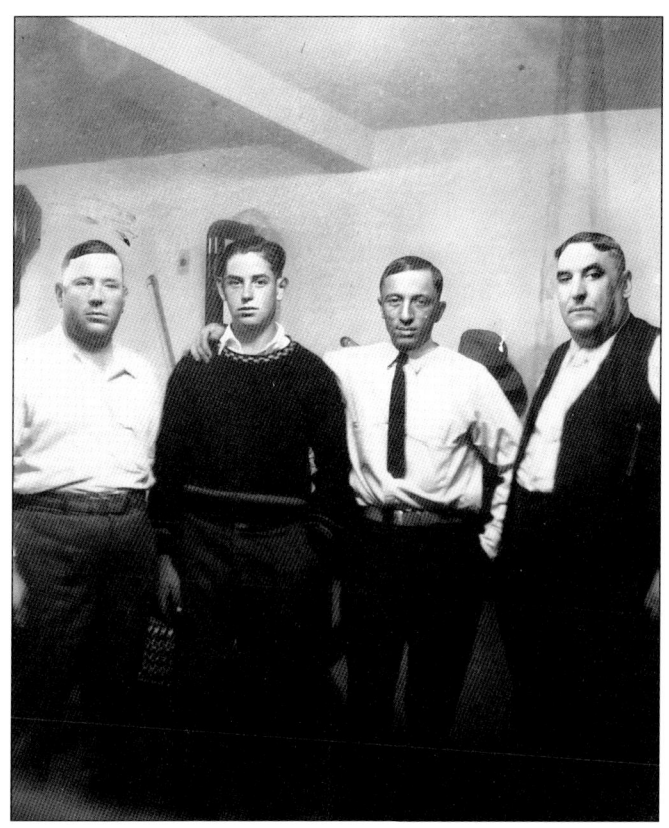

John Locurto, Frank Gairnese, and Clarence Leddy collaborated in various bootlegging operations, with Gairnese being married to Locurto's sister, establishing a familial connection between them. However, their partnership fractured when Leddy was arrested for murder and subsequently sentenced to life in San Quentin State Prison in 1928. In this photograph, from left to right, are John Locurto, an unidentified individual, Frank Gairnese, and Clarence Leddy. (Courtesy of Tony Gairnese.)

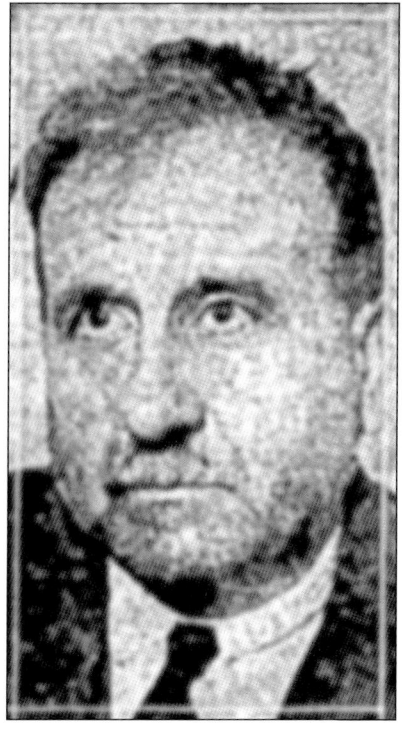

Tony Dillio, proprietor of Tony's Chicken Shack, was a familiar figure in the local courts. Since being arrested multiple times for possession of liquor, he was ordered to pay a $500 fine. Dillio was unable to pay and instead chose to spend 67 days in jail. As the justice court lacked the power to impose consecutive sentences, the first 60 days of the 67-day sentence ran concurrently with another two-month term. (Courtesy of the San Jose Public Library.)

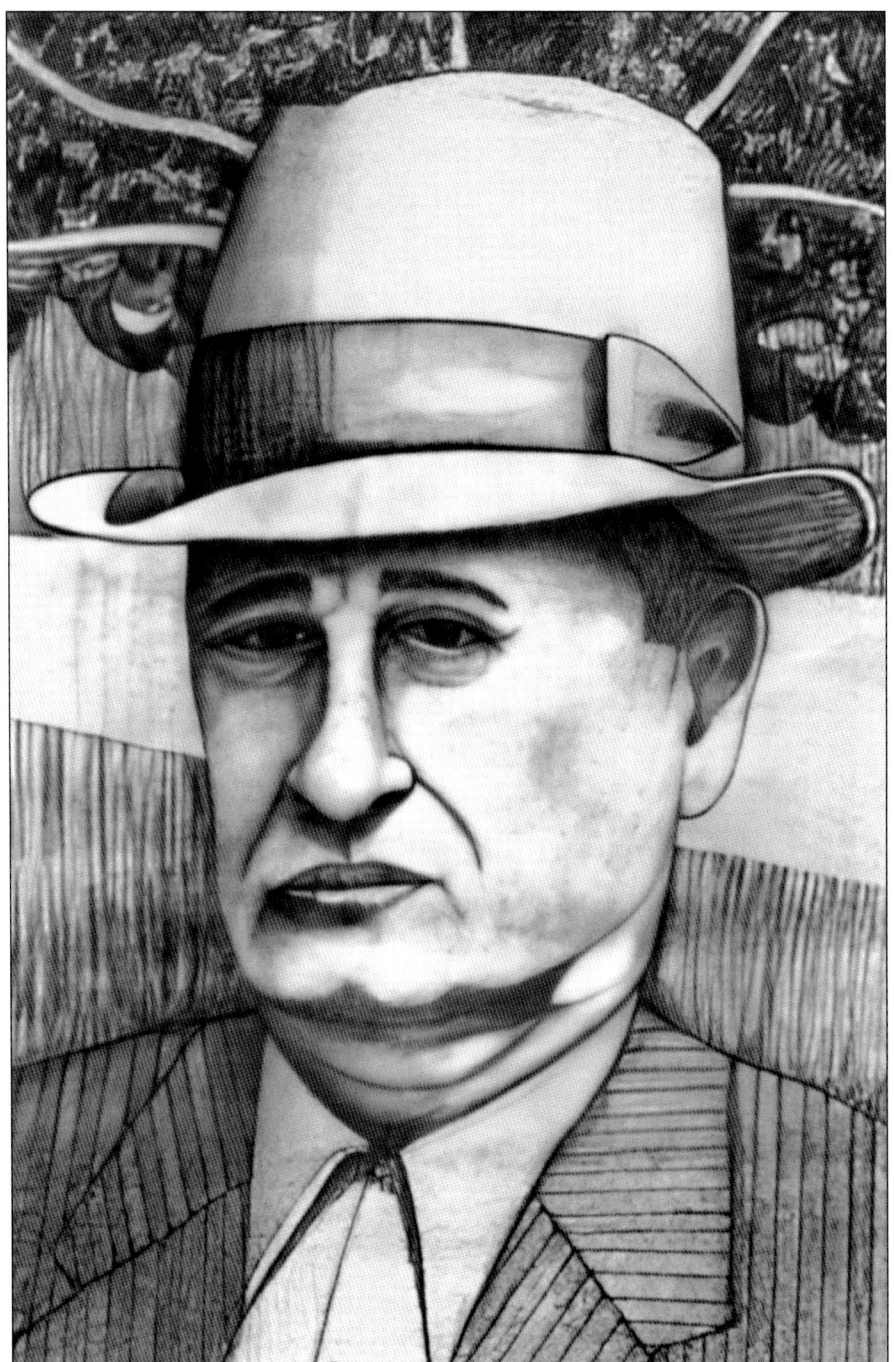

William Fenerin, also known as "Billy Finley," operated Finley's Inn. Fenerin was arrested multiple times for alcohol. During a raid in 1922, large amounts of liquor were seized by Prohibition agents. At first, Fenerin's bartender was arrested, but charges were dropped, and Fenerin was then charged. Just a month after the raid, Fenerin pleaded not guilty, and the case was transferred to federal court, where a heavier sentence would be imposed. (Courtesy of the former Waves Smoke House.)

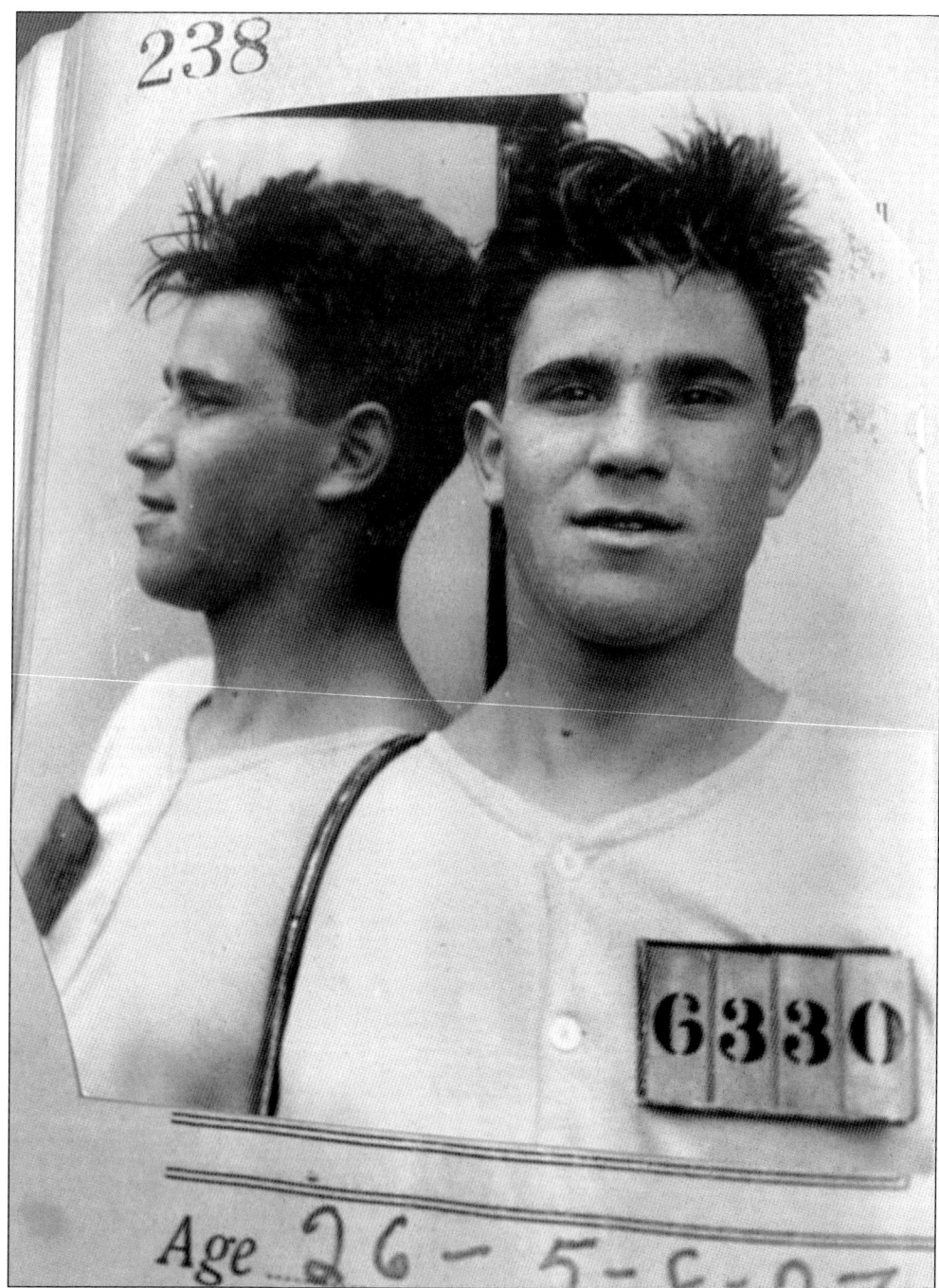

During a raid at the F. Passatino ranch near Coyote, Prohibition agents found a 500-gallon still outfitted for making jackass brandy. Operator Vito Sevino was present during the raid. He stated the still was his, but the alcohol was used to spray the trees for bugs and not for drinking. Sevino had never filed for citizenship and was later deported as an undesirable alien. (Courtesy of the Santa Clara County Archives.)

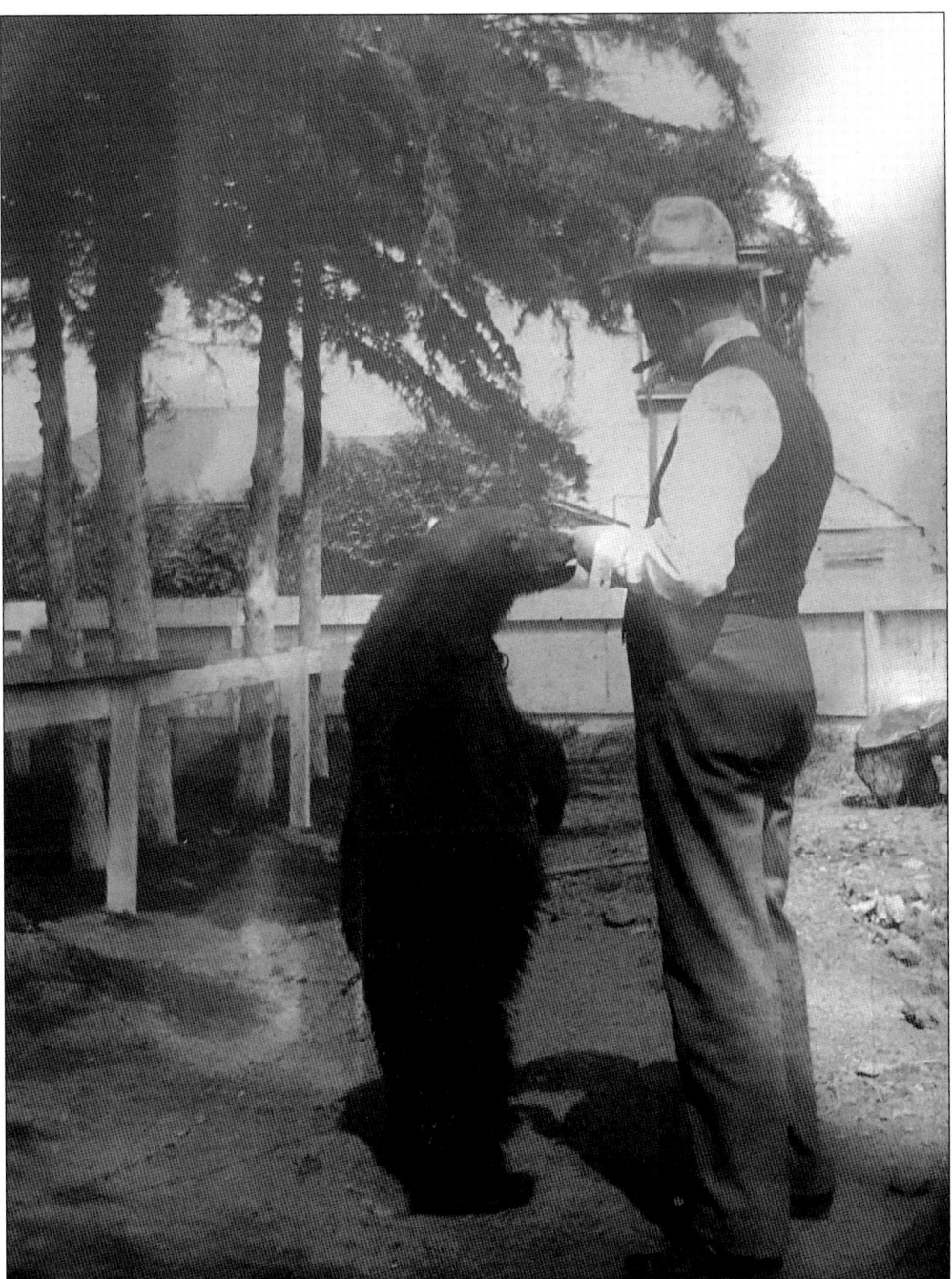
Dave Holt operated large manufacturing stills, including behind his Monterey Road residence, where a raid had found a large still, and a farm on Stone Avenue, where a 500-gallon still was found by Sheriff Emig and federal officers. This was a result of a tip of a five-ton truck with no license plate leaving Dave Holt's joint on Monterey Road and disappearing on Stone Avenue. This joint was the Palm Inn, which was considered San Jose's "high society" joint. After Prohibition, Dave Holt became the county's first licensed bail bondsman. Dave Holt is pictured here feeding a bear. (Courtesy of Linda Hancock.)

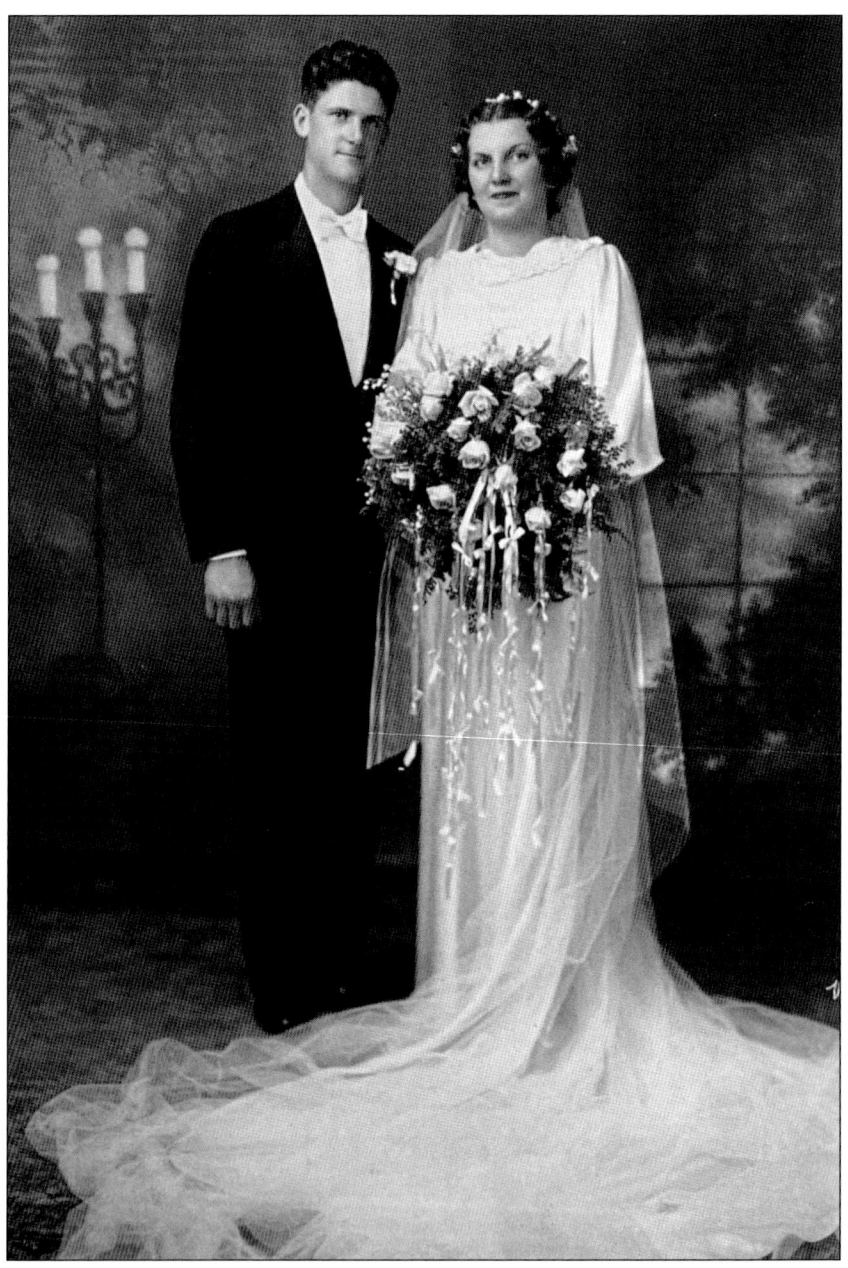

Dante Celli, born in 1911, showed a remarkable entrepreneurial spirit from a young age. By the time he was 16, he was already involved in the production of whiskey and wine, setting up his operation in the basement and garage of his parents' house at 317 Lenzen Avenue. His clientele was limited to a distributor in San Francisco, who would make monthly visits to purchase Celli's products. Celli's bootlegging venture proved to be highly lucrative, allowing him to afford a brand-new 1927 Hupmobile at a remarkably young age. He drove it to high school every day, comparable to a modern-day high school student driving a brand-new Corvette to school every day. However, Celli's illicit enterprise ended abruptly when his still exploded in the garage, leading to the discovery of his operation. Faced with the consequences, Celli promptly retired from the bootlegging business. (Courtesy of Dave and Christina Anaya.)

S. F. RUM SUPPLY AT ITS SOURCE

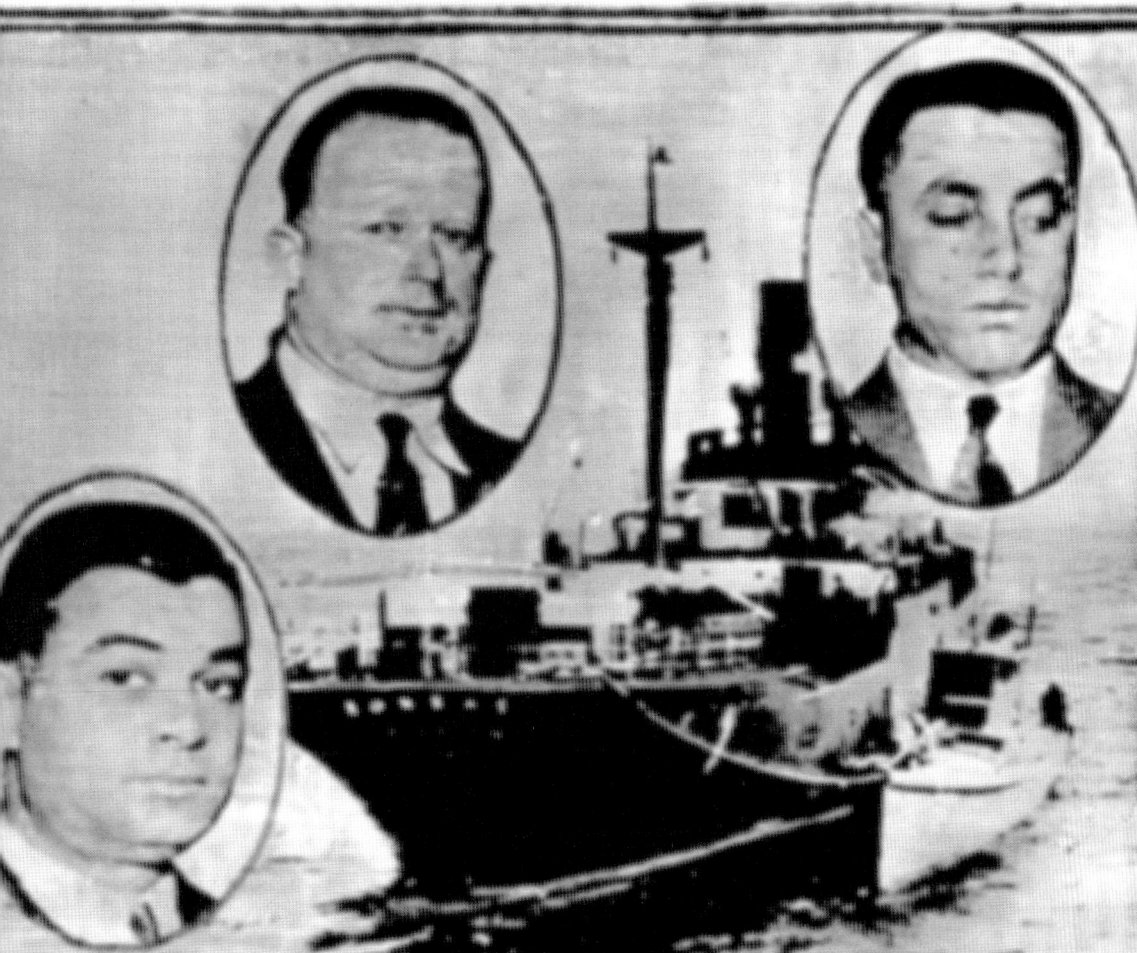

Peter Maggiore (lower left) and his brothers Harry and Quito operated roadhouses and stills in the San Jose area. They also ran the largest West Coast rum-running operation, smuggling Canadian whiskey from Canada all along the West Coast. This newspaper photograph is from the rum-running trial in November 1932 of Peter Maggiore, Harry Nelson (center), and John Marino (right). All three were charged with rum-running conspiracy. The testimony described several chases from Coast Guard cutters, one chase lasting from the Farallons down the coast to the Galapagos Islands. Many of the chases included gunfire being exchanged. Marino was considered the brains of the organization, and the Maggiore brothers were the freighters handling the liquor cargoes from Canada by land and sea. All three would be acquitted of the charges. (Courtesy of the San Jose Public Library.)

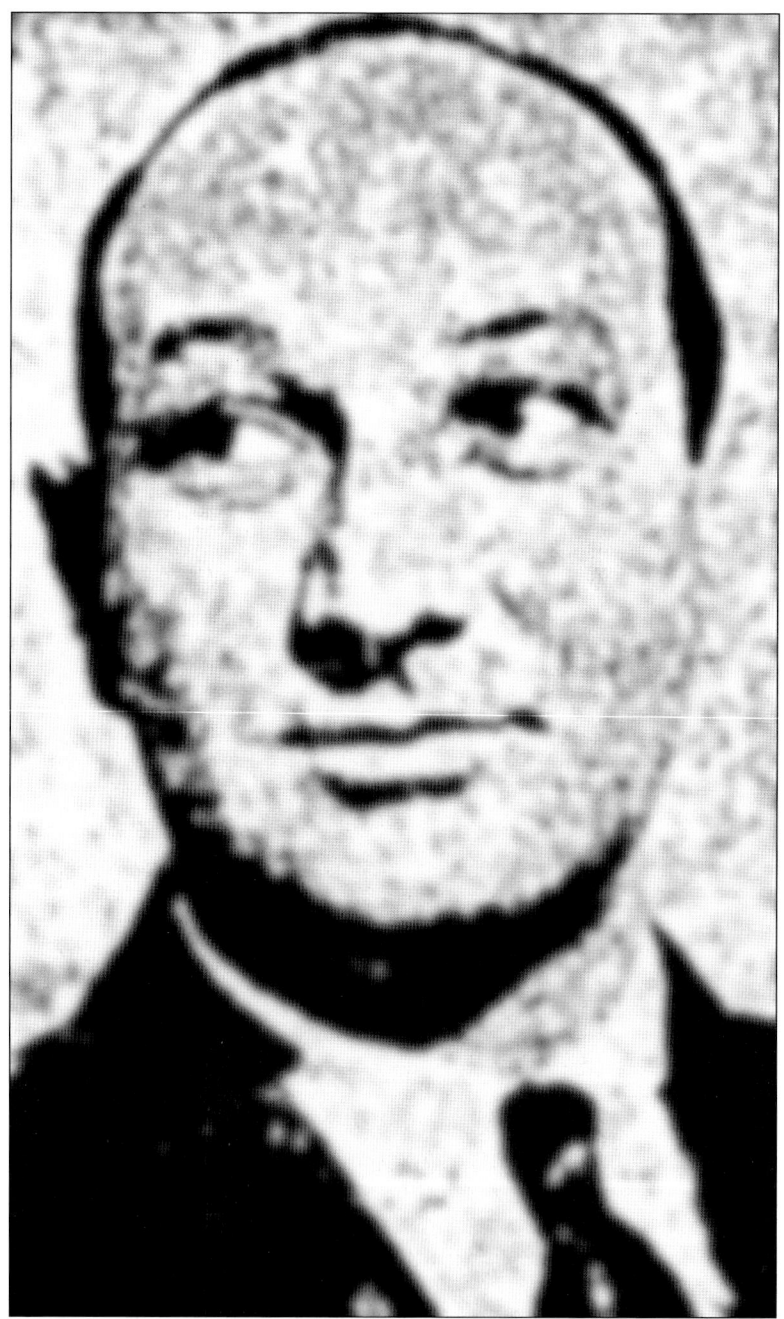

Quito Maggiore faced numerous legal troubles due to his involvement in bootlegging and rum-running operations. He and his father, V.D. Maggiore, were notably arrested for operating a massive 75,000-gallon still at the old Pacific Coast pickle factory on Monterey Road. Their illicit activities led to charges of conspiracy to violate the Internal Revenue law related to operating an illegal alcohol plant. In 1932, Quito Maggiore was charged with conspiracy once again, this time in connection with rum-running. However, he never faced trial for these charges. Tragically, a day before he was scheduled to appear in federal court for his arraignment on rum-running conspiracy charges, Quito died of a heart attack in his hotel room. (Courtesy of the San Jose Public Library.)

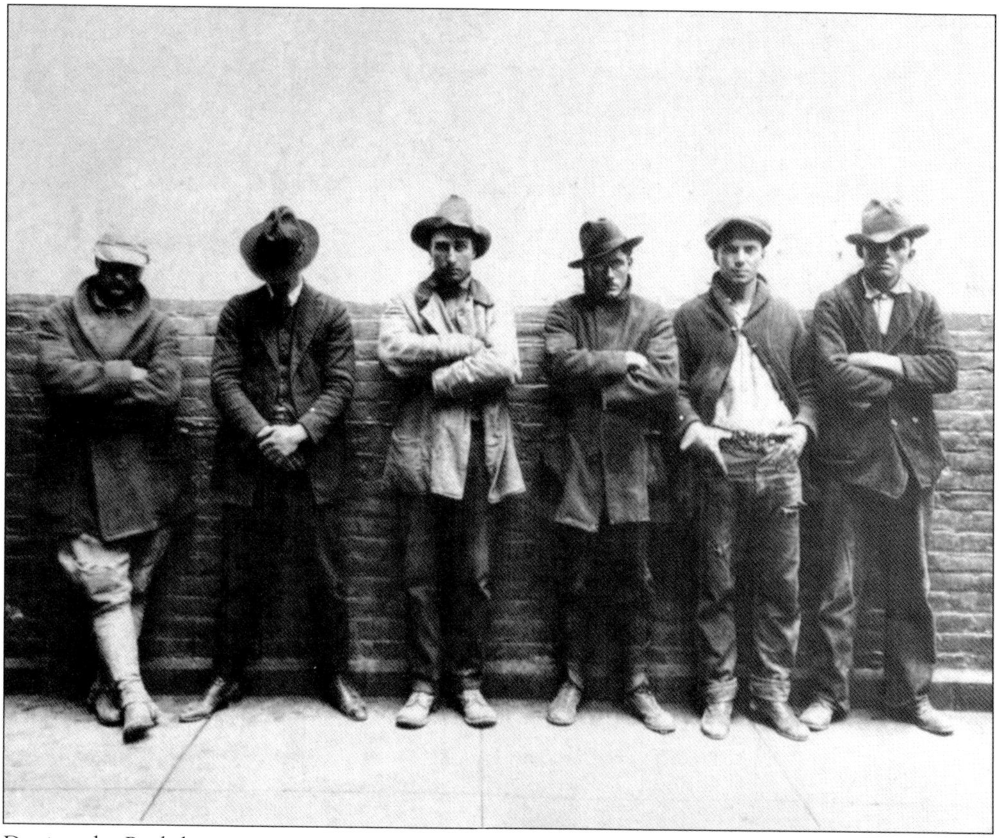

During the Prohibition era, many speakeasies and establishments serving illegal alcohol in downtown San Jose required protection from law enforcement, robbers, and extortionists. A group known as "the Market Street Boys" provided this protection. These unidentified men were instrumental in safeguarding the speakeasies and hotels serving alcohol on North Market Street in downtown San Jose, ensuring that the illicit activities could continue with some level of security and stability. (Courtesy of Ted Ramos.)

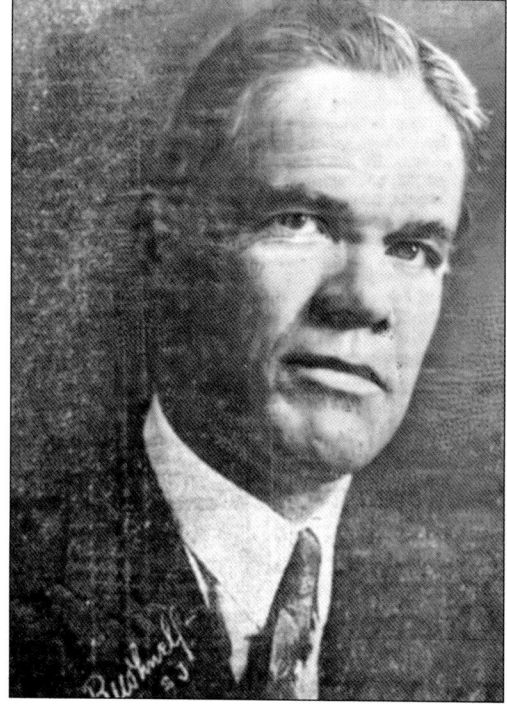

William Foley was one of the most reputable attorneys in the county during Prohibition. His client list included some of the area's most notorious bootleggers, including John Locurto during his many arrests for possession, sale, and manufacturing of alcohol, Clarence Leddy for his arrests for operating speakeasies and murder trial, and Harry Ferrari for his arrests for possession of alcohol, battery, and operating a house of prostitution and gambling. (Courtesy of the Santa Clara County Archives.)

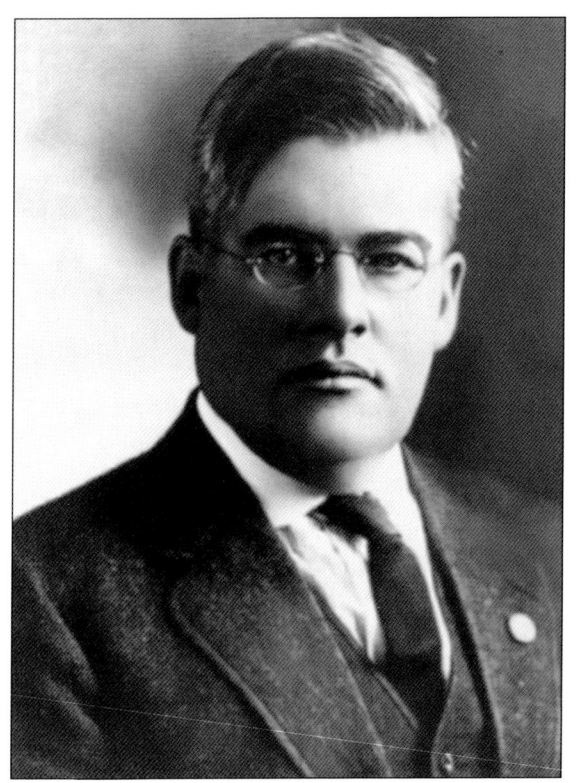

George Lyle was first voted in as sheriff of Santa Clara County in 1918, beating the incumbent sheriff. He and his deputies fought the bootleggers and still operators throughout Santa Clara County, including the unincorporated areas of San Jose. However, the public questioned Sheriff Lyle's efforts in combating the liquor laws. The local papers accused Lyle of aiding and protecting the bigger bootleggers like Clarence Leddy and John Locurto. A grand jury report contained criticism of Sheriff Lyle's enforcement of the Prohibition laws, spurring the Los Gatos Women's Christian Temperance Union and the newspaper to secure the recall of Sheriff Lyle. This pushed Sheriff Lyle to start the Santa Clara cleanup campaign, involving federal operatives and citizen constables to help. Pictured at left is newly elected Sheriff Lyle, and he is also pictured below (standing far left) with his deputies. (Both, courtesy of the Santa Clara County Archives.)

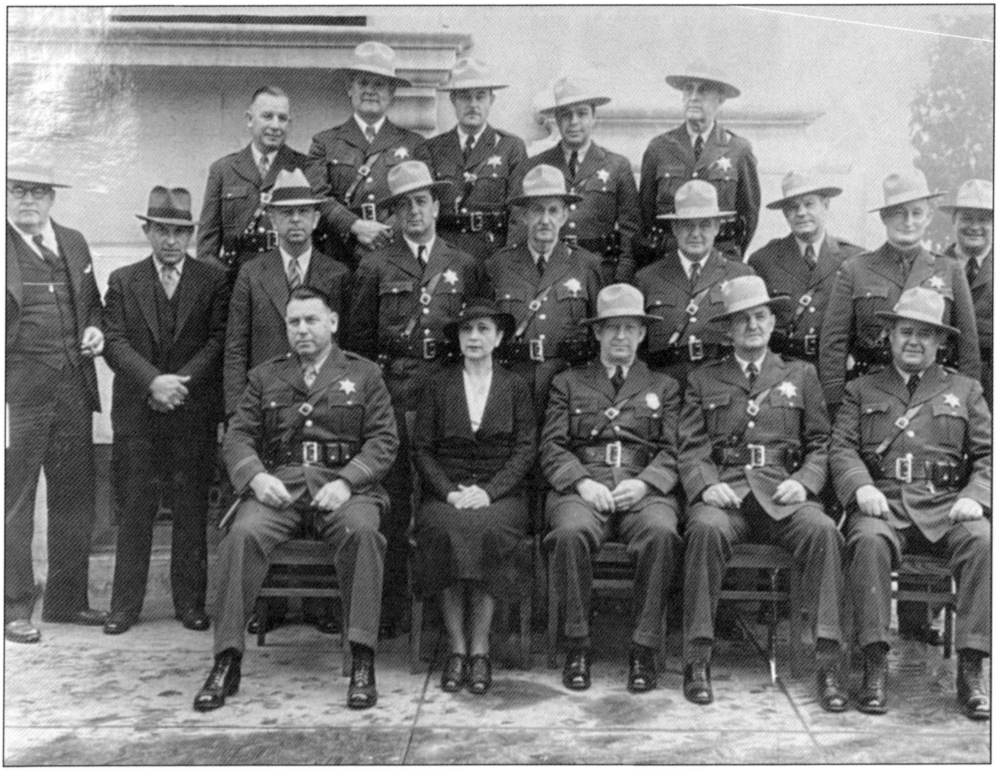

Sheriff Lyle lost re-election in 1930 to William Emig. Lyle would win back his position as sheriff in 1934 from Sheriff Emig, only to lose again to Sheriff Emig in 1938 and 1942. Pictured here is one of his many re-election campaign headquarters. (Courtesy of History San Jose.)

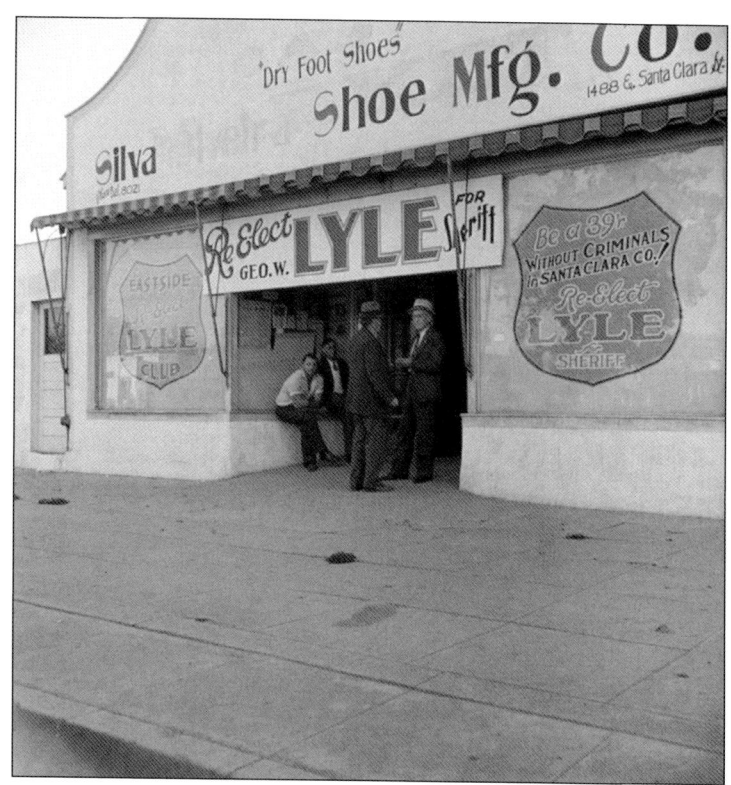

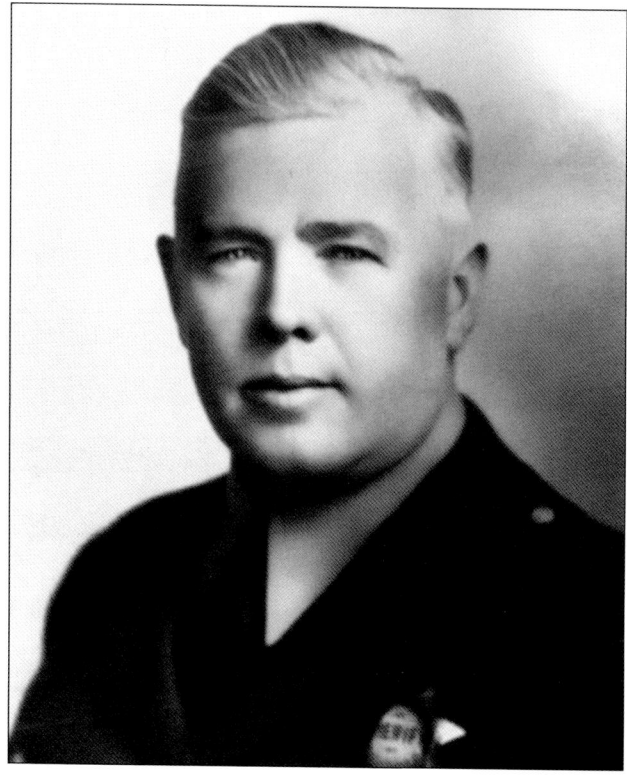

Sheriff William J. Emig was elected to office in 1930–1934 and 1938–1946. He started his career in 1920 with the Santa Clara Police Department. In 1922, he became a motorcycle officer with the San Jose Police Department. In 1930, Emig ran for sheriff on the Independent ticket and won, beating incumbent George Lyle, who was considered controversial due to his lack of action against the speakeasies and bootleggers. (Courtesy of the Santa Clara County Archives.)

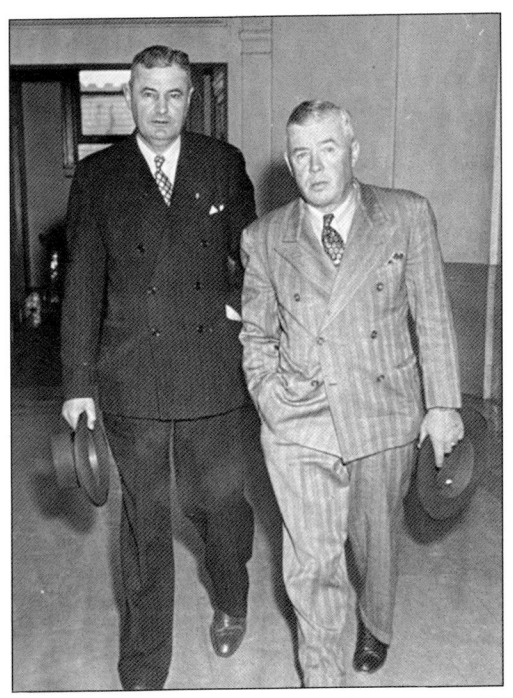

Sheriff Emig had his hands full. One deputy was killed by a bootlegger, and a couple of years later, the son of a popular department store owner was kidnapped and murdered. Emig lost re-election to former sheriff Lyle but won back his position from Lyle. Sheriff Emig resigned in 1946 when he was convicted of violating gambling conspiracy laws. Undersheriff Thomas G. Graham (left) is seen here escorting Sheriff Emig (right) to the Santa Clara County Jail. (Courtesy of Ted Ramos.)

John Newton Black was appointed chief of police for the San Jose Police Department in 1916. He complained about the lack of manpower and resources in combating Prohibition laws. This was brought up during a 1926 grand jury investigation regarding the number of speakeasies and roadhouses within San Jose and the county of Santa Clara. The grand jury came out with a report in 1928 regarding its findings and suggestions to help Chief Black. (Courtesy of the Santa Clara County Archives.)

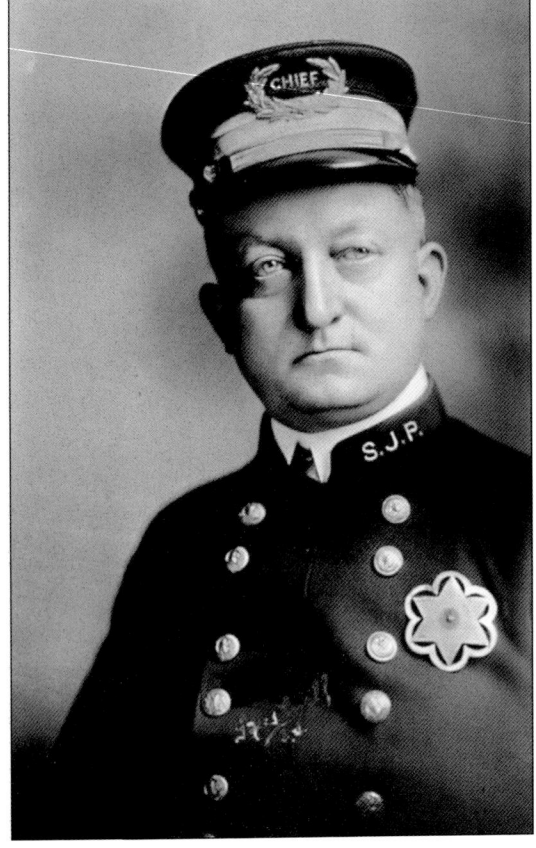

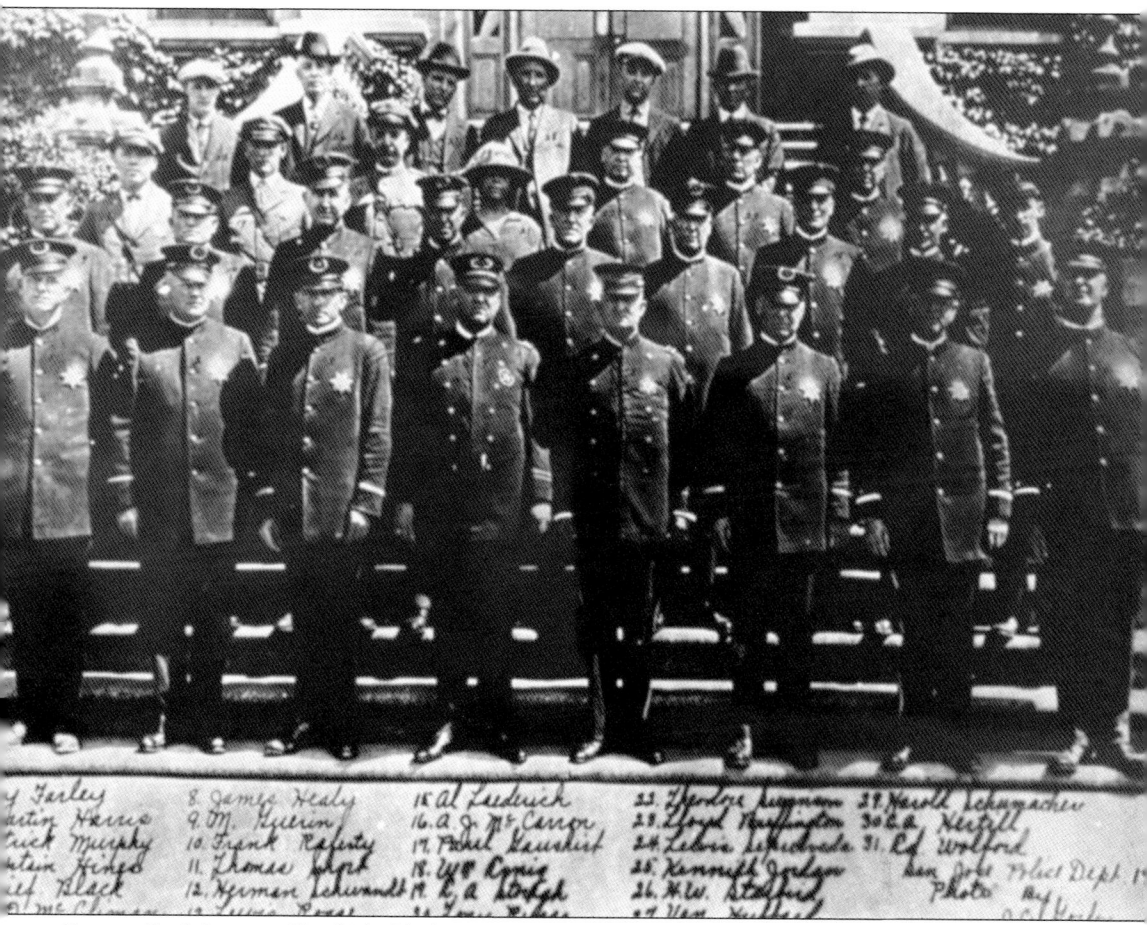

During Prohibition, Chief Black's largest issues were "blind pigs" (a Prohibition-day term for an illegal drinking place, also known as a speakeasy or roadhouse) and illegal Chinese lotteries. While claiming that the public intoxication stats were down, the number of blind pigs continued to flourish. Chief Black trained his men to combat the blind pigs. This picture depicts Chief Black (first row, fourth from right) and his police force. Some of the officers pictured here were part of most of the raids on the speakeasies and stills, as well as the arrests of the bootleggers and still operators. They include Roy Farley, John Guerin, Kenneth Jordan, H.W. Starbird, and Van Hubbard. Pictured here also is William Emig (third row, first from left) before being elected as sheriff. (Courtesy of the Santa Clara County Archives.)

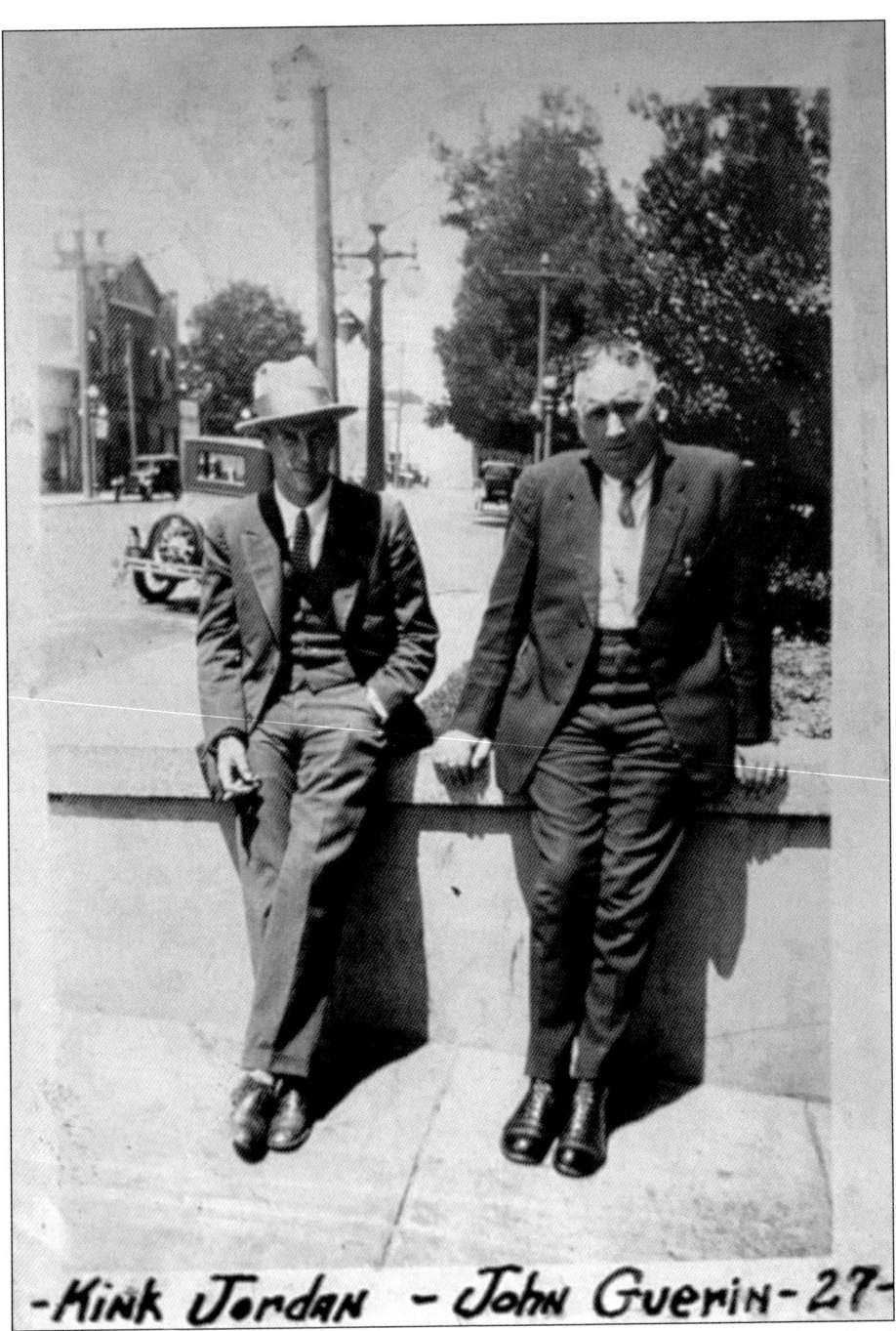

Pictured here are San Jose Police detectives John Guerin (right) and his partner Kink Jordan (left). John Guerin was appointed to head the newly created Morals Squad in 1917 to combat San Jose's vice crimes. During Prohibition, Guerin played a pivotal role in investigating the largest illegal alcohol operations in the city. His efforts included conducting raids on speakeasies and illegal distilleries, aiming to curb the rampant illegal alcohol trade and uphold the Prohibition laws. Guerin's work was essential in the ongoing battle against bootlegging and the various related criminal activities that flourished during this period. (Courtesy of San Jose Police Historical Society.)

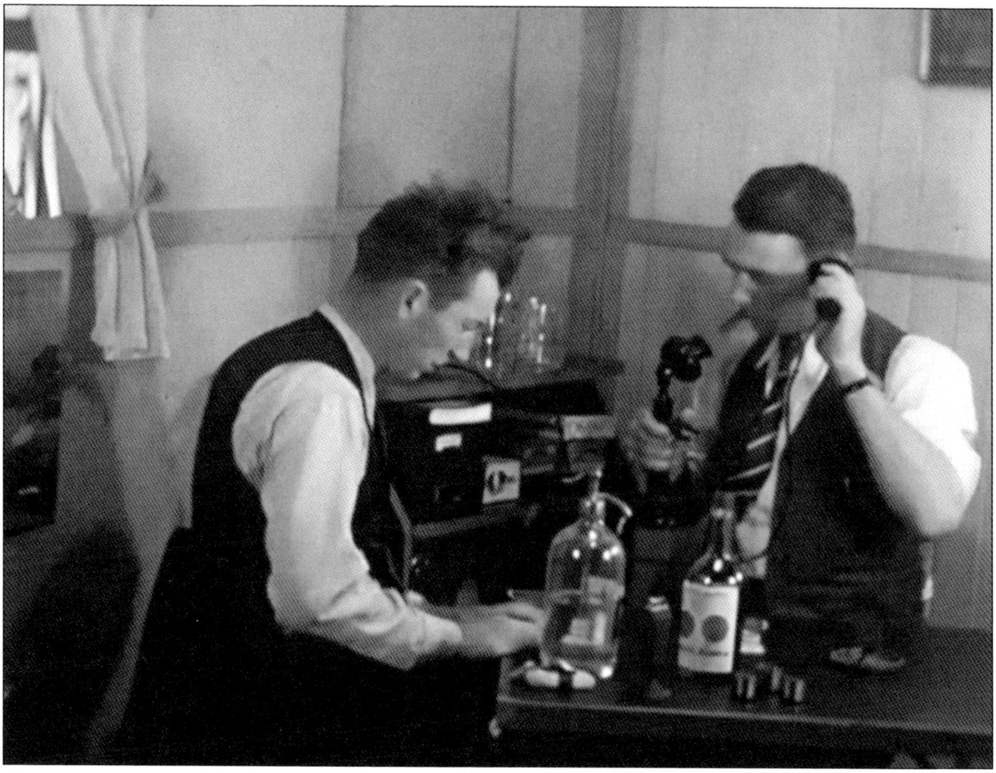

During the years of Prohibition, the San Jose Police Department created a film reel to train its officers on how to conduct investigations on violations of Prohibition laws. This included how to find the distributors and bootleggers, how to conduct a sting operation, and how to collect and handle the evidence. These photographs from the film show what a phone order to a distributor consists of (actors acting as phone order call takers) and of the police investigators discarding the evidence after the investigation is complete. (Both, courtesy of San Jose Police Historical Society.)

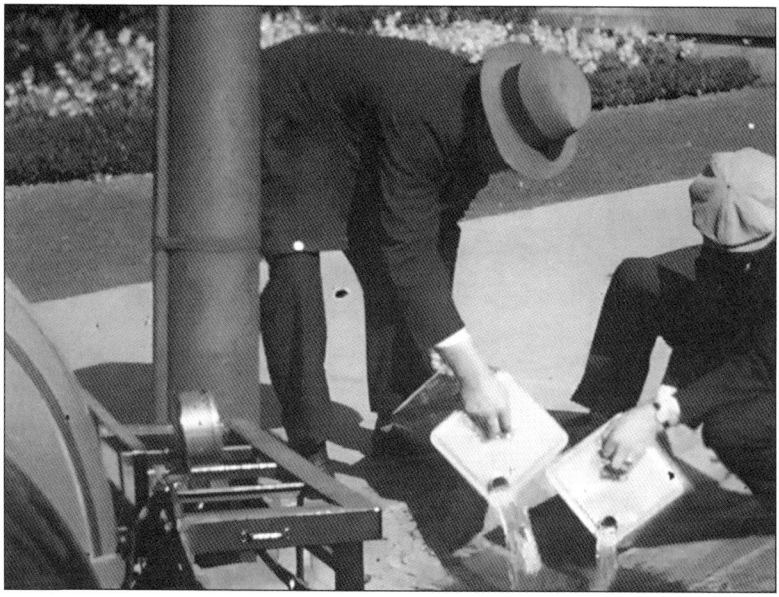

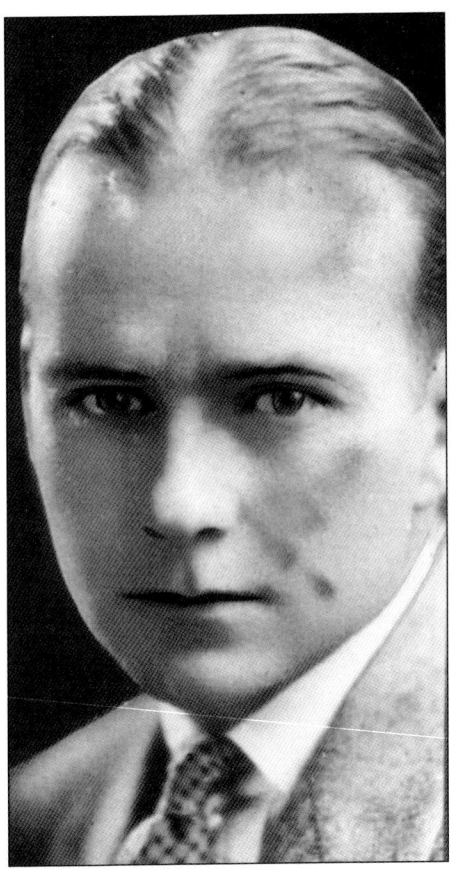

Most of the Prohibition arrests went through San Jose Police judge Percy O'Connor. After being appointed to the police court bench, he became known as a reformer for cracking down on Chinatown lotteries and still operators by issuing jail time to the offenders instead of just a small fine. Most if not all bootleggers and still operators arrested went to Judge O'Connor's court. (Courtesy of the Santa Clara County Archives.)

E.B. Bohmer was the Prohibition administrator of Northern California. He participated in raids on speakeasies and stills throughout the San Jose area. Bohmer cited a complaint that Santa Clara County had more stills operating than any other county in the state. Bohmer also complained that during planned excursions into the county, he and his agents had been blocked by a tipping off system that permitted bootleggers to close their resorts, conceal evidence, darken their places, and disappear. (Courtesy of Ted Ramos.)

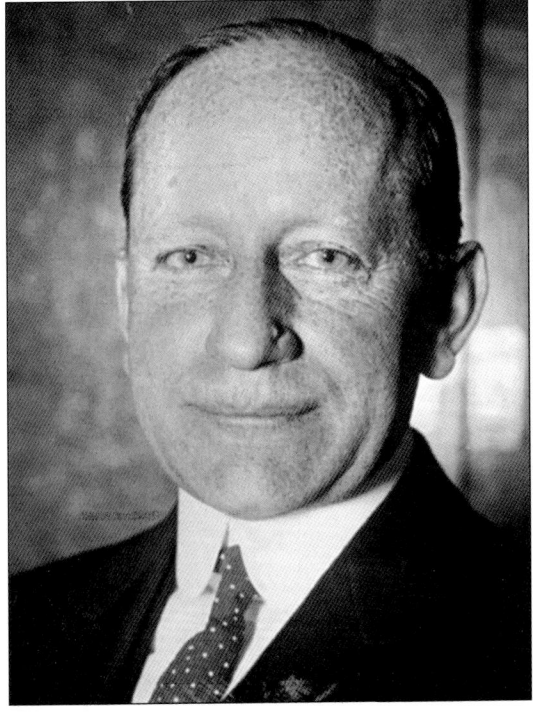

Five

A VIOLENT BUSINESS

San Jose Copper Beats Up Alleged Bootlegger

SAN JOSE, Oct. 31, (LP) Charles Fresconi, said by police to be a bootlegger, was near death here today following a fight yesterday with Police Officer Harley Adams. Adams told superior officers Fresconi resisted arrest and that he had to subdue him with a club. Fresconi had a fractured skull.

San Jose's bootlegging days did have their fair share of violence. The bootleggers fought with law enforcement and with other bootleggers. This newspaper article about known bootlegger Charles Fresconi serves as a vivid example of the consequences of resisting law enforcement. Fresconi's resistance led to severe repercussions, demonstrating the risks associated with defying authority during the Prohibition era. (Courtesy of the San Jose Public Library.)

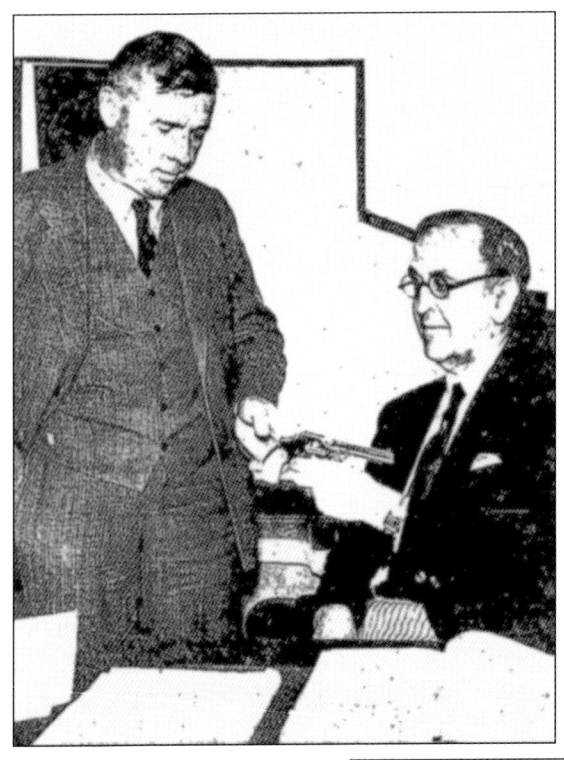

In 1931, a gathering occurred at Long Bridge Park, and many of San Jose's bootleggers and their families were in attendance, along with Constable E.C. Stamper. A fight broke out, and Constable Stamper pulled his gun. Bootleggers Frank Gairnese, Steve Mignosi, Tony Stojanovich, and John Locurto tried to prevent Stamper from shooting, but Stamper fired the gun, killing Stojanovich and wounding Gairnese and Mignosi. Stamper was charged with murder but was acquitted. Pictured here is Sheriff Emig (left) receiving the gun. (Courtesy of the San Jose Public Library.)

In 1928, Clarence "Chick" Leddy, along with his bartender Fred True, was arrested for murder during a confrontation at Leddy's Almaden Road resort. Leddy killed Robert Hill by hitting him on the head with a gardening hoe. Leddy and True were represented by attorney William Foley. True was convicted of a lesser charge and sentenced to a couple of years in prison. Leddy was convicted of murder and sentenced to life in prison. Pictured here is Leddy's mug shot. (Courtesy of California State Archives.)

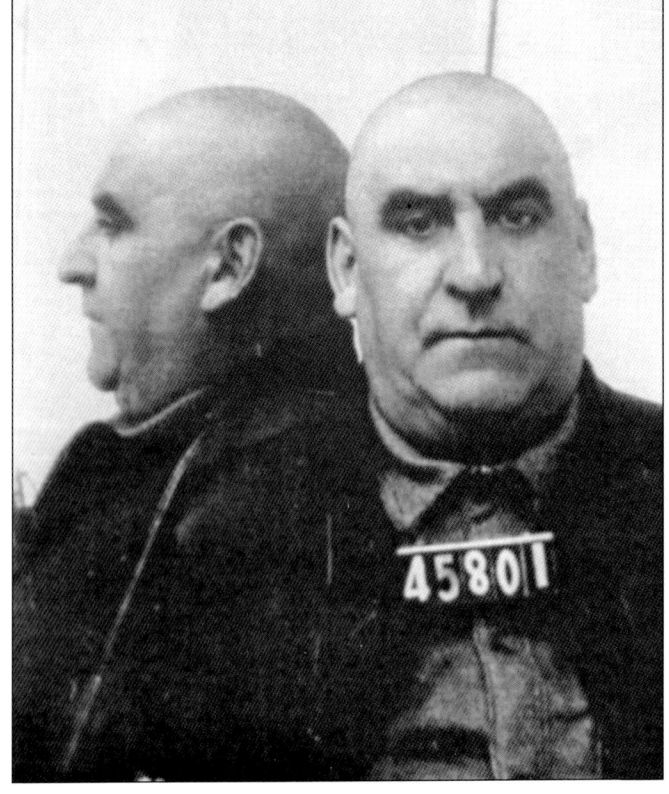

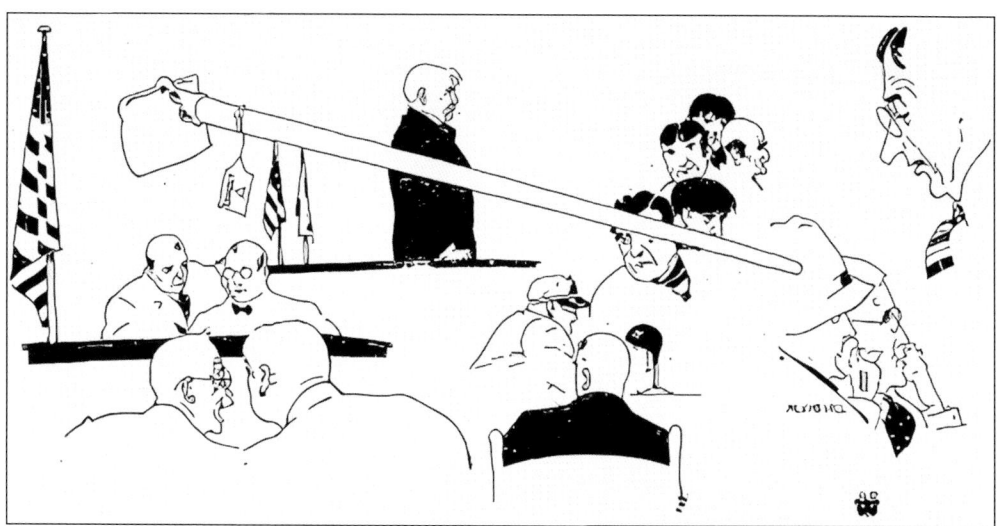

During the Leddy trial, three different stories were told regarding the motive for the killing. Robert Hill's friends testified that Leddy thought Hill was a Prohibition agent, Leddy testified that he thought Hill was going to rob him, and customers at the resort testified that Hill was winning money playing Leddy's slot machines. This courtroom artist's rendering shows the weapon used to kill Hill and others involved in the courtroom proceedings. (Courtesy of the San Jose Public Library.)

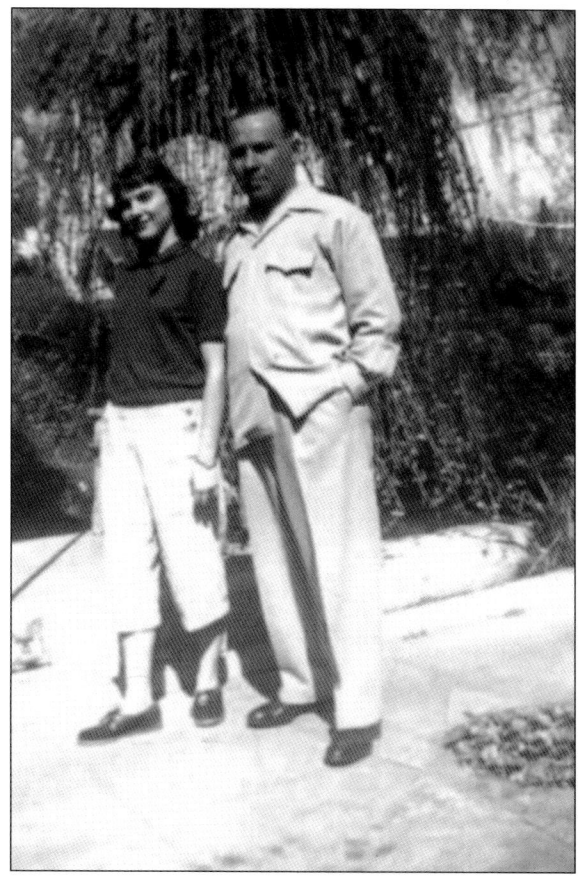

In 1930, twenty-five-year-old Jack Ciraulo and his father, Ignacio Ciraulo, were arrested at their home at 664 North Twelfth Street after a raid by police chief Black. Both pleaded not guilty in Judge Percy O'Connor's court. It was not until a jury was selected that Jack changed his mind and pleaded guilty, admitting the seven gallons of wine that were discovered were his and not Ignacio's. Believing his bootleg neighbor down the street had notified the authorities to eliminate the competition, Ignacio sent Jack and two other sons to the neighbor's house as the neighbor was getting in his car. Jack and his brothers smashed the car with clubs and pulled the neighbor out of the car and beat him. Pictured here are Jack and his daughter. (Courtesy of Charles Ciraulo.)

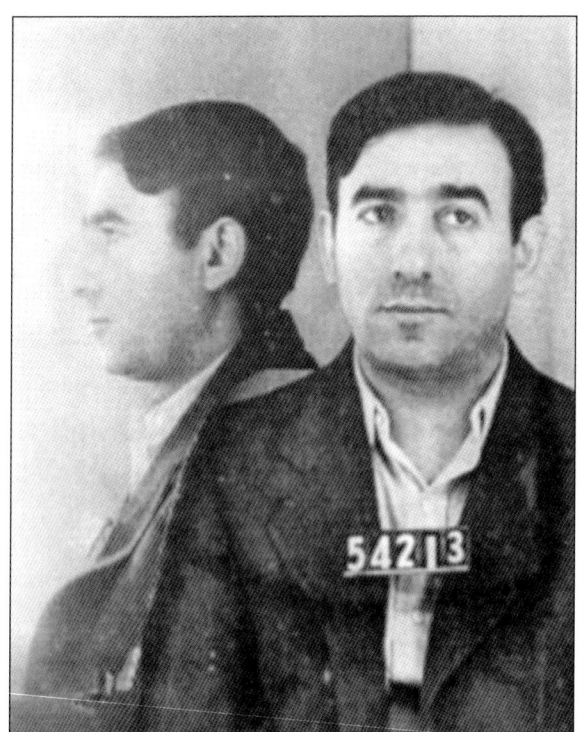

Joe Spinosa was found in the street of San Jose's Little Tijuana by bootlegger Joe Locurto. Spinosa claimed he was driving a truckload of alcohol through Little Tijuana when four men attempted to hijack the truck. During the struggle, Spinosa was shot twice. Sheriff's deputies suspected that Spinosa was hiding out in Little Tijuana to evade an impending narcotic charge in San Francisco and that his discovery was due to his own gang. (Courtesy of California State Archives.)

In 1931, a Santa Monica bootlegger and two of his partners hijacked 218 gallons of liquor at a speakeasy in Oakland, California. They fled south down the old Oakland Highway. Sheriff Emig was notified of the hijacking and sent deputies to stake out the highway through San Jose. Deputies spotted the suspect vehicle speeding by and forced it to the curb. Gunfire was exchanged, one suspect was captured, and the other suspect fled in the vehicle. (Courtesy of California State Archives.)

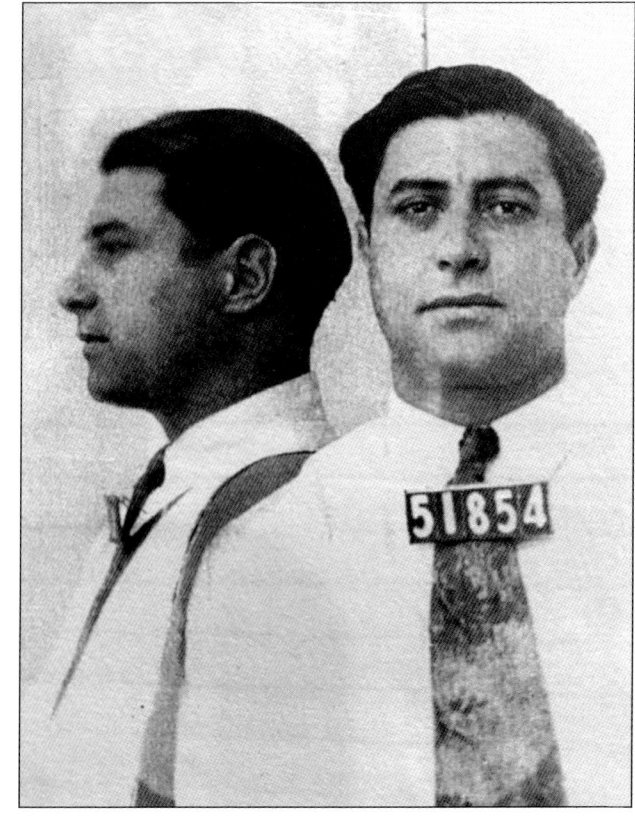

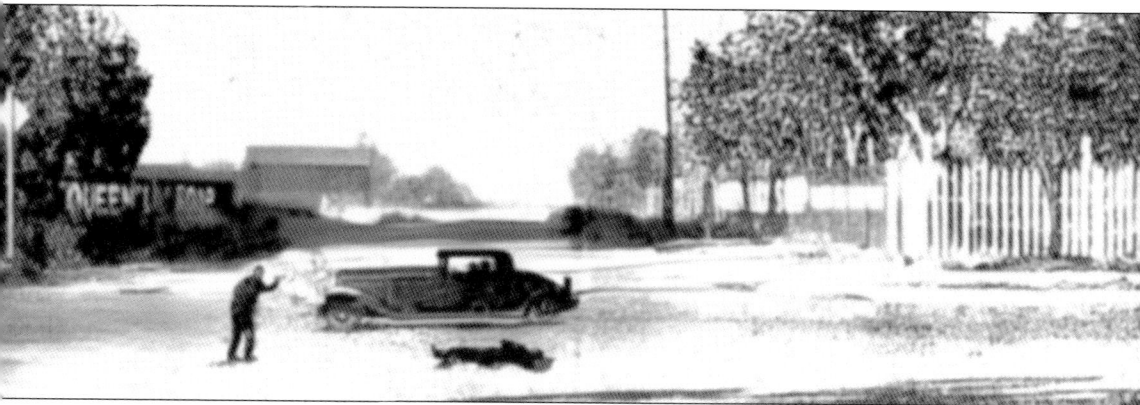

Deputies Hubert McAuley and Frank Saporito were stationed at the intersection of Oakland and Berryessa Roads when they observed a suspect vehicle speeding past. Upon stopping the vehicle, Deputy Saporito approached the passenger, Fred Hopkins, while Deputy McAuley approached the driver, Joe Teresi. During a scuffle between Saporito and Hopkins, Teresi fired two shots at McAuley, killing him instantly. This tragic incident highlights the dangers law enforcement faced during Prohibition dealing with violent criminals often involved in bootlegging and other illegal activities. (Courtesy of the San Jose Public Library.)

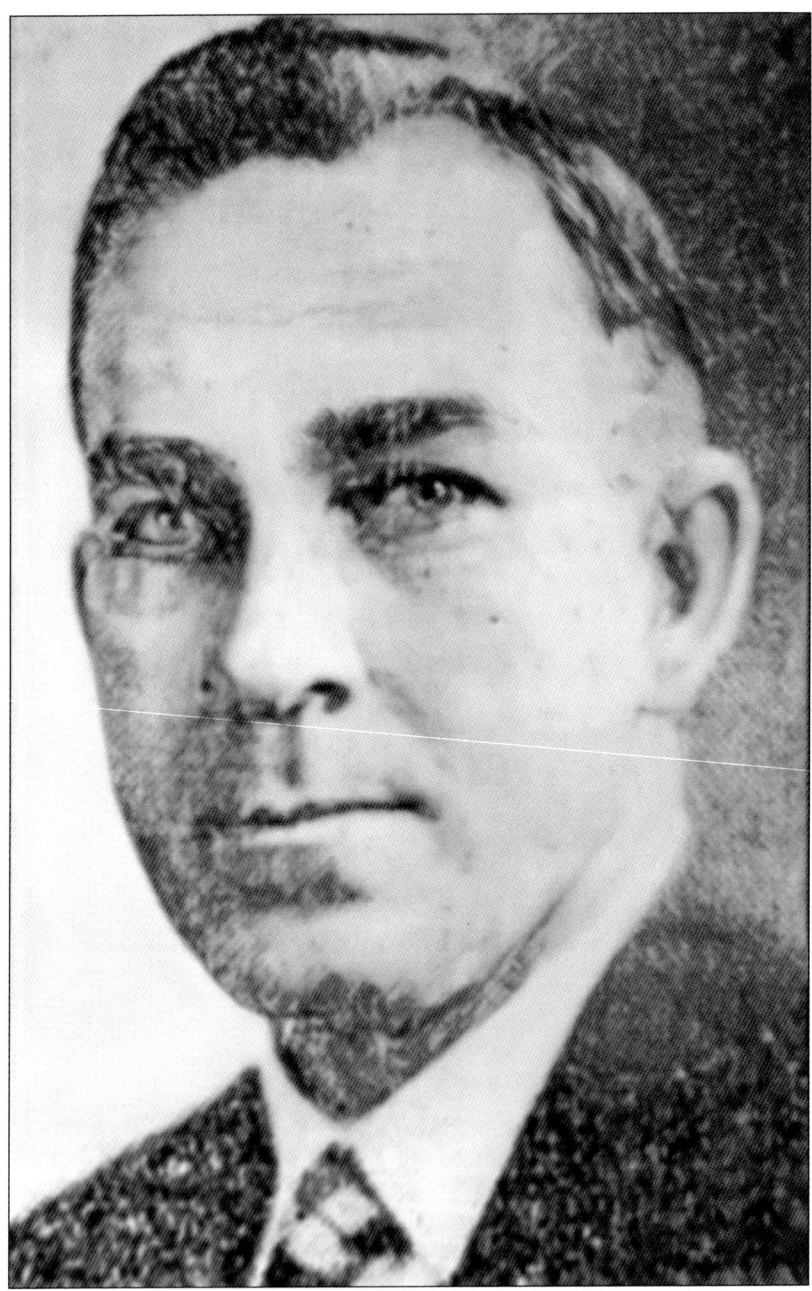

Deputy Sheriff Frank Saporito was seriously wounded during a confrontation with bootlegger Fred Hopkins. Saporito was shot once in the stomach and twice in the legs. Despite his injuries, he managed to return fire, striking and wounding Hopkins. Saporito was able to handcuff Hopkins before passing out. Joe Teresi shot Deputy McAuley and killed him before McAuley could draw his gun. When Teresi was later arrested, he was brought back down to Santa Clara County on murder charges. Teresi was found guilty in court and sentenced to life in prison. Teresi denied killing Deputy McAuley and blamed it on his two accomplices. Deputy McAuley (pictured here) was the only law enforcement officer killed in San Jose during Prohibition. (Courtesy of the Santa Clara County Archives.)

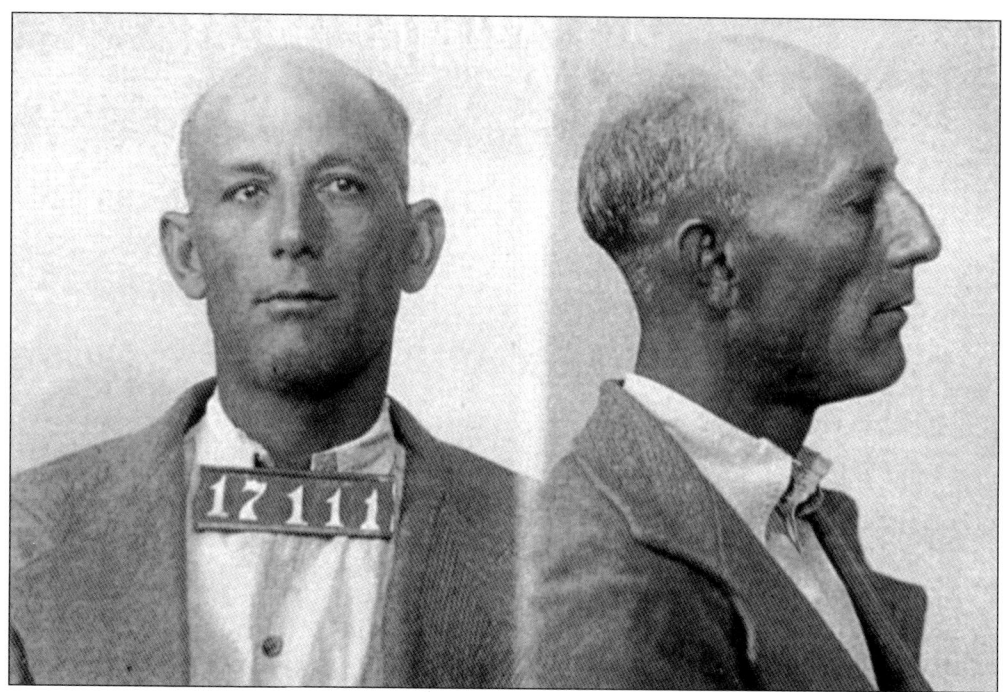

In December 1928, after Santa Clara County Prohibition agent Abel Frias had busted bootlegger Salvador Cardinelli (pictured above) for liquor crimes, Cardinelli sought revenge. Agent Frias met up with a young woman named Viola Post (pictured below) on South First Street in San Jose. Post, who was driving a car, invited Frias to join her for a ride. After driving a few blocks, Post suddenly stopped the car, and Cardinelli jumped in and was armed with a gun. They drove for a long distance along the Pacheco Pass in south Santa Clara County. The vehicle stopped, and Agent Frias was tied up. Cardinelli told Frias to forget the investigation into him. When Frias refused, Cardinelli shot Frias in the head and left him for dead along the side of the road. (Above, courtesy of California State Archives; below, courtesy of the San Jose Public Library.)

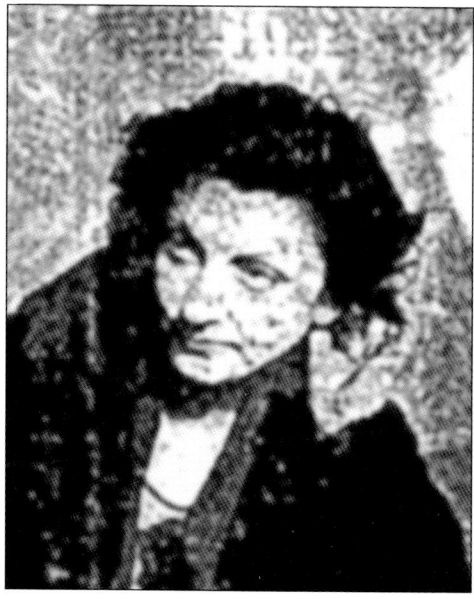

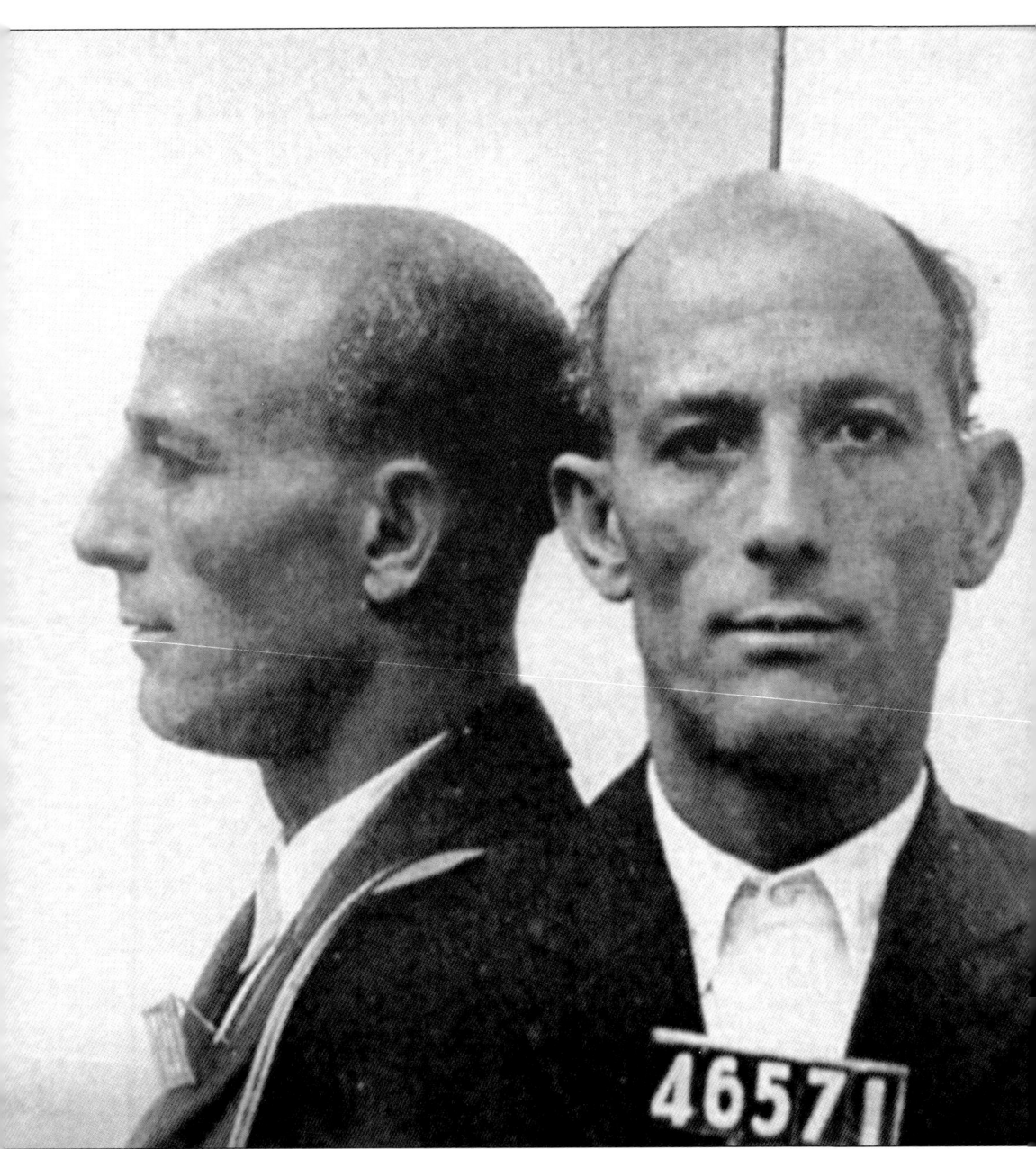

Frias was found still alive by a rancher on the side of the road and taken to a hospital in Los Banos. Frias was able to identify both Cardinelli and Post. Cardinelli was arrested and sentenced to 10 years in prison after pleading guilty to assault with a deadly weapon. Post was also arrested, but charges were later dropped. The court judge described the attack during sentencing as cowardly and cold-blooded. (Courtesy of California State Archives.)

Six
LITTLE TIJUANA

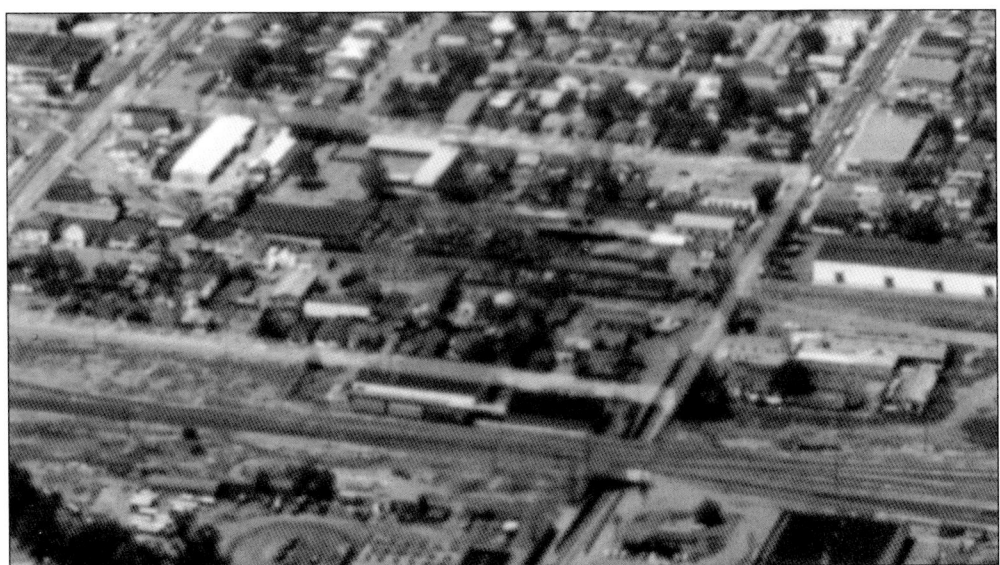

Outside San Jose city limits was an area known as "Little Tijuana" because of its wide-open speakeasies, gambling halls, and houses of prostitution. It was also home to the poorest conditions in Santa Clara County. Its location was strategic, providing proximity to San Jose customers while being beyond the stricter enforcement of the San Jose Police Department. The main boundaries of Little Tijuana were West San Carlos Street on the south, Sunol Street on the west, Park Avenue on the north, and Dupont Street on the east. Little Tijuana can be seen in the aerial photograph within the highlighted boundaries. (Courtesy of History San Jose.)

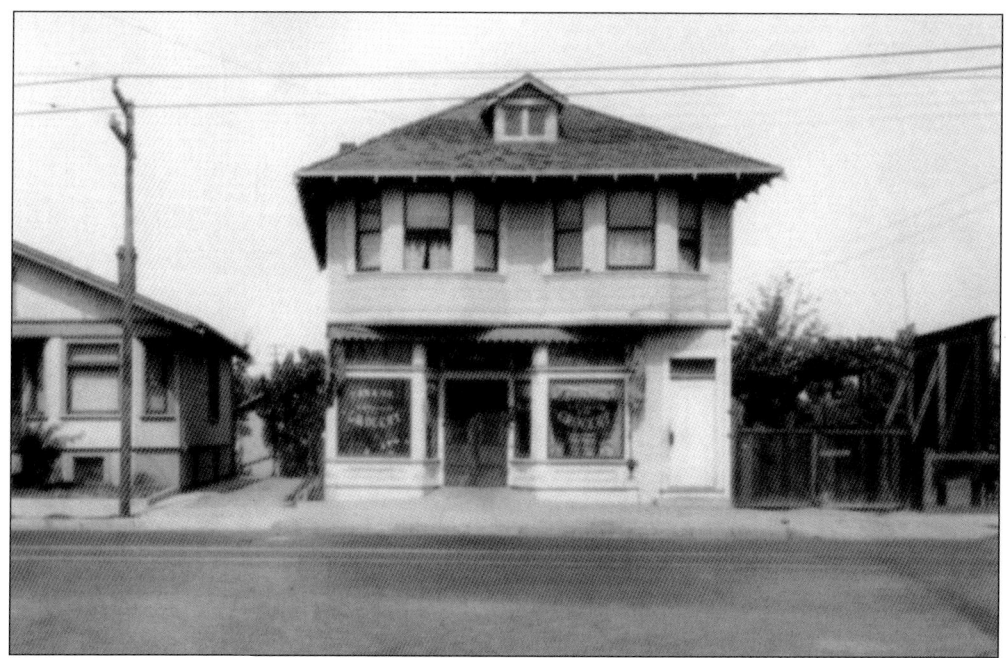

The Panama Grocery was located at 695 West San Carlos Street. In February 1925, police chief Black and officers of the San Jose Police Department raided the Panama Grocery. They found eight men gathered in a back room drinking alcohol. The men quickly smashed their glasses on the floor and ran out through the back of the building to the backyard, where officers were also waiting and took custody of the men. (Courtesy of History San Jose.)

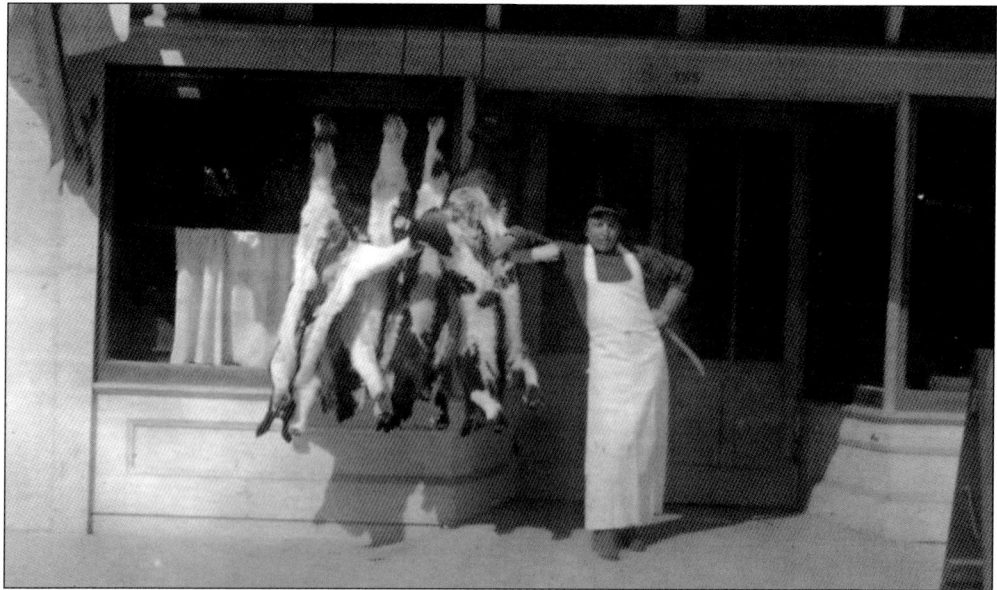

Standing in front of 755 West San Carlos Street is Frank Gairnese, who, before being a bootlegger, was a butcher at this meat market owned by the Locurto family and operated by Joe Locurto. In 1924, Joe's brother John Locurto was arrested for liquor sales. In 1927, the building was abated by District Attorney Fred L. Thomas. The building reopened and was raided multiple times for liquor sales and gambling. (Courtesy of Jeanne Rene Watson.)

Joe Locurto (pictured here) was the brother of well-known bootlegger and resort operator John Locurto. Joe faced at least five separate charges of selling intoxicating liquor, which included operations out of his store at 755 West San Carlos Street and selling liquor to undercover agents at his resort, the Press Palace, located on McEvoy Street. (Courtesy of the San Jose Public Library.)

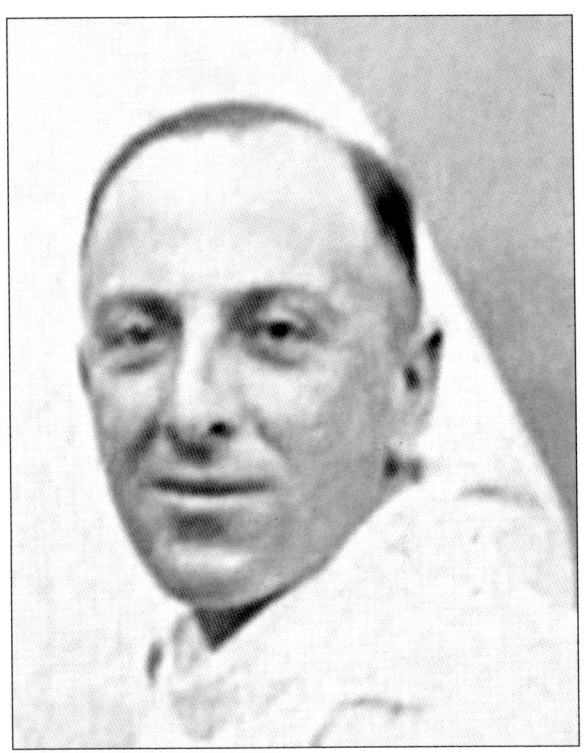

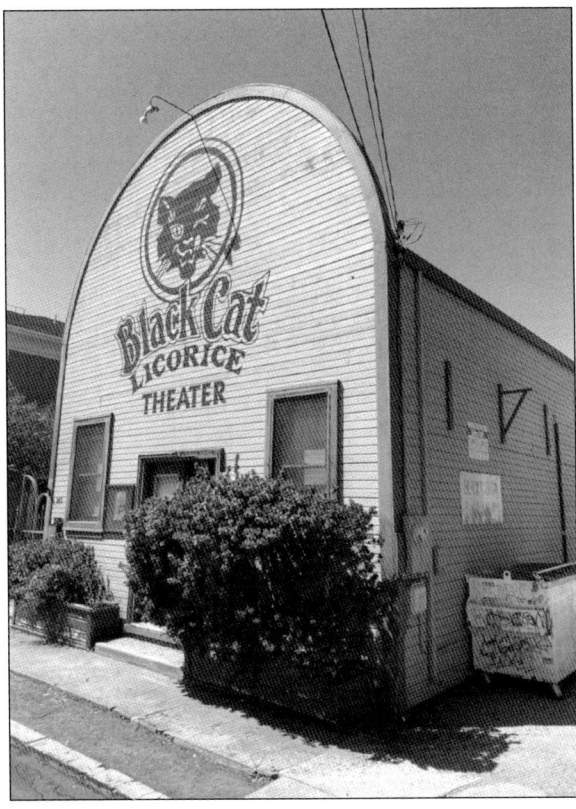

The Press Palace, located at 65 McEvoy Street and also known as the Ark Star Athletic Club, was operated by Joe and Peter Locurto and was raided multiple times by Sheriff Lyle for liquor sales and gambling. In 1928, Joe Locurto and Kenneth McBride were charged with selling and possession of intoxicating liquor. In 1930, the *Mercury Herald* sent investigators to the Press Palace. It was the most notorious liquor joint at the time. (Courtesy of Ted Ramos.)

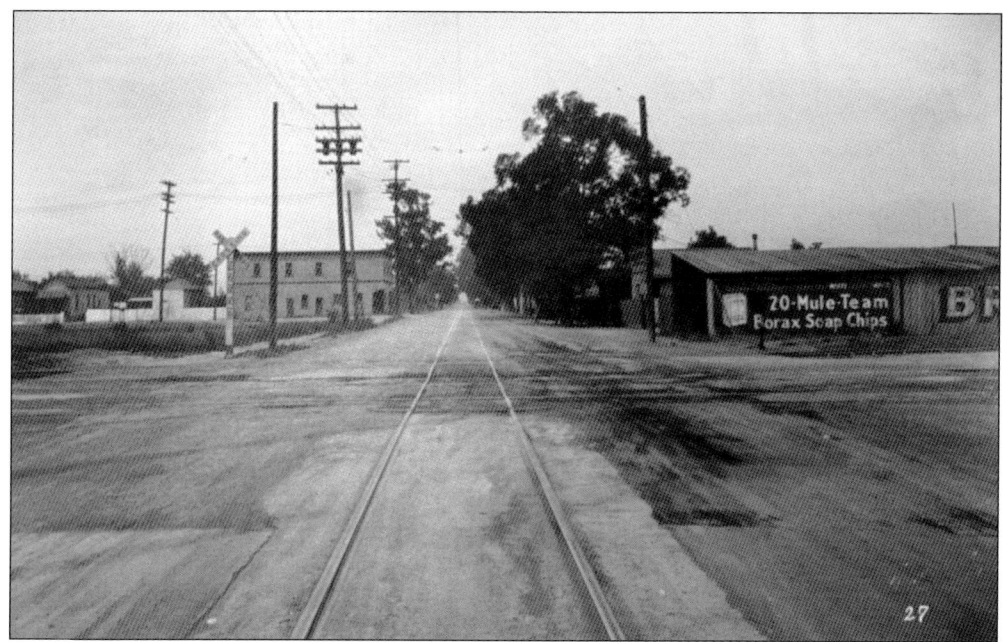

The white two-story building on the right of west-bound Park Avenue was the Westside Hotel. The Westside Hotel was owned by Frank and Margaretha Schmidt and operated by Frank Marty. In 1924, Sheriff Lyle smashed through the front doors and seized roulette tables, poker chips, blackjack tables, craps tables, and other gambling paraphernalia. The hotel was also raided after undercover agents found the hotel serving beer to cannery workers on their lunch break. (Courtesy of History San Jose.)

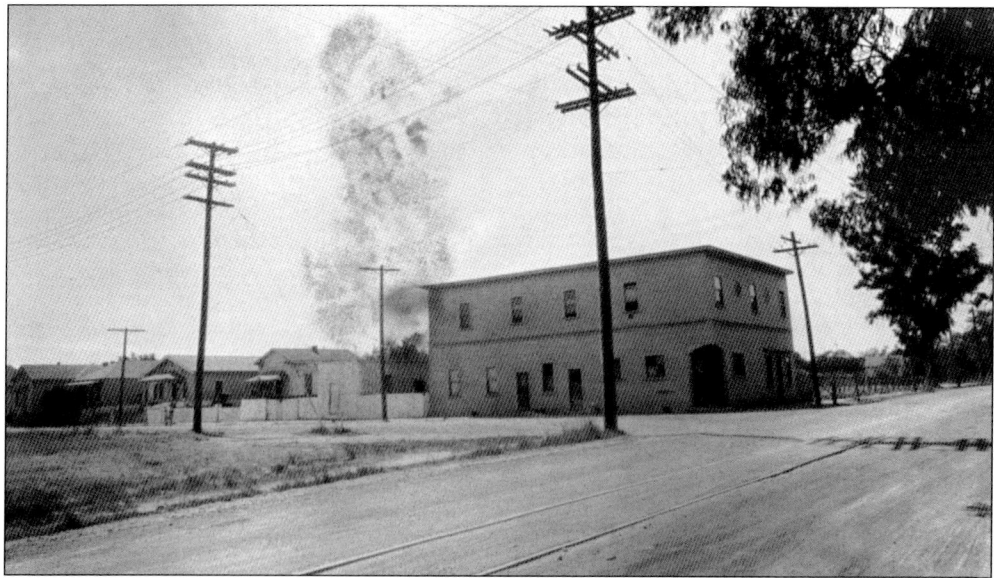

In 1930, Alberta Marino inherited the Westside Hotel from her father, Frank Schmidt, and operated it with her husband, Joe. It was moved one block over to McEvoy Street, and the name was changed to the Subway Hotel. In 1931, the Subway Hotel was raided, during which Alberta tried to hold off the officers while Joe dumped too much whiskey at one time, which did not flush down the sink before the officers reached it. (Courtesy of History San Jose.)

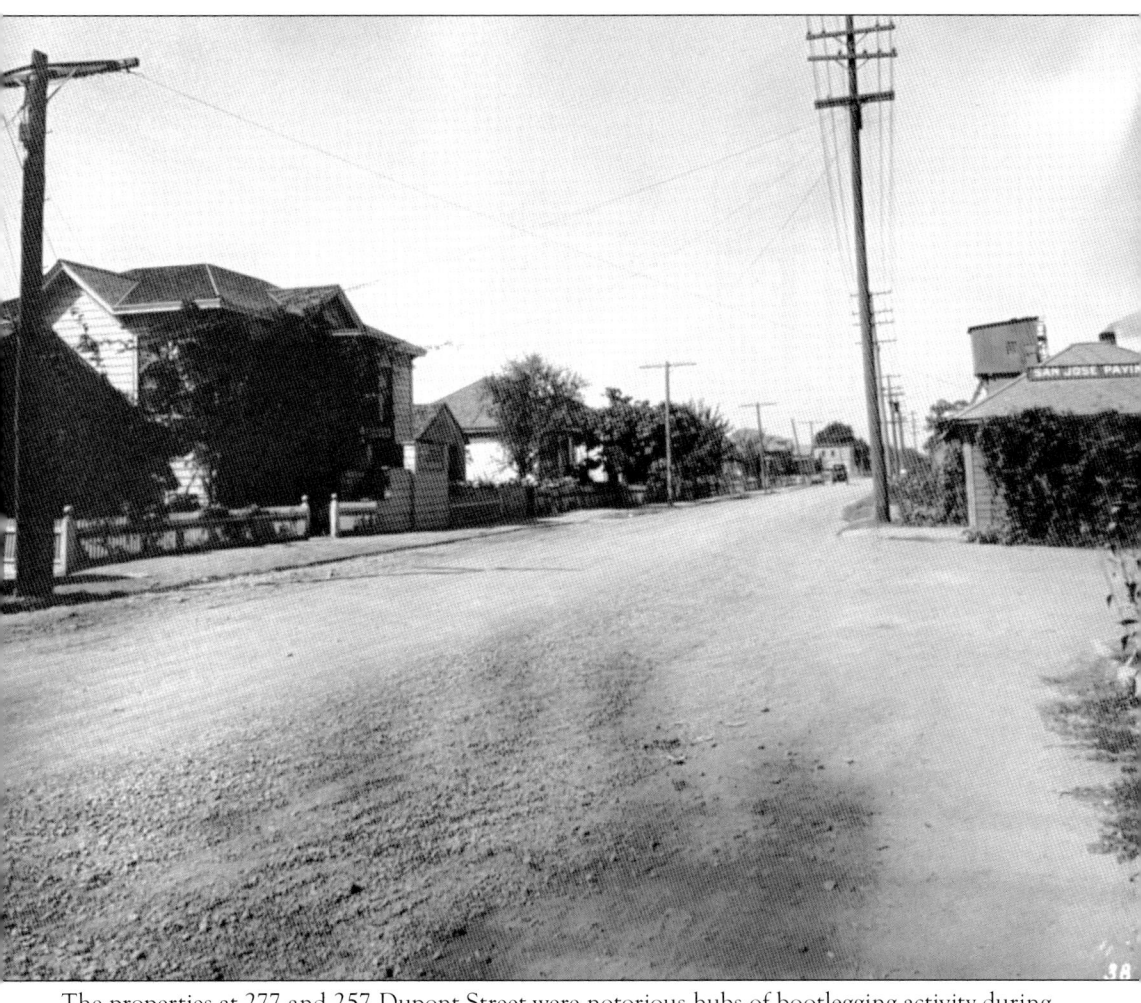

The properties at 277 and 257 Dupont Street were notorious hubs of bootlegging activity during the Prohibition era in San Jose. These locations were repeatedly raided by law enforcement, leading to the arrest and conviction of several operators for violating liquor laws. The large house at 277 Dupont Street served as a clandestine speakeasy, with its bar located in the back room. Despite multiple raids and the arrest of several operators, the establishment continued to operate, openly serving beer, wine, gin, and whiskey to patrons who entered through both the front and back entrances. In 1930, a raid conducted by Sheriff Lyle's deputies led to the closure of the resort for a year by order of a superior court judge, highlighting the efforts of law enforcement to combat illegal alcohol sales at this location. Two houses down from 277 Dupont Street, 257 Dupont Street was home to another notorious speakeasy known as Hazel's Joint. Operating as a full bar located in the basement of the residence, Hazel's Joint was raided multiple times, leading to its closure and padlocking by the county in 1930. Following the closure, the bar relocated to a barn behind the residence, where it operated under the name the Red Barn. (Courtesy of History San Jose.)

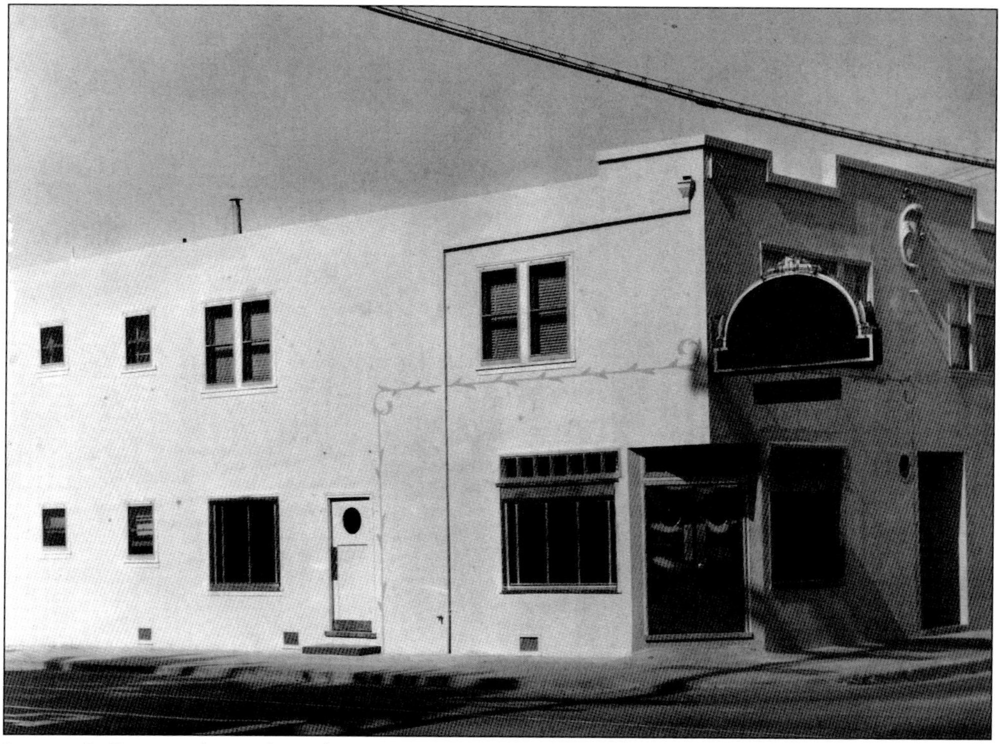

Loproto's Grocery, located on the corner of West San Carlos and Sunol Streets, was owned and operated by Sam Loproto. In 1929, an undercover federal agent with sheriff's deputies searched Loproto's grocery store with a search warrant obtained by prior liquor sales. Individual pint bottles of whiskey were found. Loproto was arrested and pleaded guilty. He was fined $1,000 for possession of liquor with a prior conviction and given the opportunity of serving a day in county jail for each $10 of the fine. Loproto paid the bulk of the fine, and the rest was paid through jail time. The judge stated that if the place were a rowdy or resort-type place, Loproto would have been given the full 90-day maximum jail sentence. (Both, courtesy of Tom Loproto.)

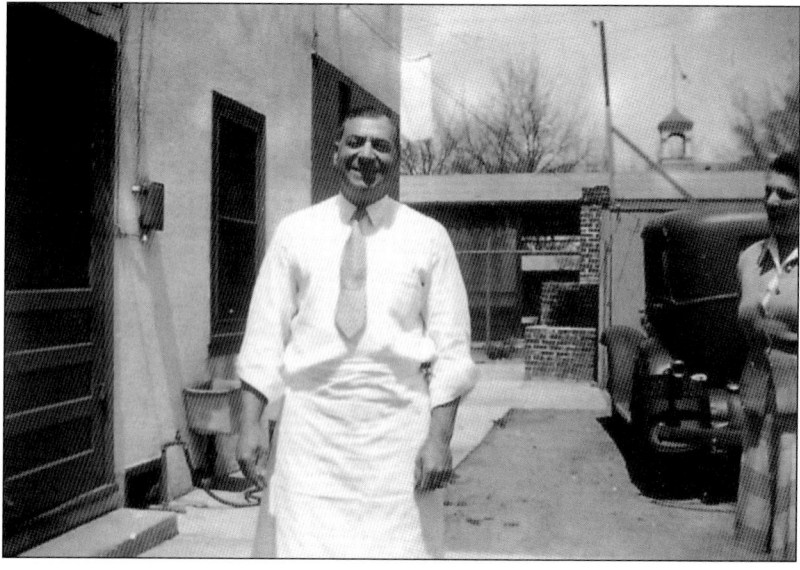

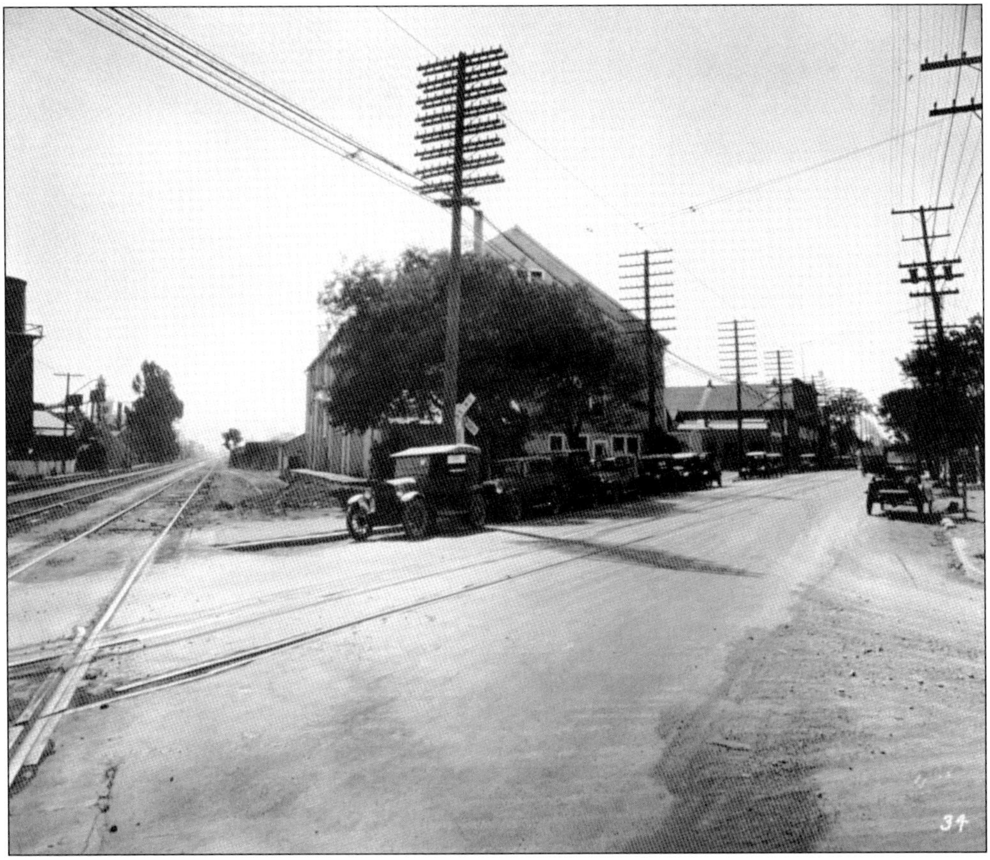

In Little Tijuana, Ton's was a Chinese gambling house located on the corner of West San Carlos and Dupont Streets. Ton's gained notoriety for its illegal activities, particularly the sale of alcohol to federal agents during frequent raids. Ton's was also known for selling lottery tickets, further adding to its reputation as a hub of illicit gambling and vice. Despite law enforcement crackdowns and repeated raids on Ton's, the establishment continued to operate. (Courtesy of History San Jose.)

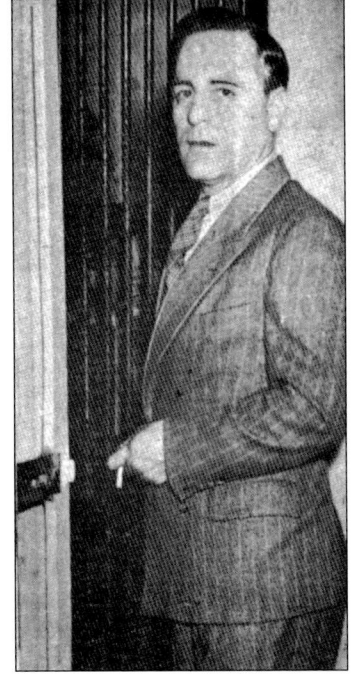

Harry Ferrari was one of the more notorious bootleggers in San Jose. He operated two resorts on Dupont Street that mostly consisted of prostitution. Ferrari had operated many resorts in San Jose and in other Bay Area cities. Ferrari had been arrested twice in Alameda for operating two resorts, Bucket O' Blood and the Hornets' Nest. Both were later closed through abatement. (Courtesy of Tony Gairnese.)

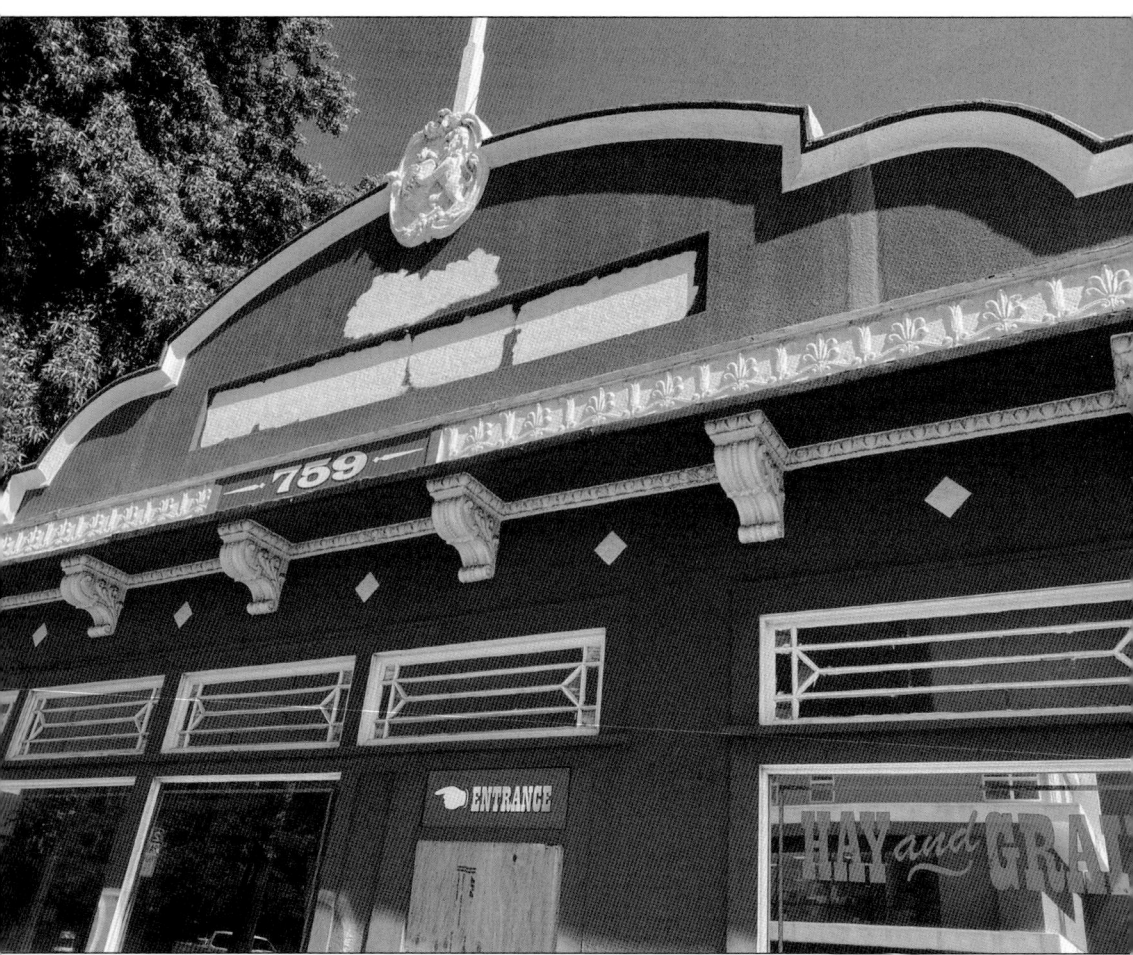

A car garage located at 759 West San Carlos Street was owned by John Locurto as one of his buildings for his automobile sales and service business. In June 1925, after running down clues picked up during a series of liquor raids, federal agents found 5,000 gallons of illicit wine of good quality worth $10,000 in this building. The wine was found in the main garage area and in the cellar beneath. Locurto had just finished a 90-day jail sentence for a prior conviction of violating the Volstead Act. (Courtesy of Ted Ramos.)

Seven
THE LOCURTOS

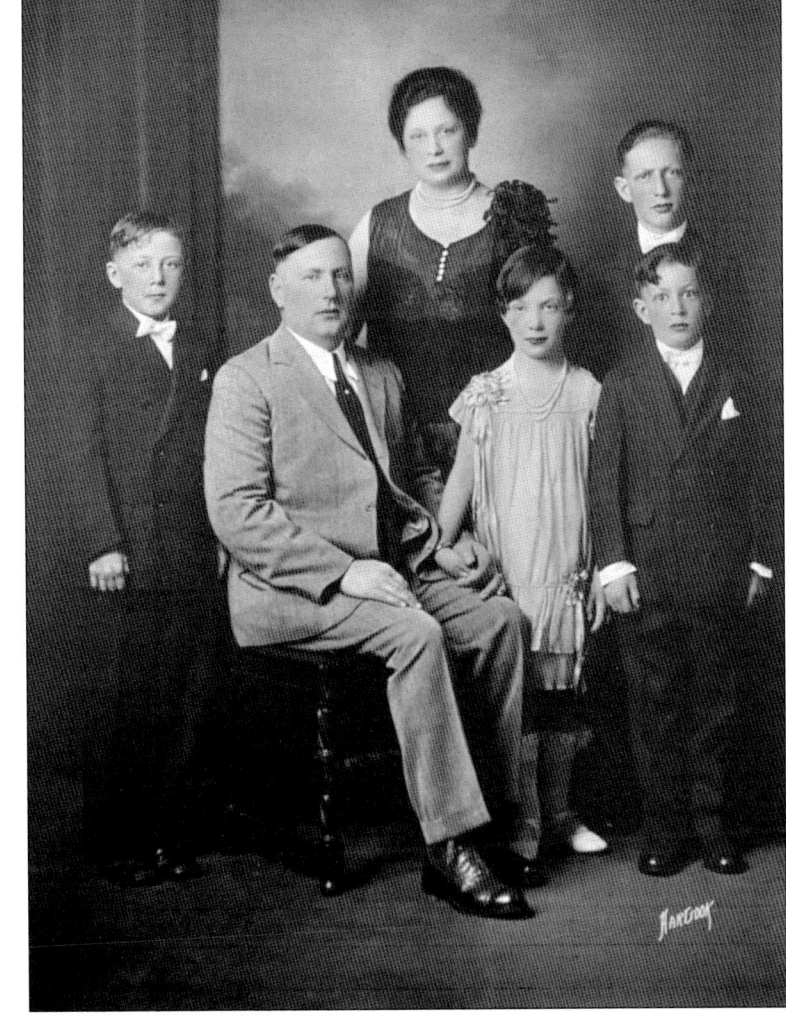

John B. Locurto arrived in San Jose from New York in 1905. John became a rancher and had a pig farm near the Curtner Avenue area. John then opened a butcher shop at his family's market on West San Carlos Street. John, along with his brothers Joe and Peter, operated businesses at the corner of West San Carlos and McEvoy Streets. John is pictured here sitting on the chair with his family. (Courtesy of Darlene Bursch.)

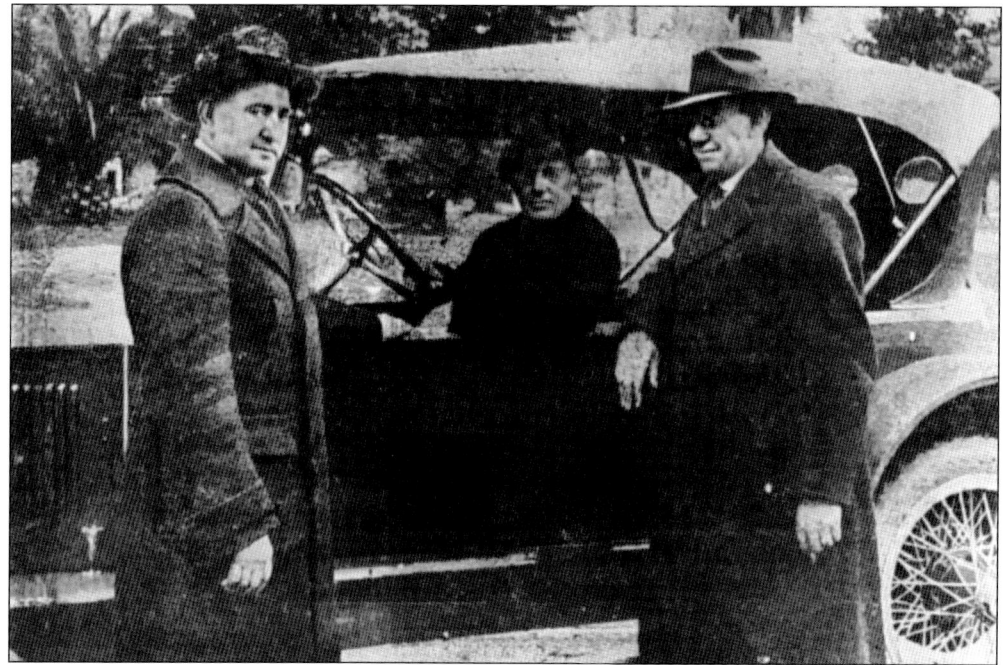

In 1921, John Locurto bought the Consolidated Garage on North Market Street. John then opened a car dealership on South First Street called Locurto Motors. His success in the automotive business gave him the funds and the business knowledge to use in his future bootlegging enterprise. John Locurto is pictured here sitting in one of his dealership's cars. His sales manager, W.G. Barton, is on the left, and salesman Charles Steel on the right. (Courtesy of the San Jose Public Library.)

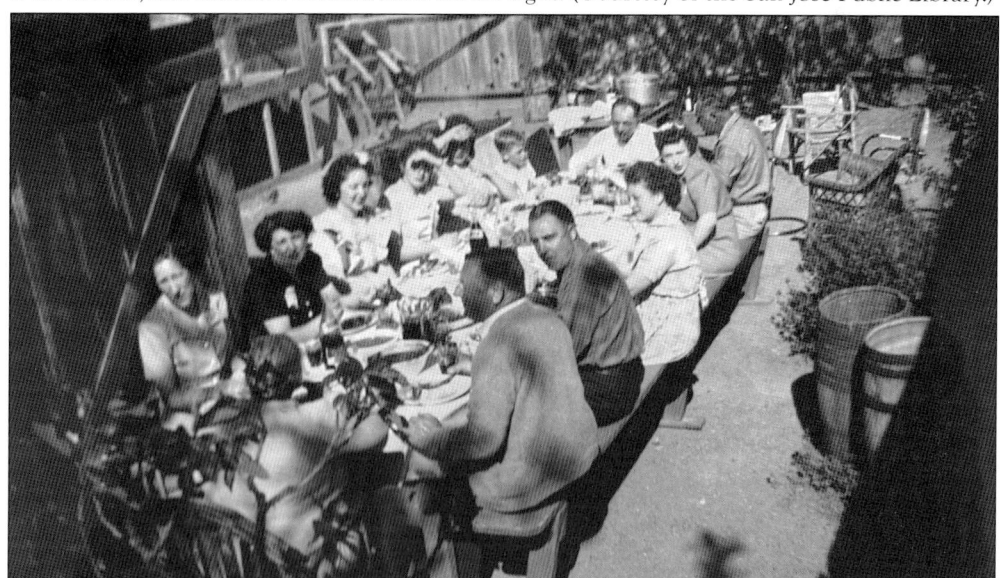

The 410 Club was located at 410 Race Street and was a house occupied by the Gairnese family. Operator John Locurto had been arrested by undercover federal agents at this basement club after enough evidence was found to prove that John was the proprietor of the club and was illegally selling alcohol. Operator Frank Gairnese is seen here in the back yard of 410 Race Street sitting at the end of the table with family. Locurto is on the other side. (Courtesy of Darlene Bursch.)

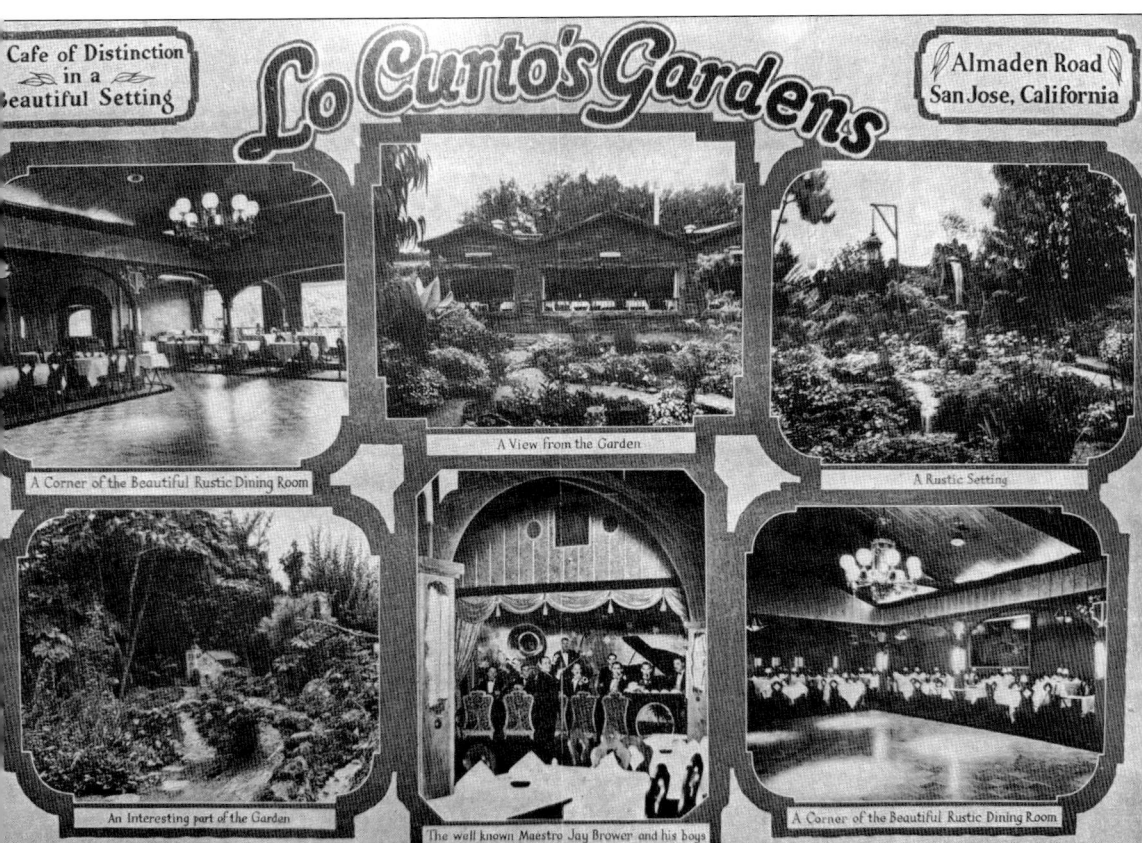

From the time Prohibition began, John Locurto had been arrested multiple times and was issued numerous fines and given multiple jail sentences from 45 days to one year. In 1928, Locurto's partner, Chick Leddy, was arrested and sent to life in prison for murdering a customer at Leddy's resort on Almaden Road. Leddy turned over the resort to Locurto with the promise that Locurto would give Leddy's wife $100 a month while Leddy was in prison. Locurto took possession of the resort's property but never sent Leddy's wife any money as agreed. Locurto then built a Tudor-style home on the resort property and moved his family to live in the new home. Locurto then opened his own resort and called it Locurto's Gardens. (Courtesy of Tony Gairnese.)

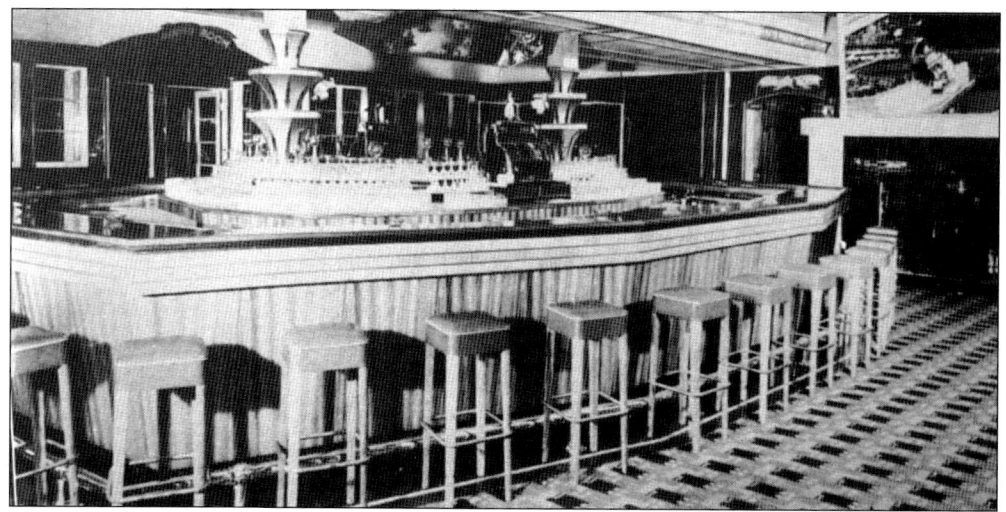

Located at 515 Almaden Avenue near Alma Street, Locurto's Gardens stood as one of John Locurto's most extravagant speakeasy resorts during the Prohibition era. This establishment was an example of luxury that characterized some of the more prominent speakeasies of the time. At the heart of Locurto's Gardens was its 80-foot bar, a grand centerpiece that exuded elegance and sophistication. The bar was surrounded by expensive stools, chairs, and beautifully decorated walls adorned with mirrors, creating an atmosphere of luxury and exclusivity. The sheer value of the bar alone amounted to an impressive $16,000, reflecting the investment and attention to detail that went into creating this lavish speakeasy experience. Locurto's Gardens was not just a place to obtain illicit alcohol; it was a destination for socializing, entertainment, and indulgence, offering patrons an escape from the constraints of Prohibition-era regulations. (Both, courtesy of Ted Ramos.)

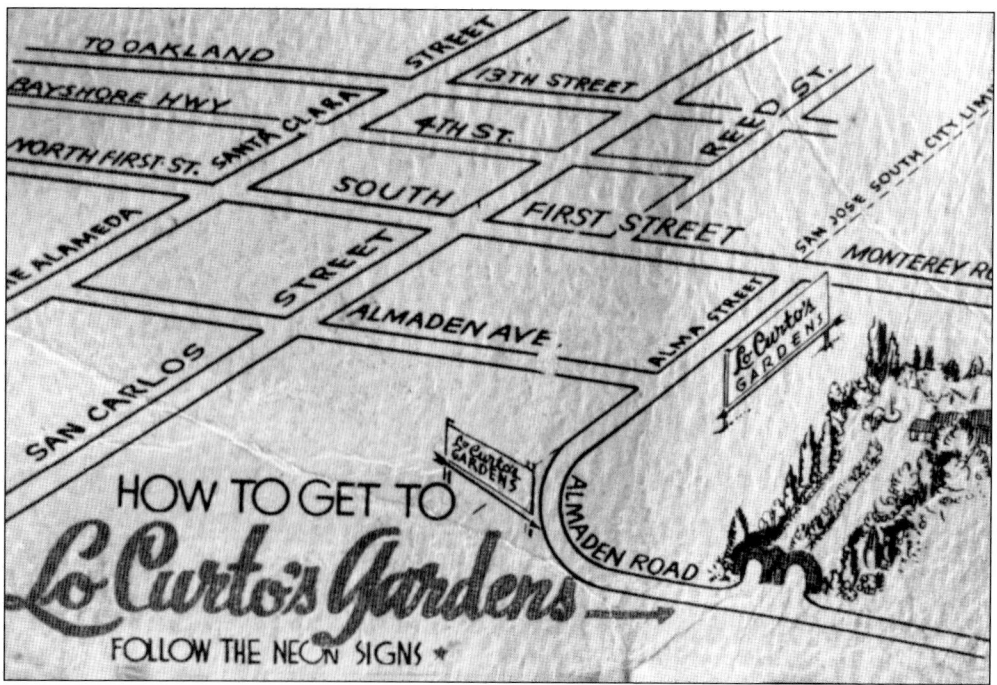

After Prohibition was repealed, Locurto continued to operate Locurto's Gardens with illegal gambling in the back. Locurto was also still manufacturing and selling alcohol. In 1936, federal agents raided Locurto's property, which included the Gardens and his home. They found 1,500 gallons of untaxed whiskey and alcohol, parts of a dismantled still, and counterfeit tax stamps and whisky labels. This news article shows some of the large barrels found in the basement of Locurto's garage. (Courtesy of Tony Gairnese.)

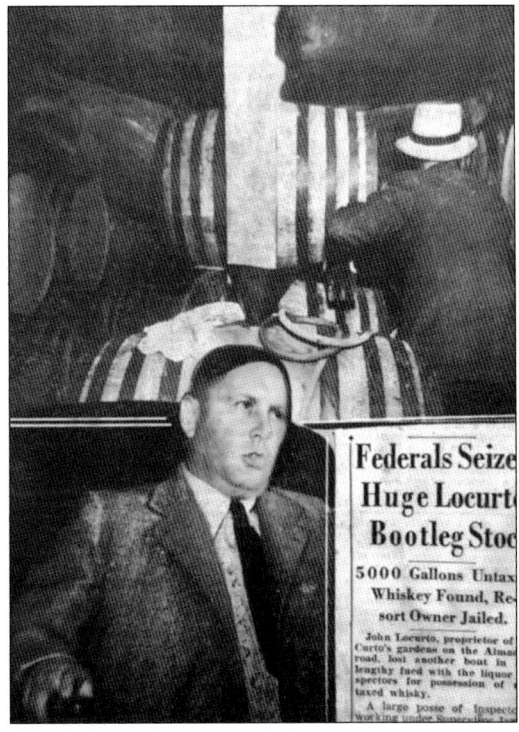

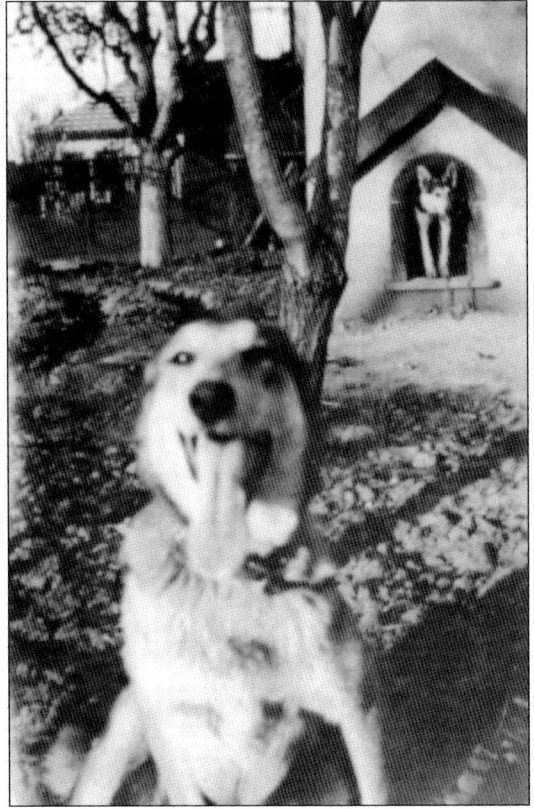

During the same raid, federal agents discovered a doghouse adjoined to a garage behind the resort. A sliding panel was concealed at the rear of the doghouse. Behind the panel, agents found a staircase that led to the garage basement. It was in the basement where agents found barrels of untaxed whiskey and counterfeit tax stamps. Pictured here is the doghouse that concealed the hidden passageway to the garage basement. (Courtesy of Jeanne Rene Watson.)

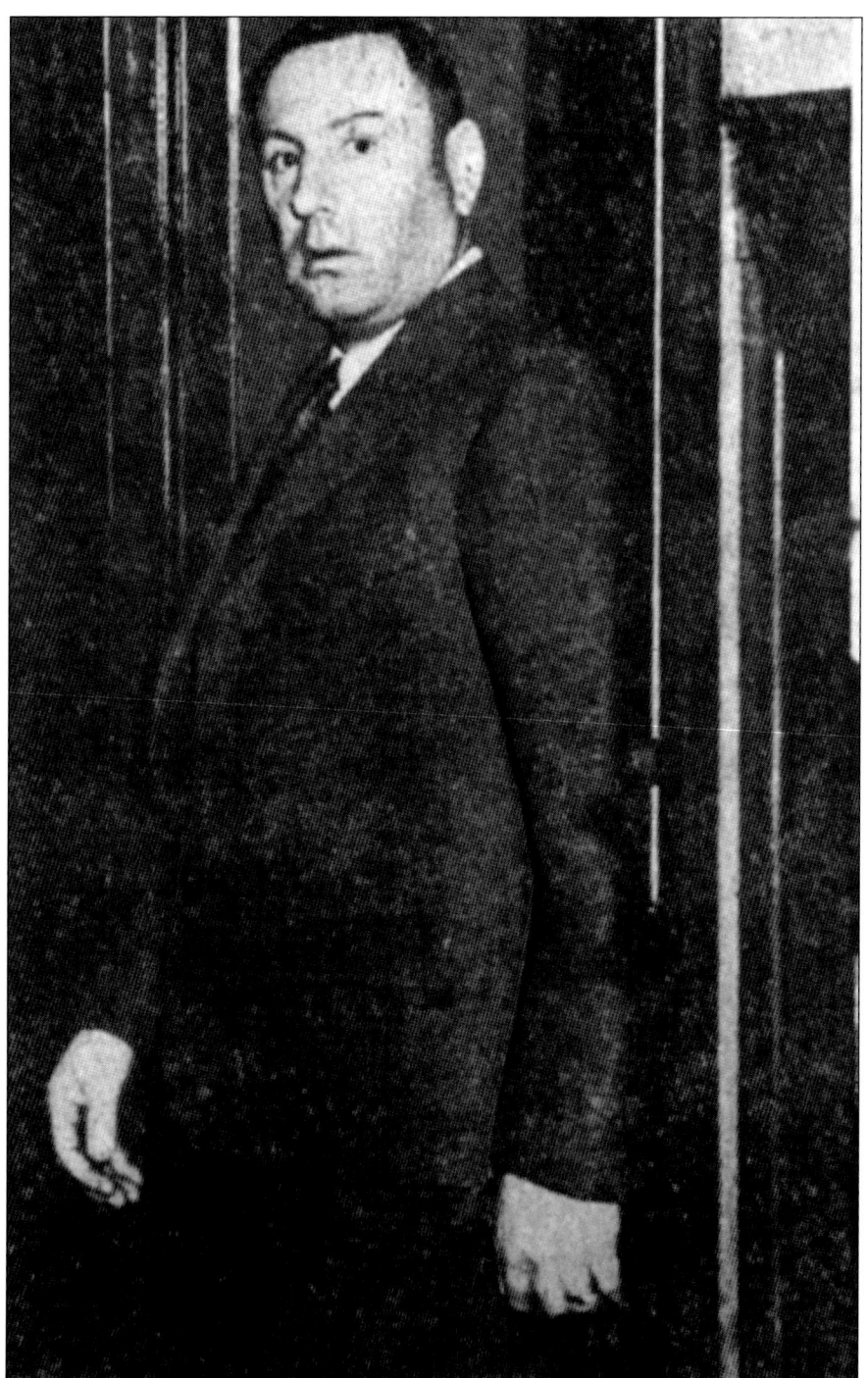

In 1937, a federal grand jury in San Francisco indicted John Locurto on 13 counts of possession of counterfeit tax stamps. Locurto pled guilty to possessing untaxed liquor and was sentenced to one year in jail and fined $5,000. A dozen other indictments were dismissed. It was calculated that Locurto owed $4,337.77 in taxes on the liquor found at the resort during the raid. Locurto is pictured here walking into court. (Courtesy of Tony Gairnese.)

After the raid at Locurto's Gardens, John Locurto sold the license to Will R. Conway. The name was changed to Olympic Gardens. Not even two weeks after the license was granted, Sheriff Lyle's deputies raided the resort. Seventy-five men and women were grouped around the blackjack and craps tables, and the dealers were arrested. Four slot machines were also found. (Courtesy of the San Jose Public Library.)

Sheriff Raids Locurto, Holds Three Dealers

75 Patrons Routed From Hot Spot, Now Called 'Olympic Gardens.'

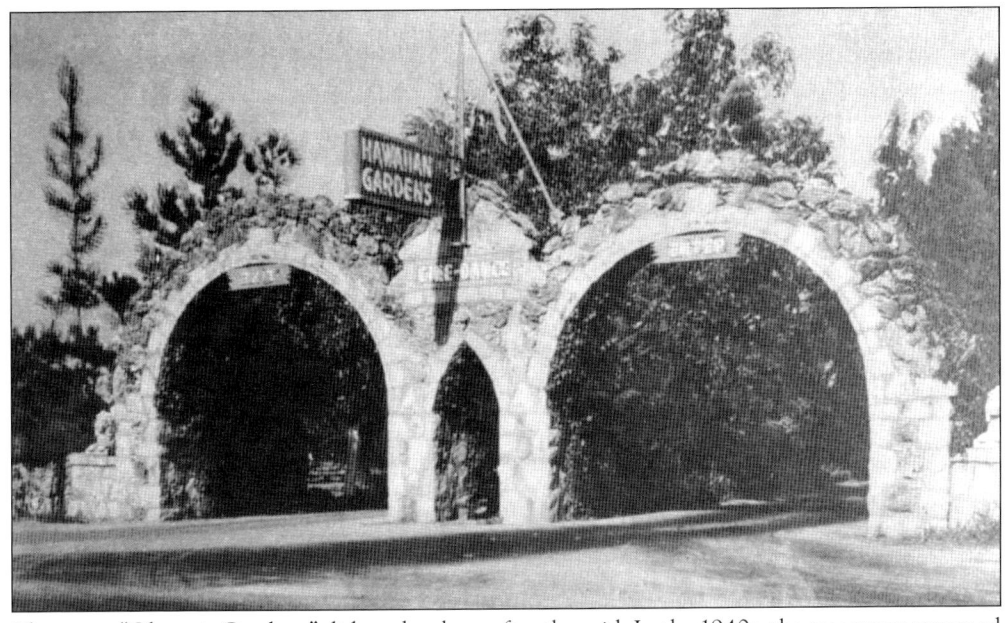

The name "Olympic Gardens" did not last long after the raid. In the 1940s, the resort was renamed Hawaiian Gardens and came under the ownership and management of Baron Long. The entrance to Hawaiian Gardens featured two Gothic arches modeled after the Dobois Castle. The Locurto name was removed and replaced with the words "Dine-Dance." A new sign reading "Hawaiian Gardens" was installed, matching the neon lights running along the two arches. (Courtesy of Ted Ramos.)

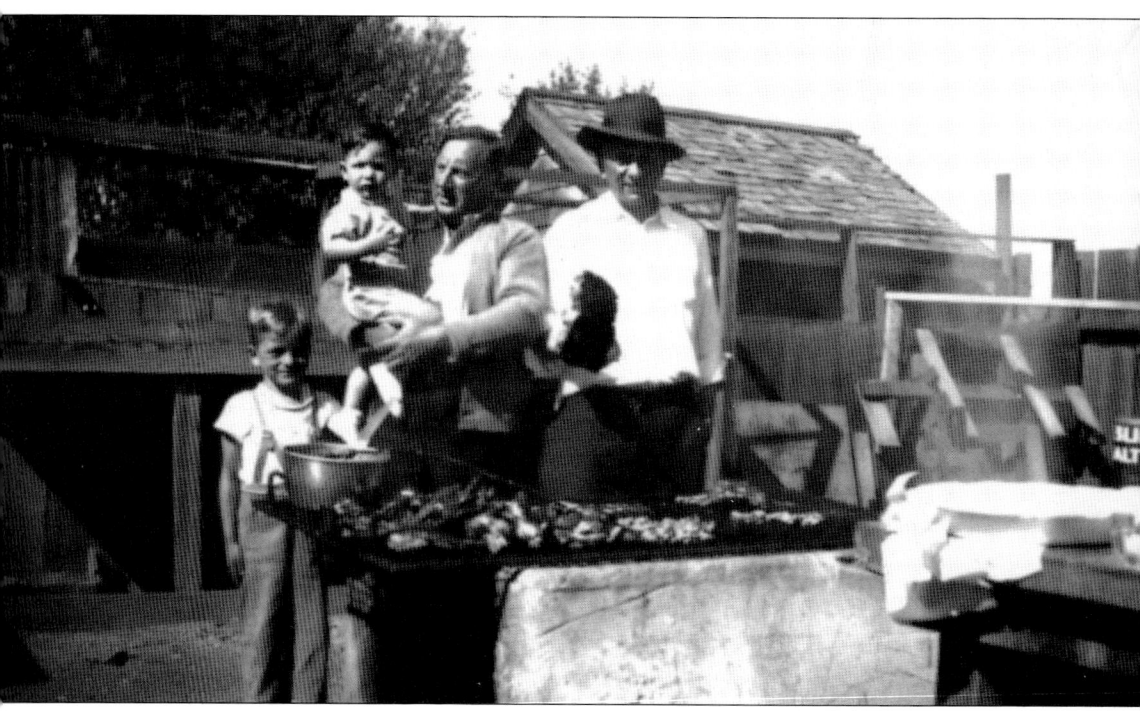

By the time Hawaiian Gardens was operated by Baron Long, John Locurto had retired. He spent his time with his family and grandchildren, having concluded his days in the liquor business and as a resort operator. On January 3, 1957, Locurto, known as the "Liquor King" of Santa Clara County, passed away at the age of 69. In this photograph, Locurto is pictured with his two grandsons and his brother-in-law Frank Gairnese. (Courtesy of Jeanne Rene Watson.)

Eight
Post-Prohibition

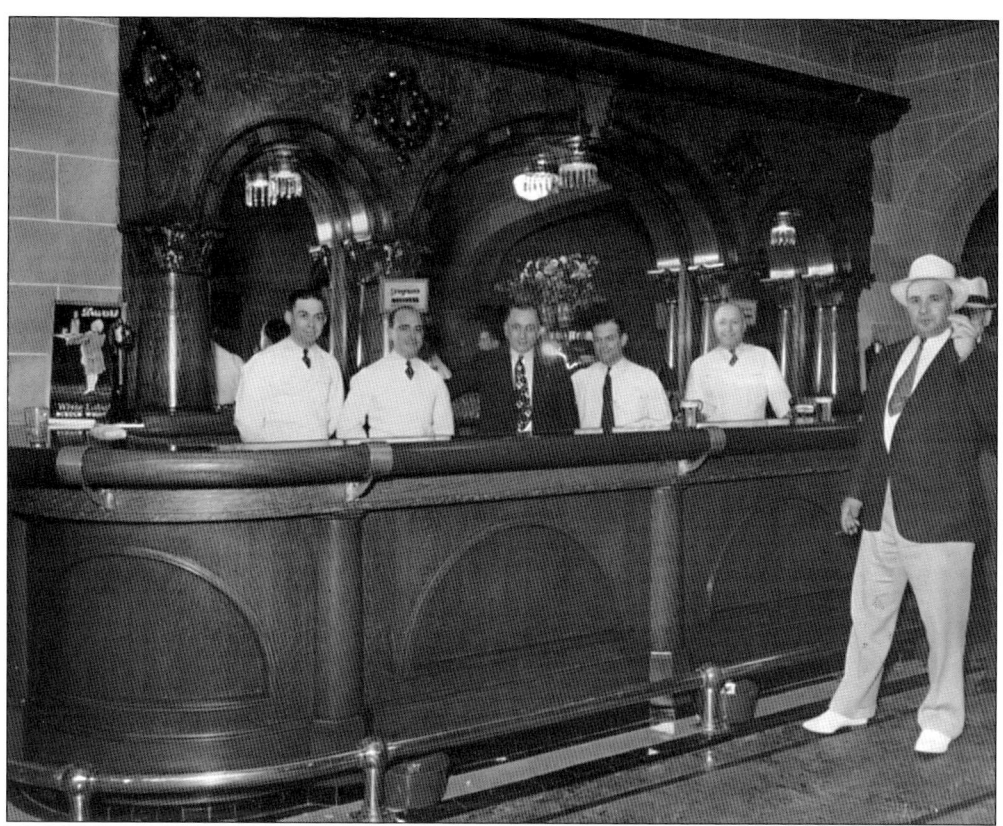

On December 5, 1933, Prohibition was officially repealed. It did not take long for those who had operated speakeasies and roadhouses to find new work. In this photograph from 1935, former bootlegger and resort operator Frank Gairnese (behind the bar in a dark coat) stands with his bartenders on the opening night of his new establishment, Frank's, located at North First and St. John Streets. (Courtesy of Tony Gairnese.)

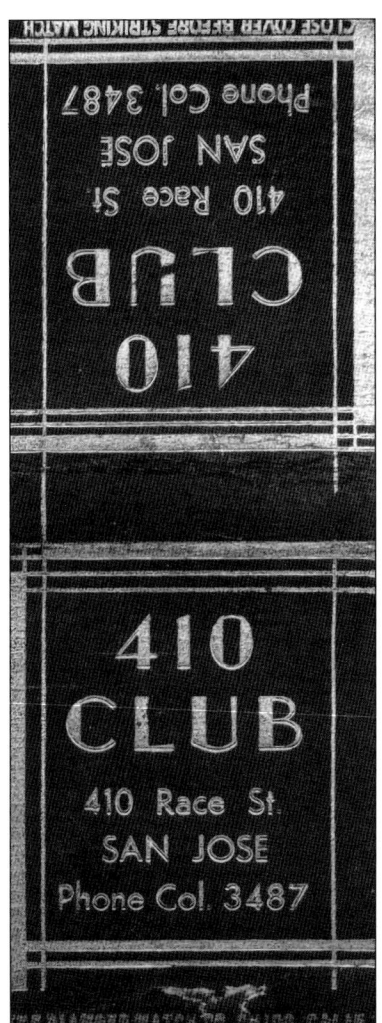

As soon as Prohibition was repealed, Frank Gairnese transformed the 410 Club from an underground speakeasy into a legitimate resort serving licensed beer and hard liquor. The club featured live musical entertainment, including jazz and Dixie music. In 1935, Frank Gairnese transferred the 410 Club's operating license to Elven Johnson. He then went on to open a new bar in downtown San Jose called Frank's. In 1941, Frank Gairnese reopened the 410 Club after the California Board of Equalization revoked Johnson's liquor license in 1937. However, Gairnese also faced trouble with the State Board of Equalization for selling drinks after the 2:00 a.m. curfew, resulting in a 15-day license suspension. By 1942, the 410 Club closed permanently. (Left, courtesy of Ted Ramos; below, courtesy of the San Jose Public Library.)

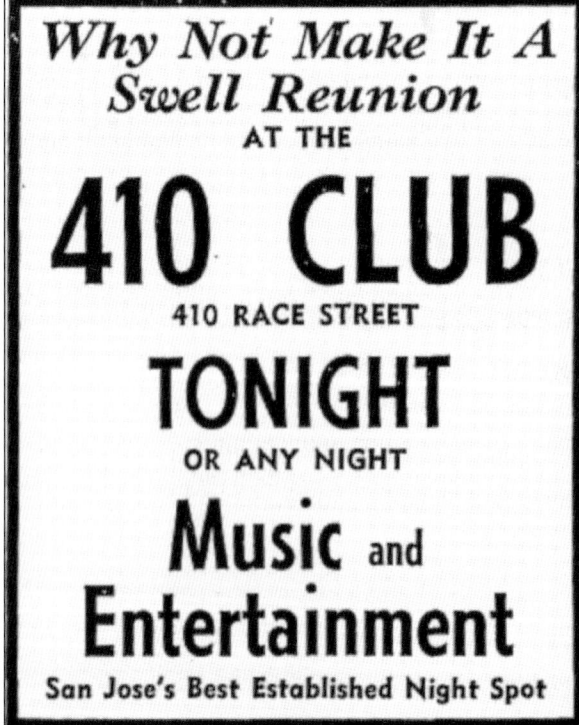

In 1935, after giving up the license for the 410 Club, Frank Gairnese opened his new bar, Frank's. Located on the southwest corner of North First and St. John Streets, next to St. James Park and the downtown post office, Frank's boasted a more extravagant location and interior than any of his previous establishments. It featured a long, beautifully crafted bar and marble floors with the letter "F" for Frank engraved into them. This photograph of the exterior was taken after Frank had sold his bar. The building was torn down by developers in 1972. (Right, courtesy of History San Jose; below, courtesy of the Sourisseau Academy.)

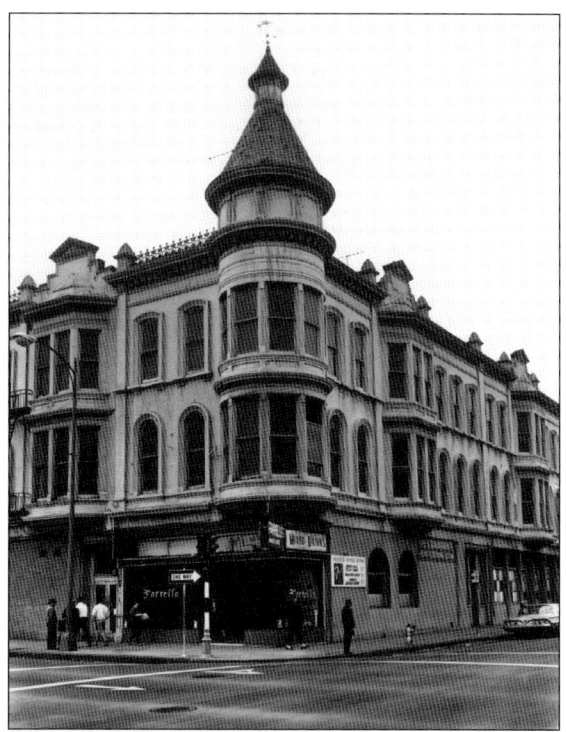

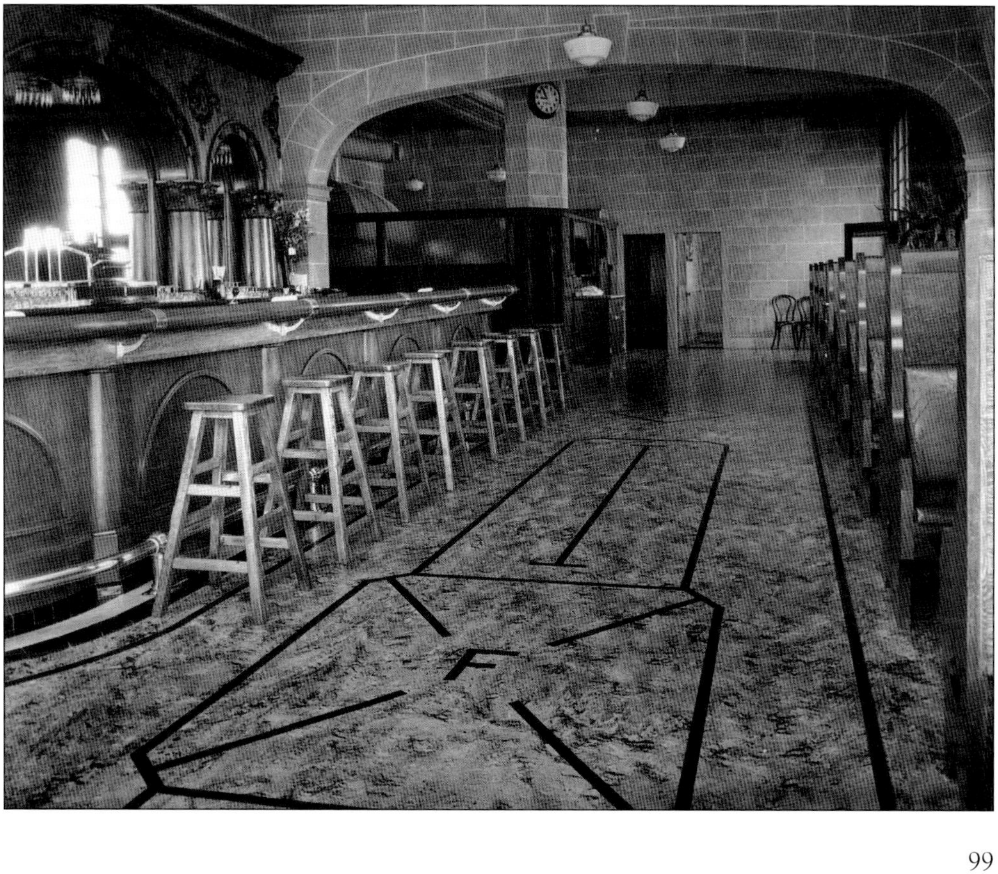

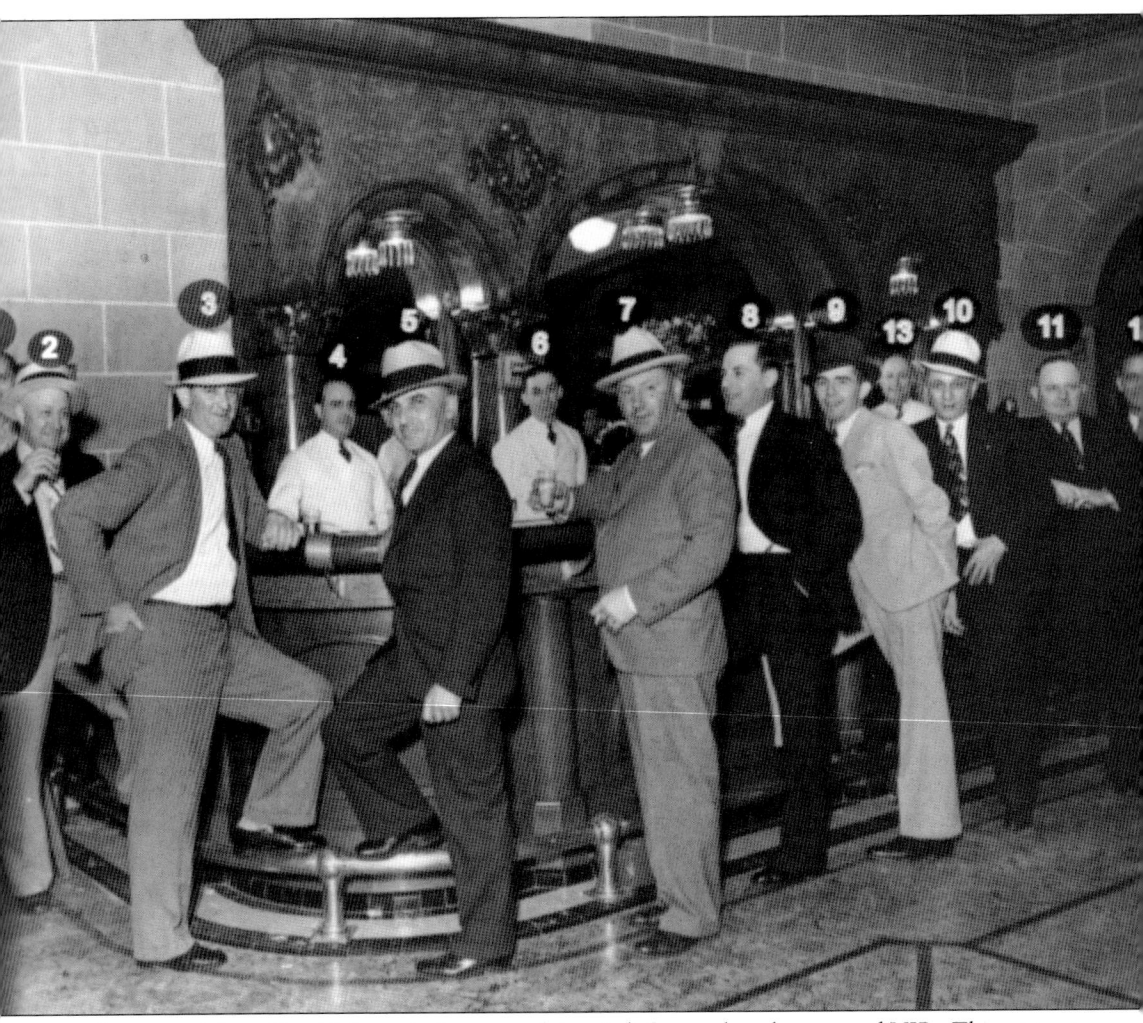

Opening night at Frank's brought in some of the city's former bootleggers and VIPs. This picture features the following gentlemen standing in front of the bar celebrating opening night: (1) unidentified, (2) Frank Chapman, (3) Vince Armetta, (4) Ted Martinez, (5) Vincent Moscarella, (6) Mike Musso, (7) John Locurto, (8) Harry Ferrari, (9) Jimmy Mills, (10) Frank Gairnese, (11) unidentified (possibly Charles Bigley), (12) unidentified, and (13) Henry Rogers. (Courtesy of History San Jose and Tanner Ramos.)

In 1941, Frank Gairnese sold Frank's and reopened the 410 Club. Frank's eventually became Farrell's, which also became a popular bar downtown until 1972, when the city tore down the building. This matchbook was from Frank's and was available to customers. (Courtesy of Ted Ramos.)

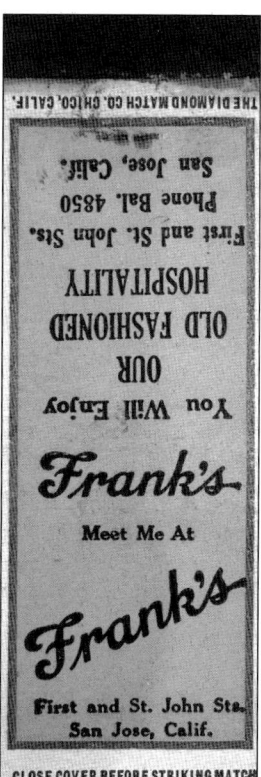

On February 28, 1942, after permanently closing the 410 Club, Frank Gairnese opened the San Carlos Club, the last bar he operated before retiring. Located at the corner of West San Carlos Street and Lincoln Avenue, the San Carlos Club became a popular neighborhood staple known for its good music and entertainment, just like all of Gairnese's previous establishments. (Courtesy of the San Jose Public Library.)

FRANK GAIRNESE'S NEW
SAN CARLOS CLUB
OPENING TONIGHT!

(Corner Lincoln and San Carlos Avenue)

- Music and Entertainment Nightly
- A Place to Meet Old Friends
- Al Meyers to Serve You

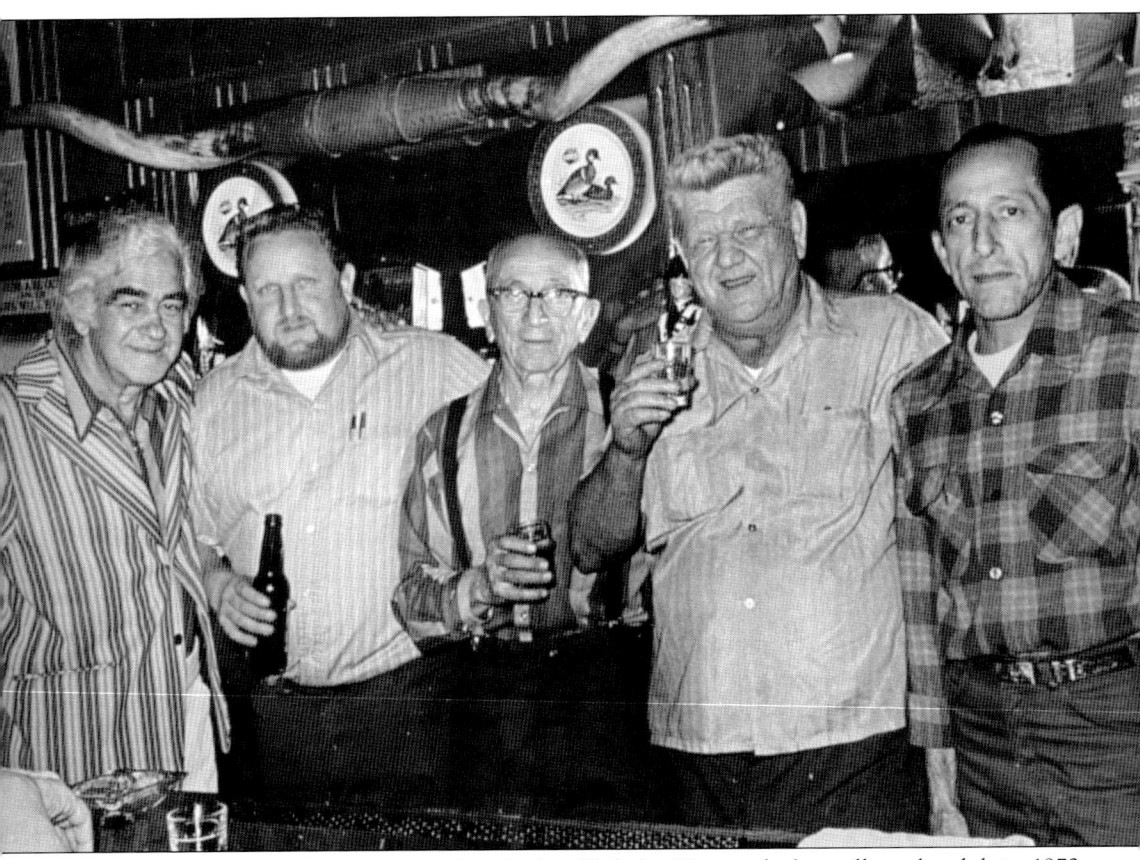

Frank Gairnese would operate the San Carlos Club for 30 years before selling the club in 1972 and officially retiring from the liquor business. Despite all his arrests during Prohibition and troubles with the California Board of Equalization afterward, Gairnese joined the Bartenders Union Local 577 and was viewed as a good member ever since. Gairnese is pictured here (center) behind the bar with his family and friends at the San Carlos Club. (Courtesy of Tony Gairnese.)

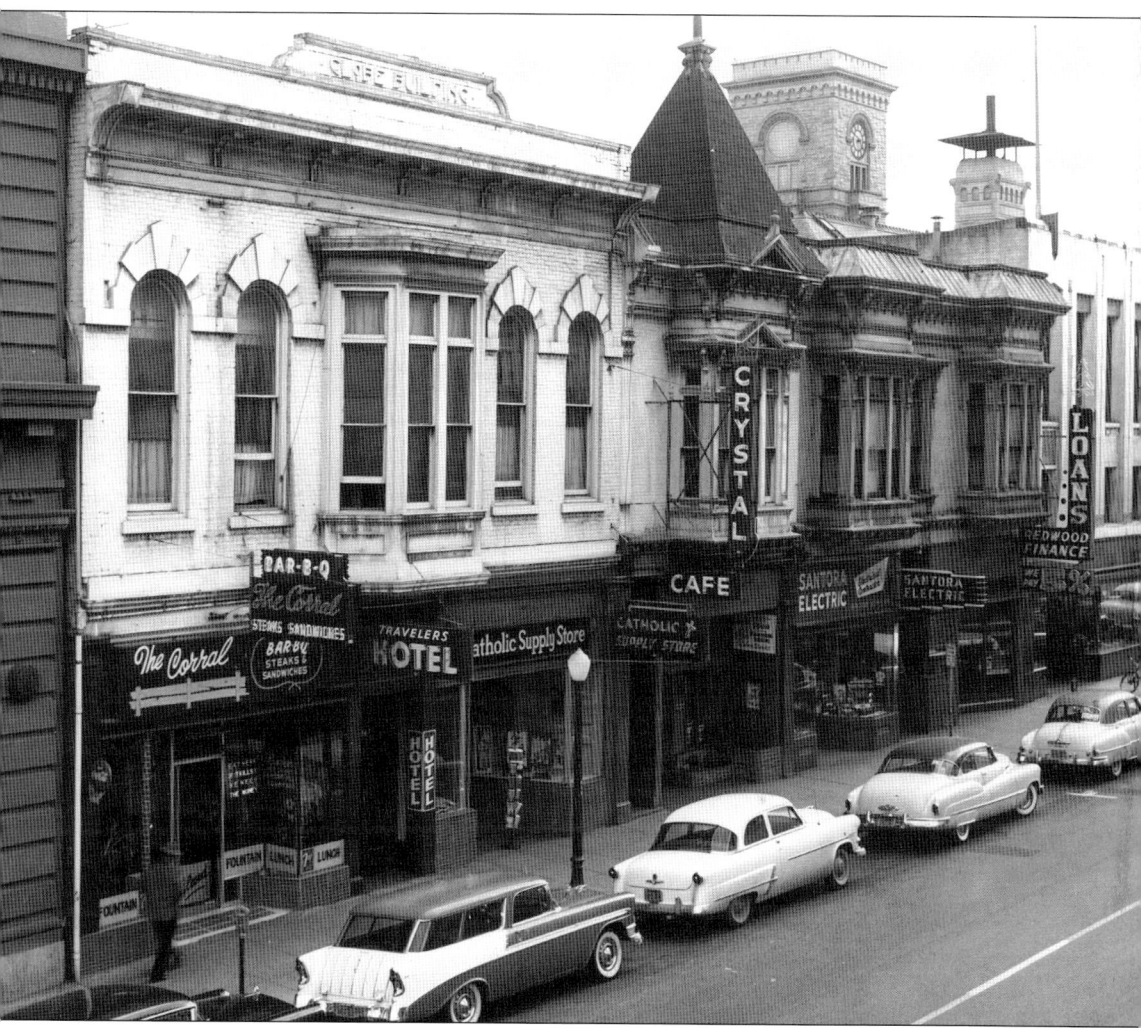

After Prohibition ended, the Crystal Café resumed its business as a bar and café. It also continued its gambling operations with a horse racing betting parlor in the back room. Regardless of all its liquor raids during Prohibition and gambling raids after Prohibition, the business remained open until the mid-1970s, when the city redevelopment demolished the entire block. (Courtesy of History San Jose.)

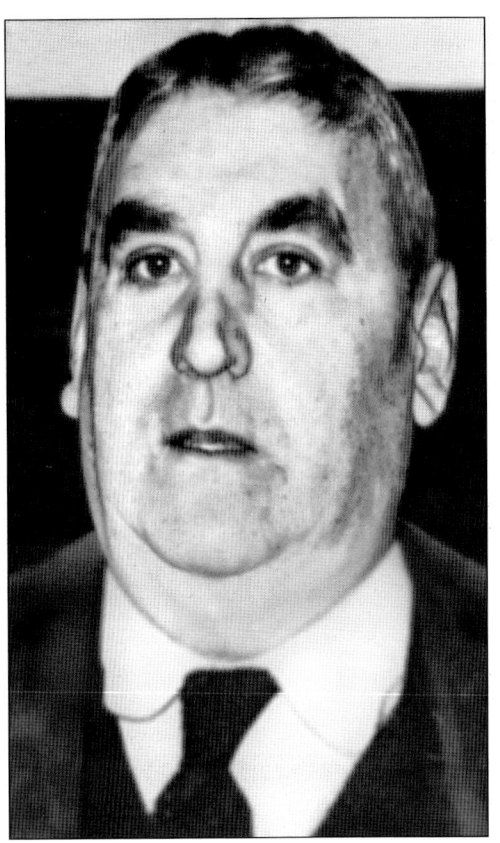

In 1938, Chick Leddy was paroled and pardoned by the governor after serving 10 years of a life sentence for murdering a customer at Leddy's Almaden resort in 1928. Subsequently, the governor's aide was investigated for bribery amid rumors that Leddy had paid him for his release. (Courtesy of the San Jose Public Library.)

After Chick Leddy was pardoned from prison after serving 10 years for murder, he opened the Alma Bar at 198 Alma Avenue. This location was near the speakeasy resort he operated during Prohibition. Leddy operated the bar with his son Clarence Jim Leddy until Chick died in 1950. The bar later got in trouble for liquor law violations. (Courtesy of History San Jose.)

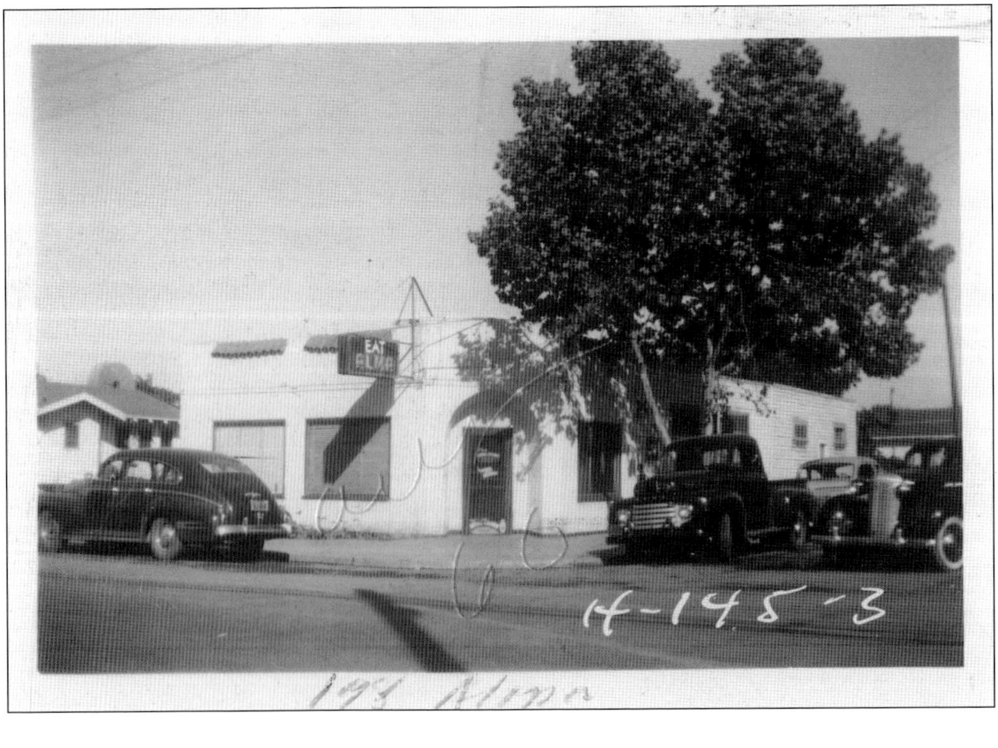

Jim Leddy continued to operate the Alma Bar after his father's death. In 1959, the Alma Bar's liquor license was suspended for serving alcohol after 2:00 a.m. The Alma Bar closed shortly thereafter. This matchbook was given to the customers at the bar. (Courtesy of Ted Ramos.)

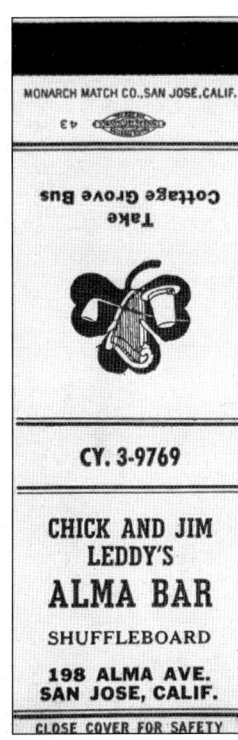

After Prohibition, Sam Loproto transitioned from the grocery business to opening a tavern and a barbershop behind the building. The tavern, known as Sam's Cavern, was operated by Sam and his son Frank. Sam worked as both a bartender at the tavern and a barber at the barbershop. In the 1940s, Sam brought in Mildred Nelson, who made the best tamales in town, transforming Sam's Cavern from a local pub into a popular bar and restaurant. (Courtesy of Sam Loproto.)

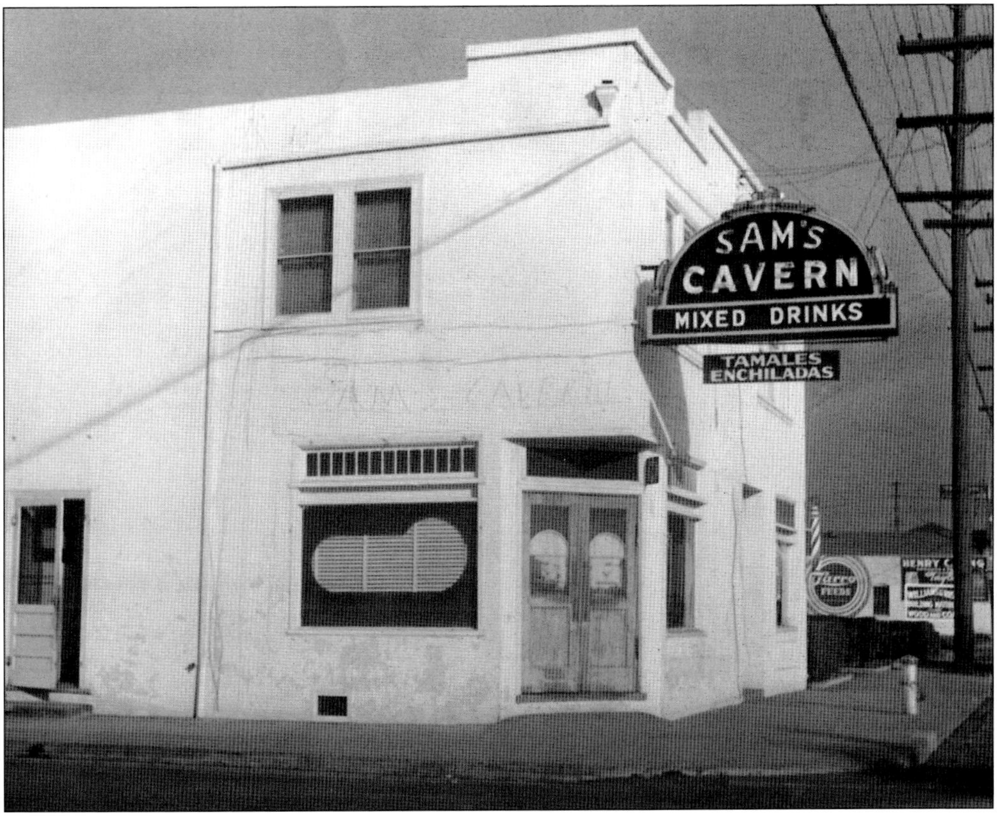

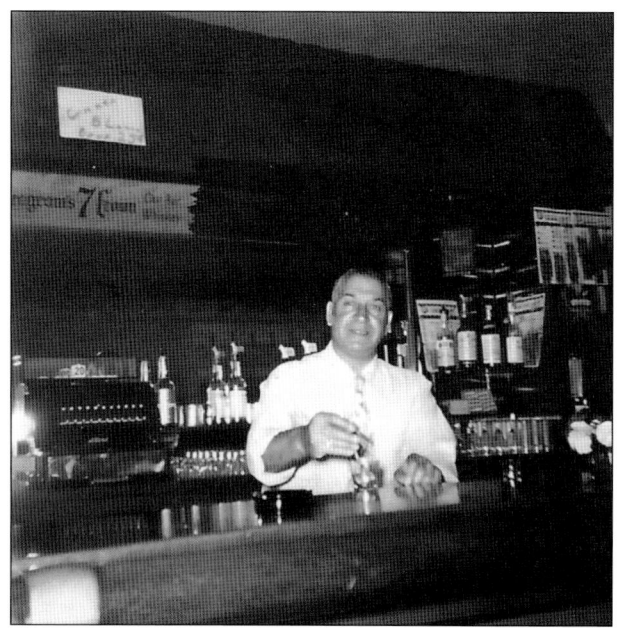

Sam Loproto's son Frank entered World War II, during which time Sam remodeled the building, including its exterior. When Frank returned from the war, he rejoined his father in running Sam's Cavern. By the 1950s, Sam's Cavern was thriving and had become a local favorite. However, in 1958, Sam passed away, and despite the tavern's popularity and success, it began to struggle in the 1960s, becoming a target of crime and robberies. Eventually, Frank sold the bar and opened a new establishment called the Red Coach Lounge. Pictured at left is Sam behind the bar, and the image below shows Sam with his son Frank. (Both, courtesy of Sam Loproto.)

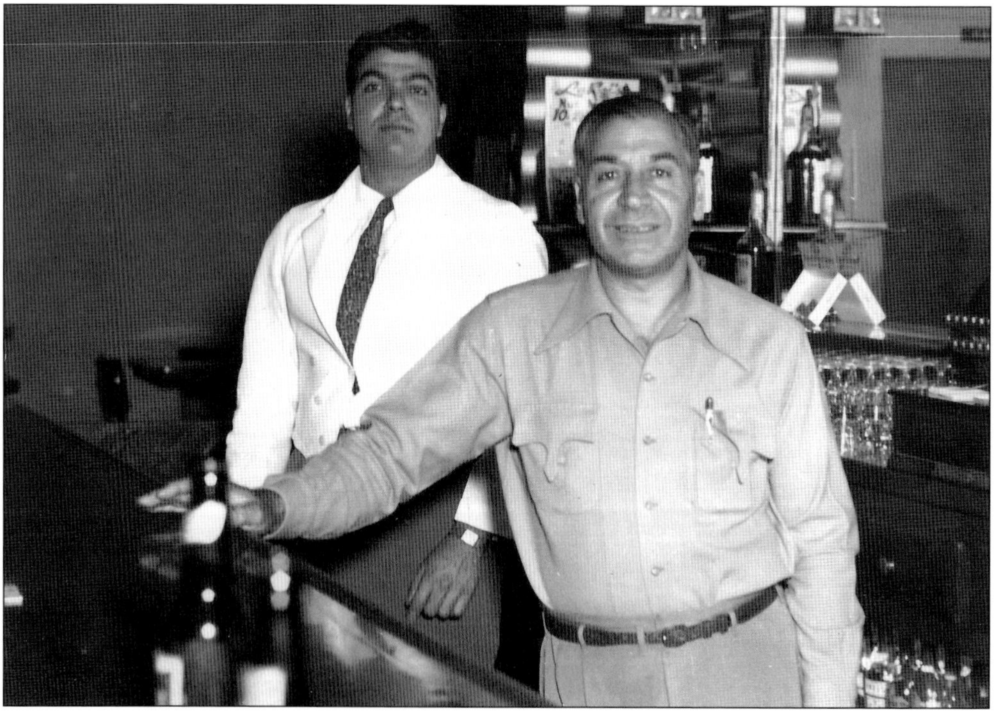

Martin "Bert" Haley operated a bar and liquor store at 79 Post Street after Prohibition. During Prohibition, he drove a limousine to deliver liquor to customers. In 1921, he was caught and arrested, and the federal government confiscated the limousine. In 1922, he was arrested again during a liquor raid at the Newland Hotel. In 1959, Haley was arrested for selling heroin with another ex-bootlegger, Joe Parente. This drew the attention of the Alcohol Beverage Control (ABC) Agency, which investigated Haley's liquor license at his 79 Post Street tavern. The investigation revealed that another Prohibition-era bootlegger, Frank "Dingo" Mendoza, was a silent partner, leading to the revocation of Haley's license. (Both, courtesy of Ted Ramos.)

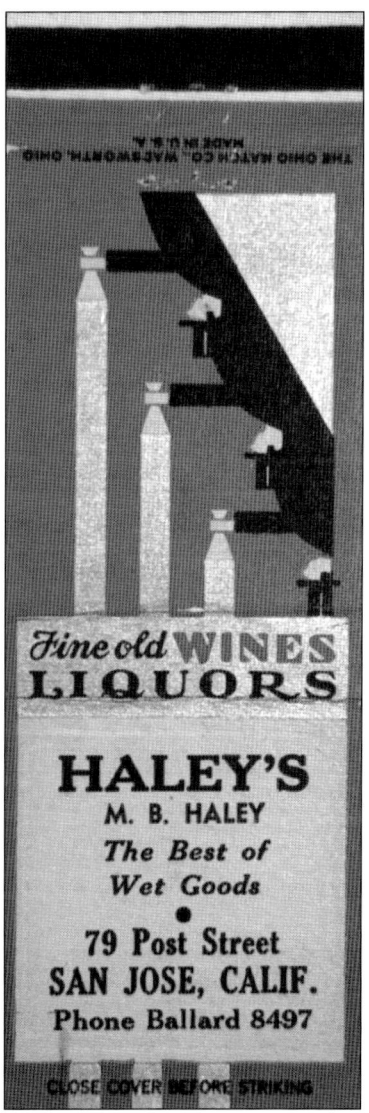

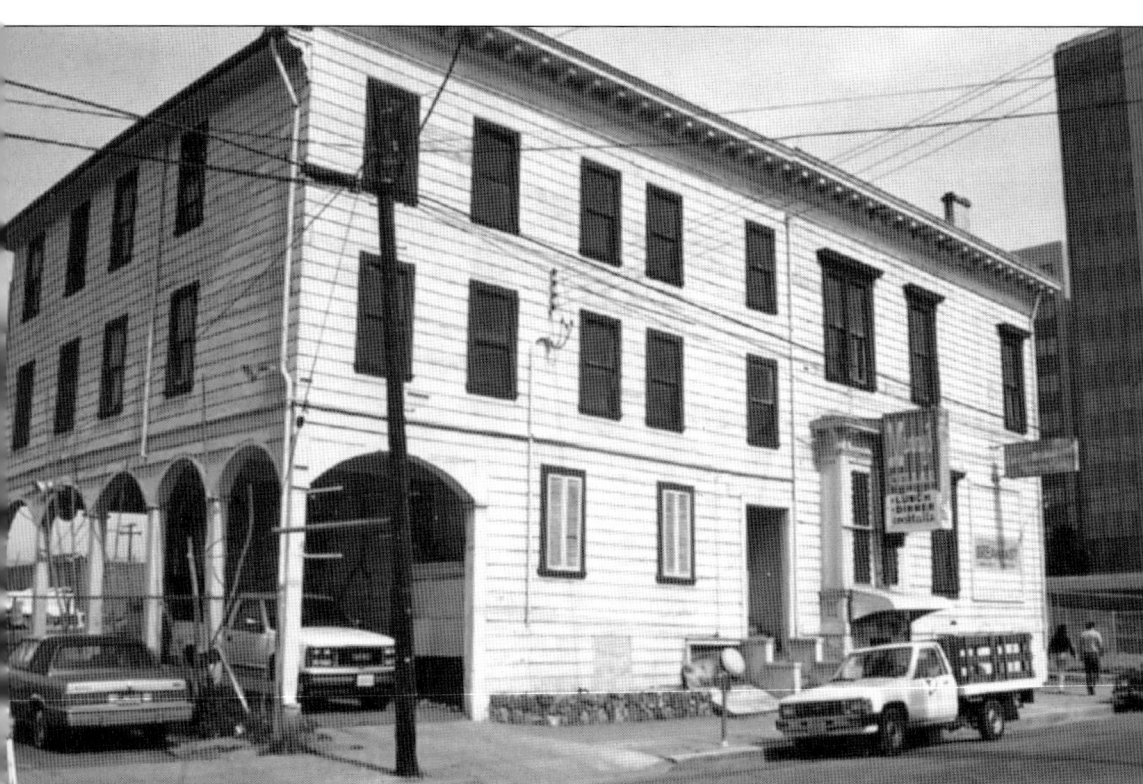

The Italian Hotel, which had its share of raids during Prohibition, became one of San Jose's favorite watering holes. It was not until 1962 that the bar Manny's Cellar opened in the old Italian Hotel. Operated by Manny Pereira and Tom Taylor, it remained a San Jose favorite until it closed in 1990. Today, the sign is still being preserved at History San Jose, and the building has been restored as a museum. (Courtesy of History San Jose.)

BIMBO'S GRILL
Eighth and Taylor Streets
Dancing Every Saturday Nite
THREE-PIECE ORCHESTRA
American and Italian Dinners
Tommy Aristo Serving at the Bar

Tommy Aristo, who was a bartender for Frank Gairnese and operated a speakeasy resort near King and Story Roads, later used his skills and experience to tend bar at Bimbo's Grill at Eighth and Taylor Streets. This popular destination for nearby cannery workers offered Italian dinners and live entertainment. Bimbos later became Bini's, which remained a favorite spot for locals and employees of the city and county buildings. (Above, courtesy of the San Jose Public Library; below, courtesy of History San Jose.)

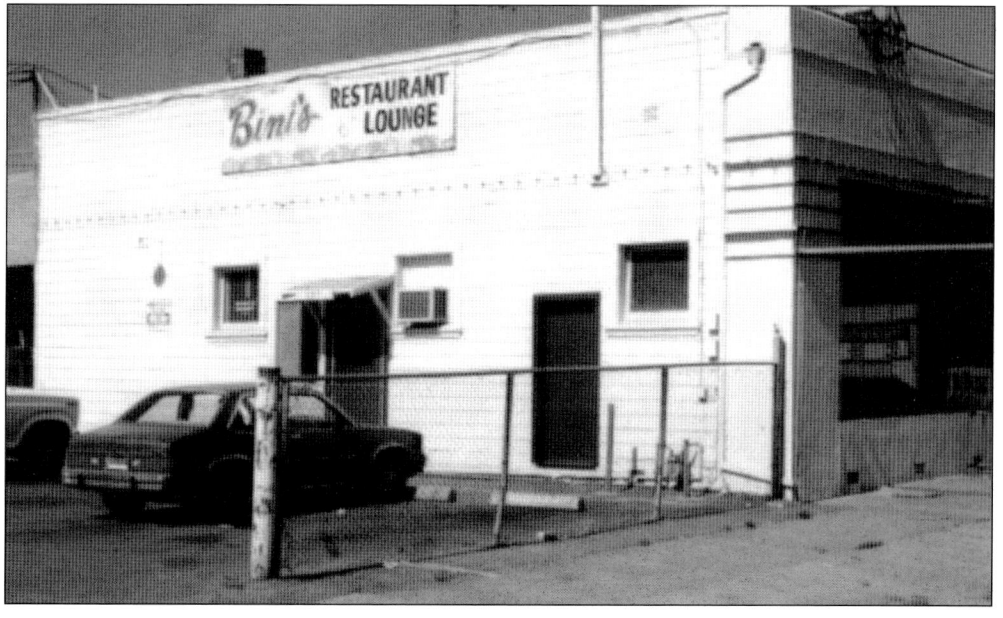

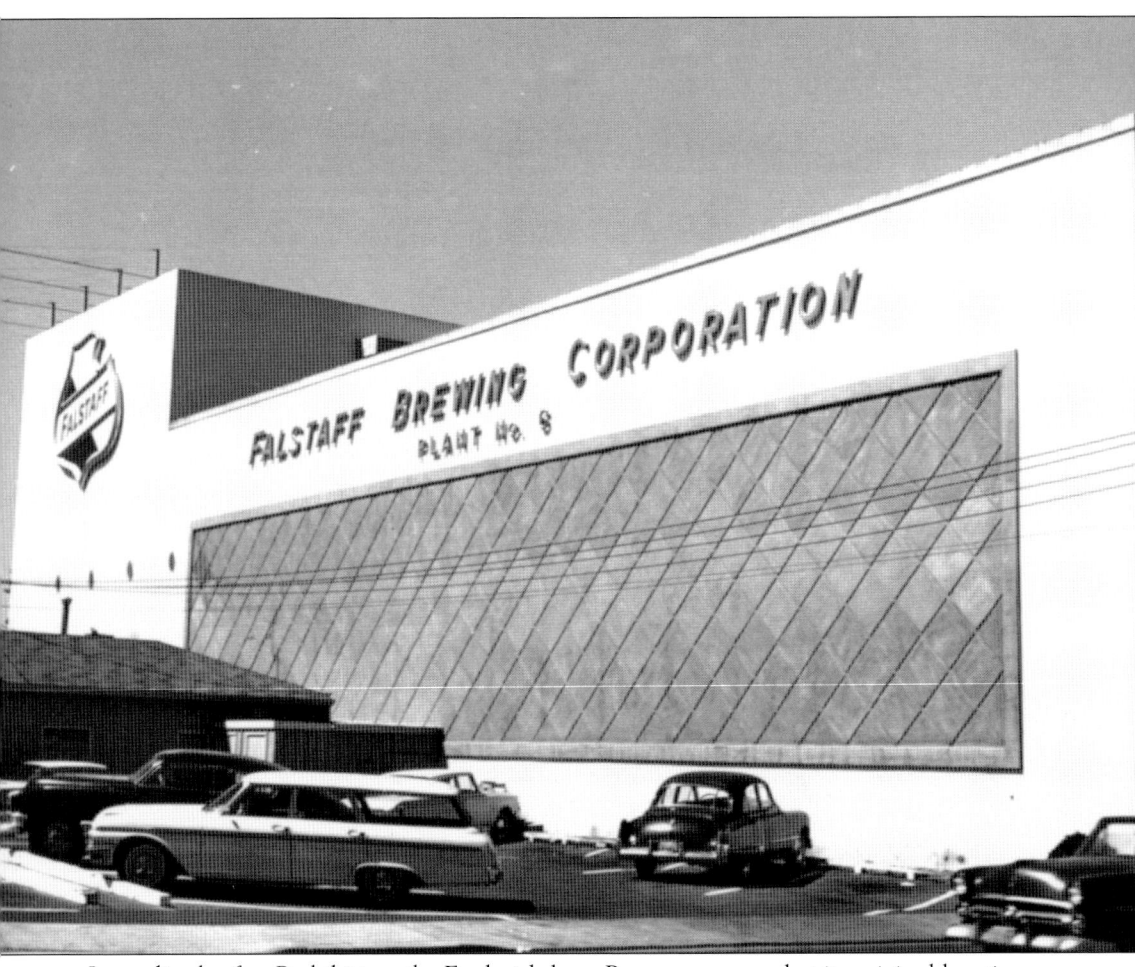

Immediately after Prohibition, the Fredericksburg Brewery reopened at its original location near Alameda and Cinnabar Streets. It continued operating until 1936, when the Pacific Brewing and Malting Company purchased the site. In 1952, the Pacific Brewing and Malting Company was acquired by the Falstaff Brewing Corporation. This brewery was the last remaining one in San Jose from the pre-Prohibition era. The building was demolished in 1980. (Courtesy of History San Jose.)

Dave Holt, who operated one of San Jose's most popular speakeasy resorts on Monterey Road, turned his resort into a legitimate business, continuing the name as the Palm Inn. He also ran a restaurant called Holt's Buffet on West San Fernando Street, and Holt became San Jose's first licensed bail bondsman. In 1937, Dave Holt offered his bail bond services to former bootlegger and speakeasy operator Harry Ferrari, who had been arrested for assault at one of his prostitution houses on Dupont Street in Little Tijuana. Ferrari jumped bail and fled to Mexico, leaving Holt with the $3,000 bond. (Both, courtesy of the San Jose Public Library.)

-Announcing-
the Reopening of
-PALM INN-
Dine, Dance, and Be Merry

Specializing in Southern Cooked Chickens, Steaks and Dinners

We Pride Ourselves on Barbecued Sandwiches!
DANCE AS LONG AS YOU LIKE

We Cater to Private Parties and Banquets

PHONE FOR RESERVATION, Ballard 8464
(Three Miles South on the Monterey Road)

Real Southern
Home Cooked
DINNER
50c
Holt's Tavern
Monterey Road
(Formerly Palm Inn)

Dancing - Refreshments

For Reservations Call
Bal 9F23

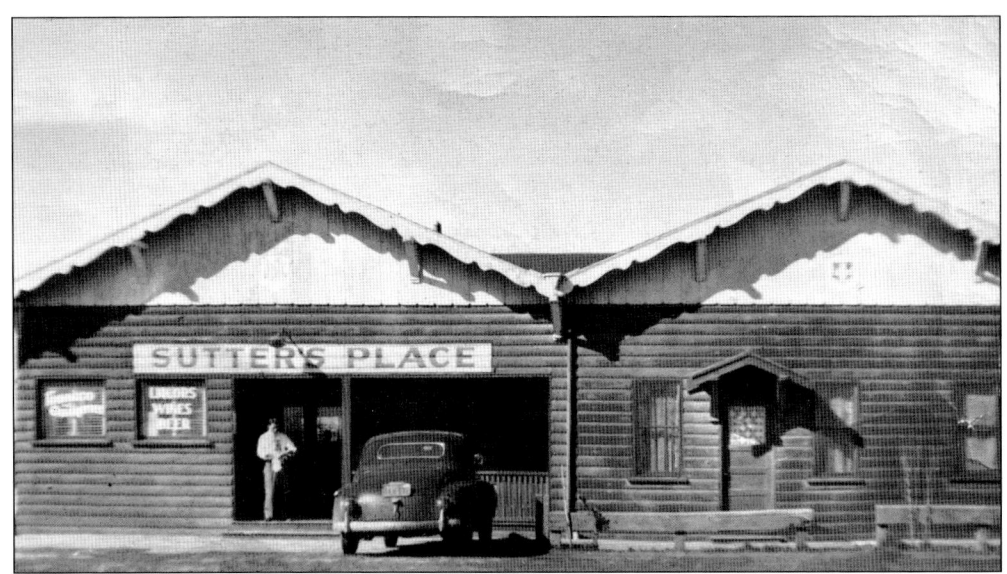

Joseph Sutter Sr. purchased the Panama Inn and renamed the establishment Sutter's Place, which became a favorite in the town of Alviso. Sutter Sr. operated Sutter's Place until his death in 1948. His son Joseph Sutter Jr. returned from the war and took over the operations. Sutter Jr. ran the club until it was forced to close and relocate in 1992. Sutter's Place transformed into Bay 101, one of the largest cardroom casinos in Northern California. (Courtesy of Charlene Sutter Arvizu.)

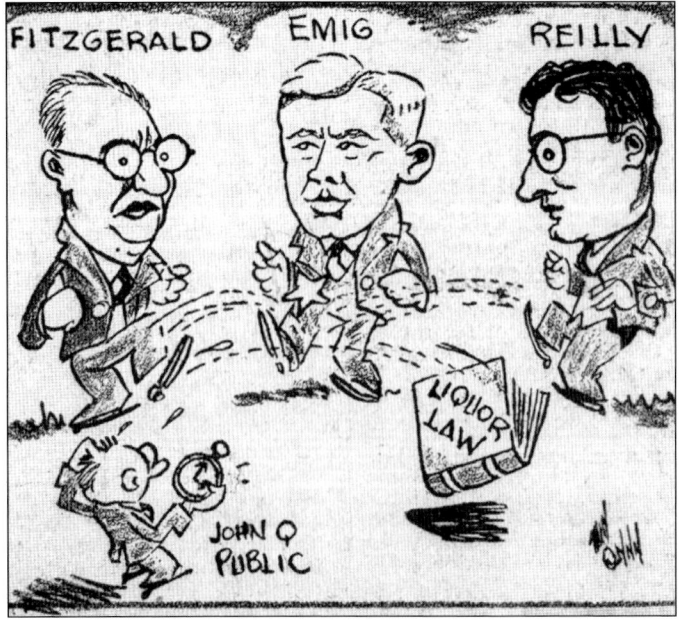

In 1941, San Jose faced issues with bars selling alcohol after curfew. District Attorney John Fitzgerald claimed his office was only responsible for prosecuting cases after they were presented to him. Sheriff Emig asserted that it was not the duty of his deputies to enforce closing hour violations, placing the responsibility on the State Board of Equalization. George Reilly, representing the State Board of Equalization, responded by stating that he had hired more personnel to enforce these laws. (Courtesy of Tony Gairnese.)

Nine
REMAINING RELICS OF PROHIBITION

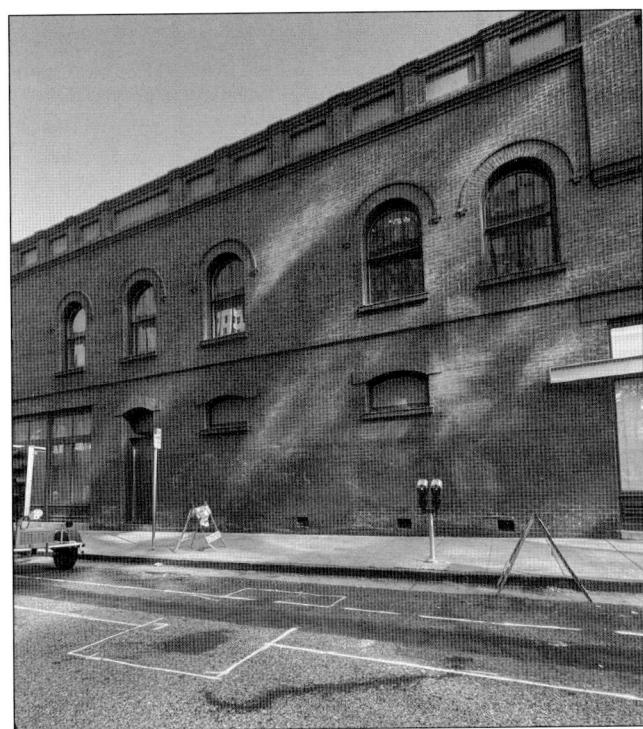

Jim Salata's contributions have been significant in preserving historical architecture in San Jose and have helped maintain some of the city's historical character. Norm Koepernik has been instrumental in preserving several old buildings in San Jose. He has ensured that some historic sites remain intact, providing valuable links to the past. The Preservation Action Council of San Jose has been and continues to be an important organization in ensuring that the city's historical sites are recognized and maintained. This photograph of the Alcantara Building, located at Post and Market Streets, is an example of successful preservation. The building housed the Arc Café, which was the speakeasy owned by Clarence Leddy. (Courtesy of Ted Ramos.)

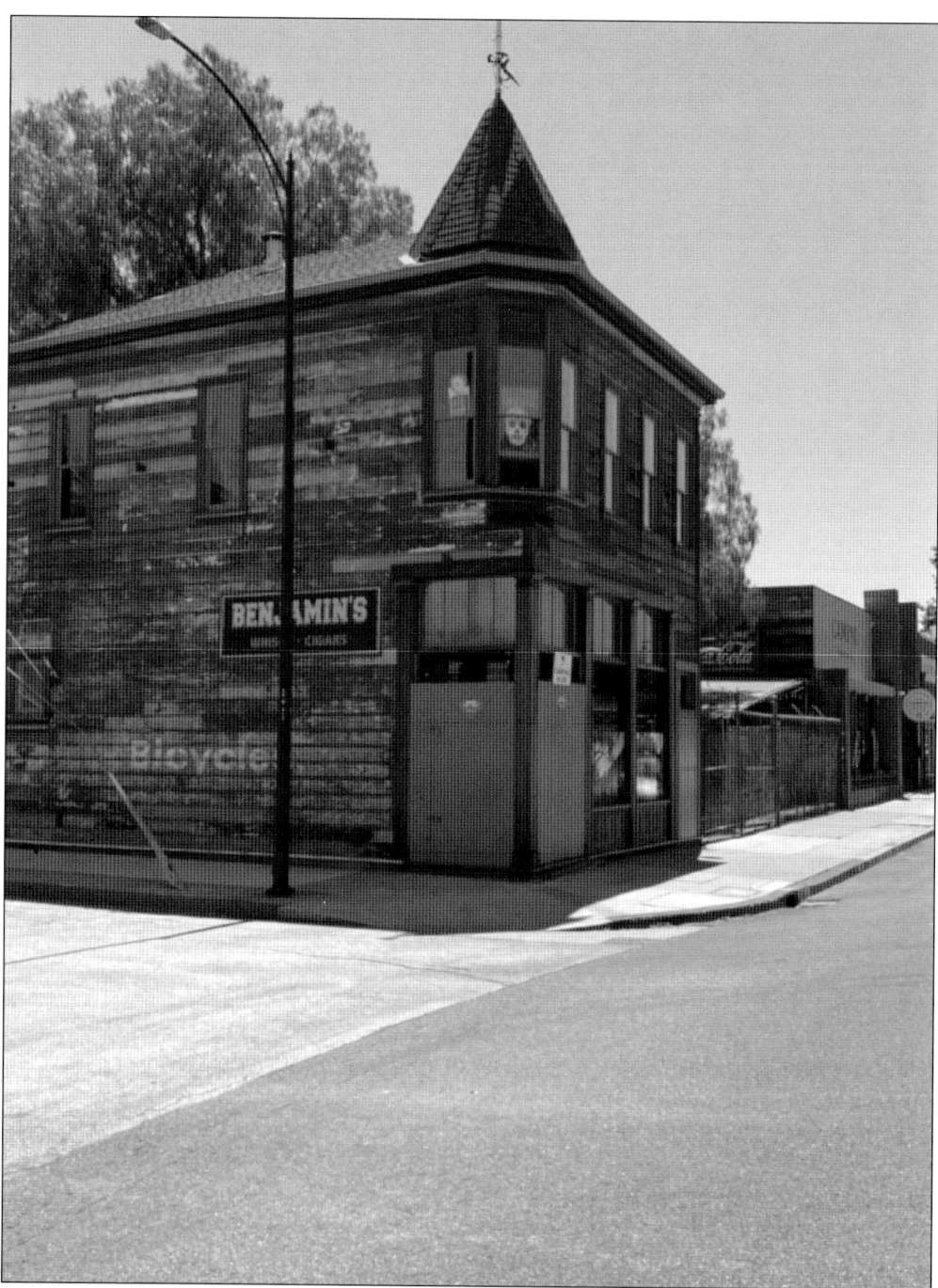

The building located on the corner of South First and Martha Streets, once known as the Fabery Bicycle Shop after its time as a grocery store operated by the Benjamin brothers, was slowly deteriorating due to neglect before being nearly destroyed by a fire. Jim Salata of Garden City Construction has beautifully restored this building, which will soon be ready to serve drinks once again. (Courtesy of Ted Ramos.)

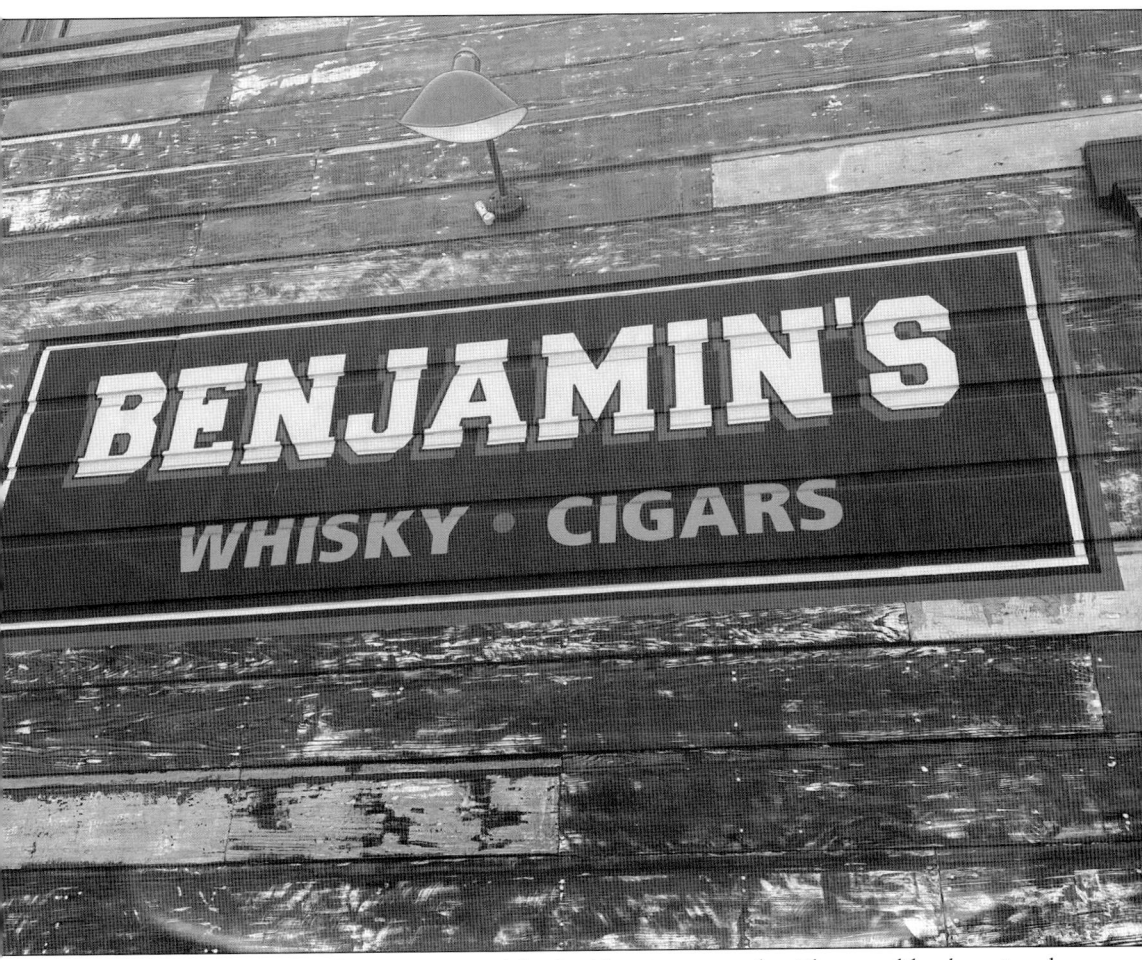

The attention to detail in the restoration of this building is spectacular. Elements like the painted advertising sign on the side of the building pay homage to its past, when the Benjamin brothers sold cigars at their store. This building looks to be reopening as a beer garden with artifacts of San Jose's history in the outdoor plaza. A special thank-you to the owner of this building for restoring it for future display. (Courtesy of Ted Ramos.)

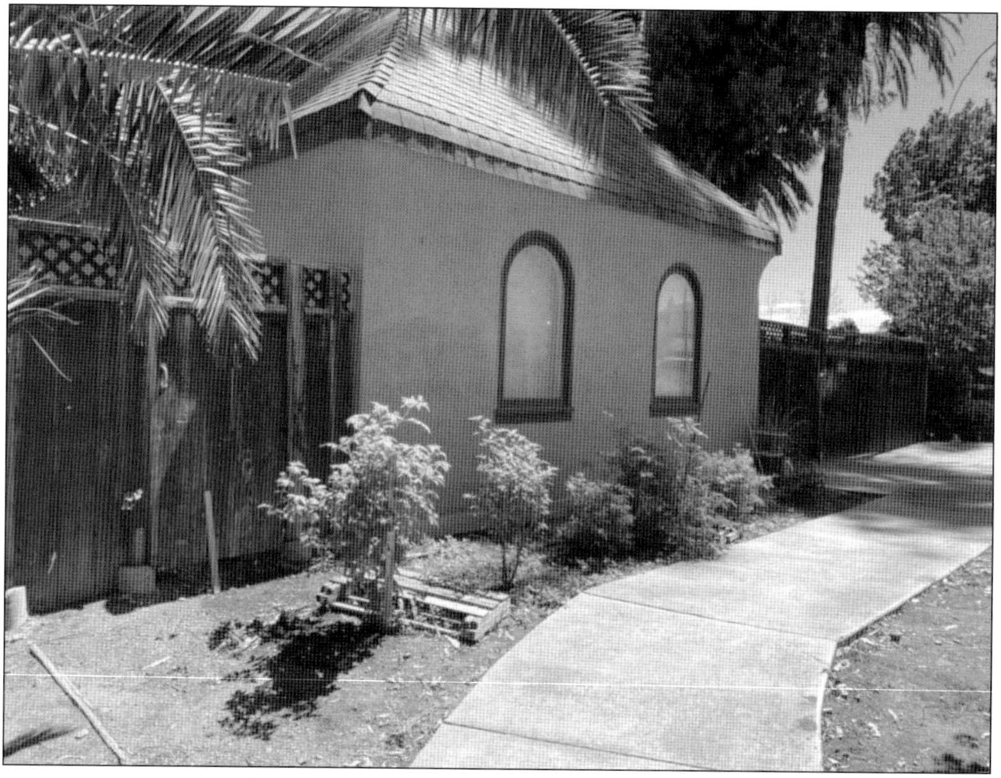

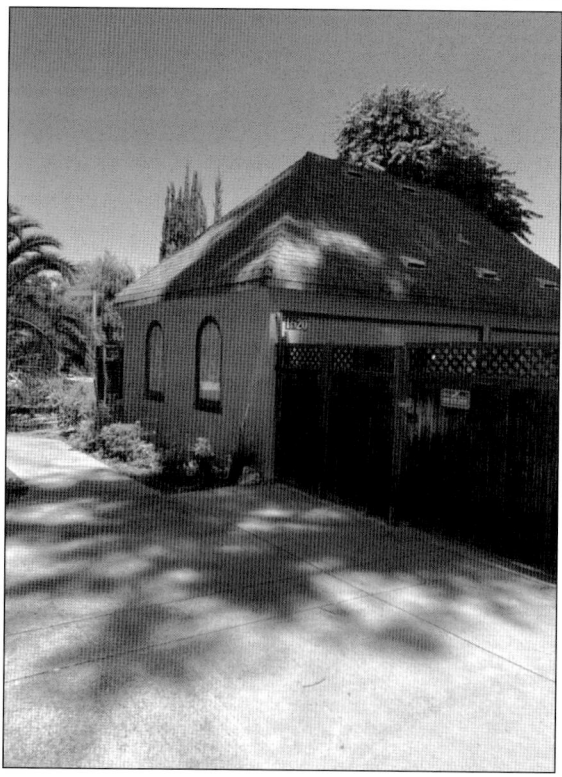

Locurto's Gardens may have faded into memory, but the Locurto residence still stands, serving as a leasing office for the apartments that now occupy the property. Adjacent to the house is the detached garage, which holds its own intriguing history. It was in this very garage that federal agents made a startling discovery: thousands of gallons of whiskey hidden in the basement. An additional curiosity is the doghouse connected to the garage, concealing a secret staircase that leads down to the basement. (Both, courtesy of Ted Ramos.)

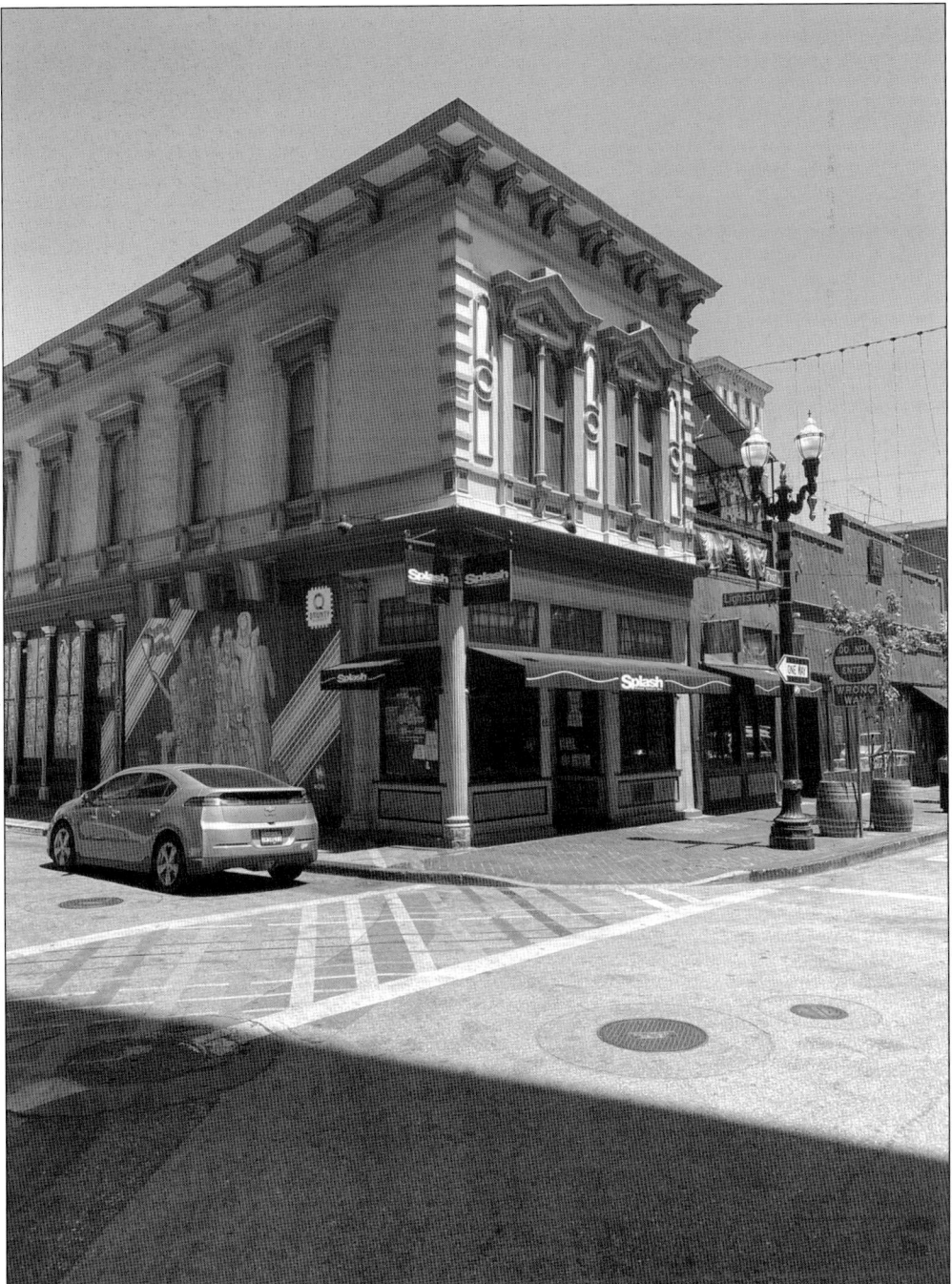

The building where Billy Finley operated Finley's Inn still stands today on Post Street. It is considered one of San Jose's oldest commercial buildings and has undergone various transformations over the years, housing businesses like Ace Loan pawn shop. Today, it operates as a bar, serving alcohol just as Finley once did in the building—but now legally. (Courtesy of Ted Ramos.)

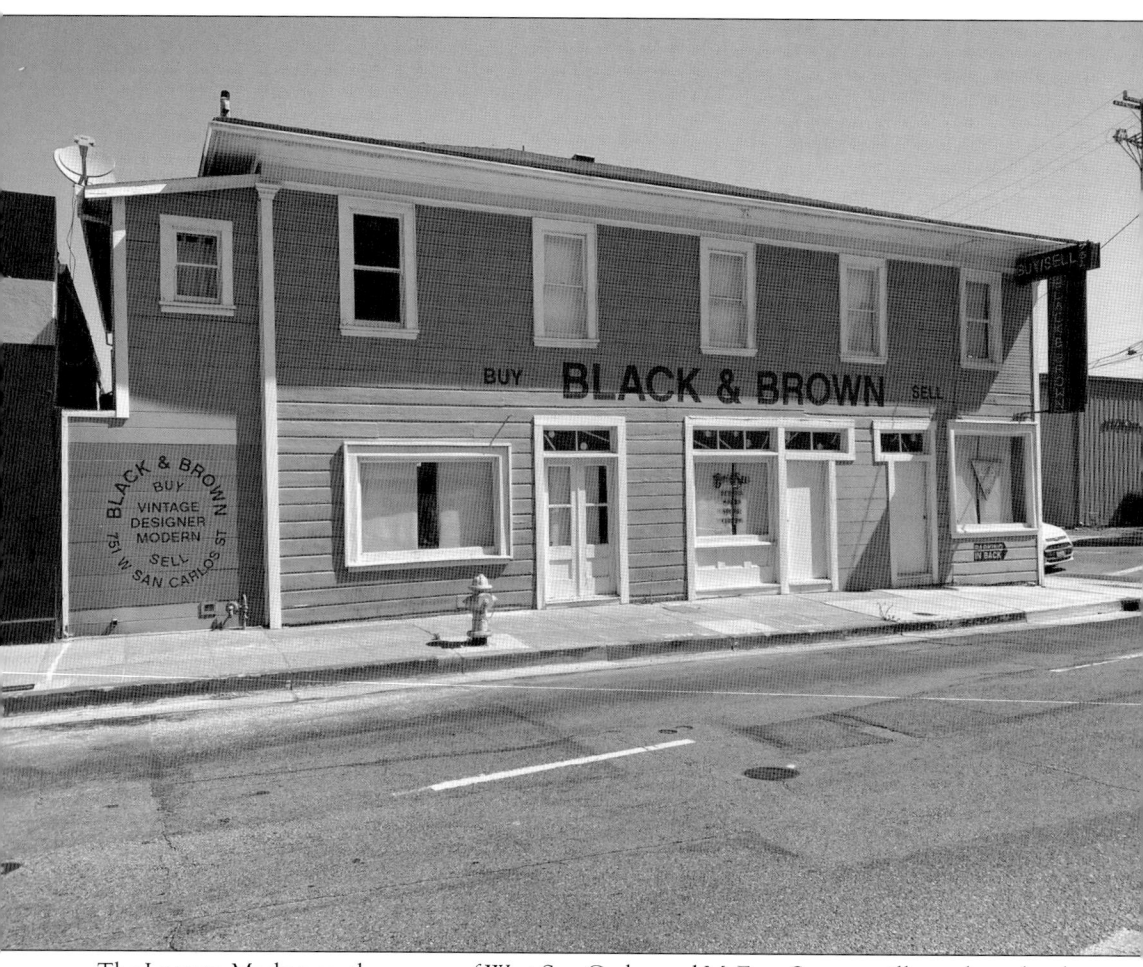

The Locurto Market, on the corner of West San Carlos and McEvoy Streets, still stands under the ownership of another San Jose building preservationist, Norm Koepernik. Upon acquiring the building, Koepernik embarked on a restoration. Today, it is leased as a vintage clothing store. The basement retains remnants of its early days, with meat carving devices from when the Locurto family and Frank Gairnese worked as butchers at the market before their bootlegging endeavors began. (Courtesy of Ted Ramos.)

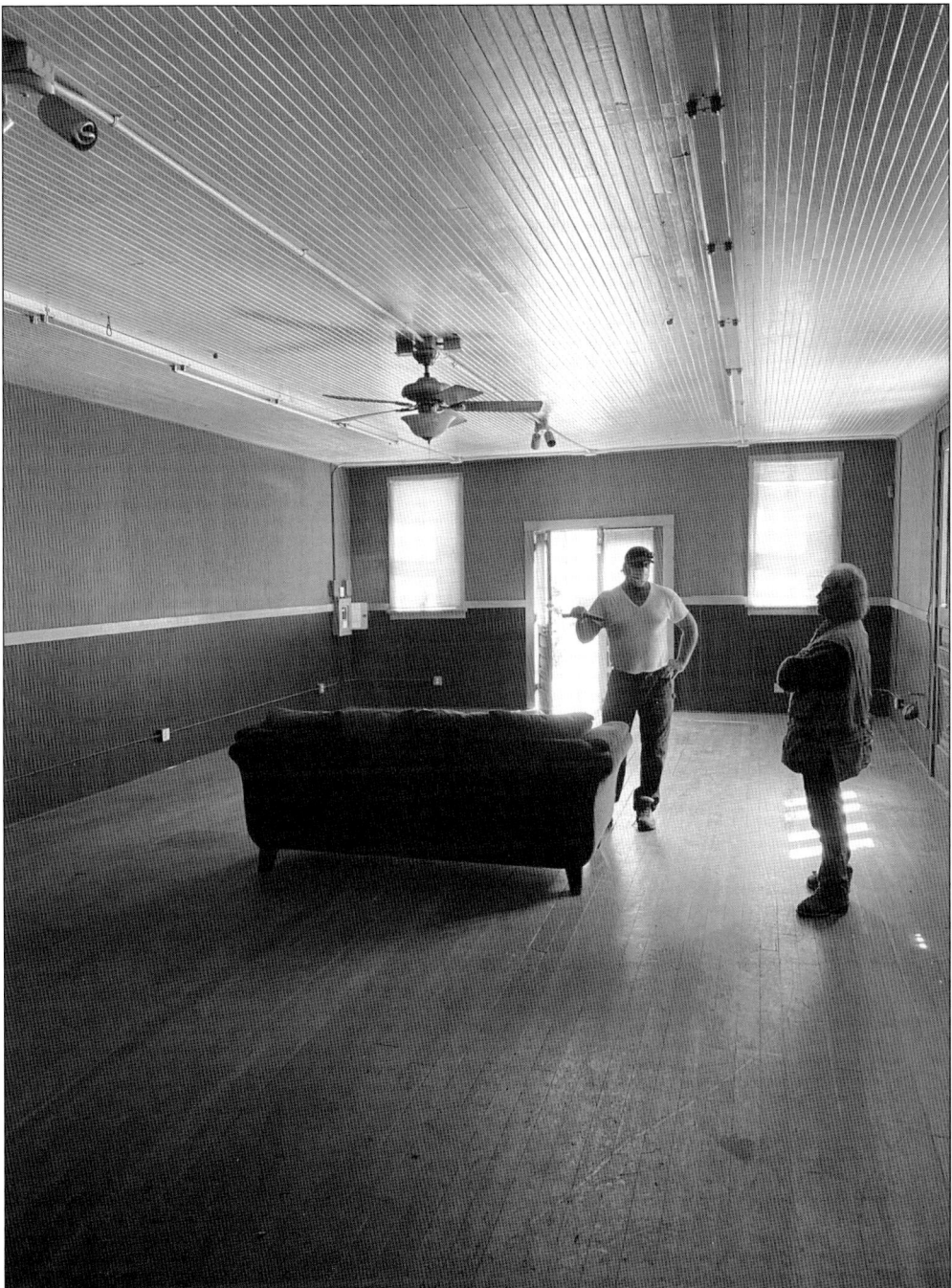

Next to the Locurto Market stands another gem restored by Norm Koepernik: the Press Palace, another speakeasy resort once operated by Joe Locurto in Little Tijuana. Today, the building boasts a large cat painted on its facade with the name Black Cat Licorice Theater. Norm Koepernik is seen on the right with Mark Cozzalio. The building's history includes accounts of a long bar on one side of the room and gaming tables. (Courtesy of Ted Ramos.)

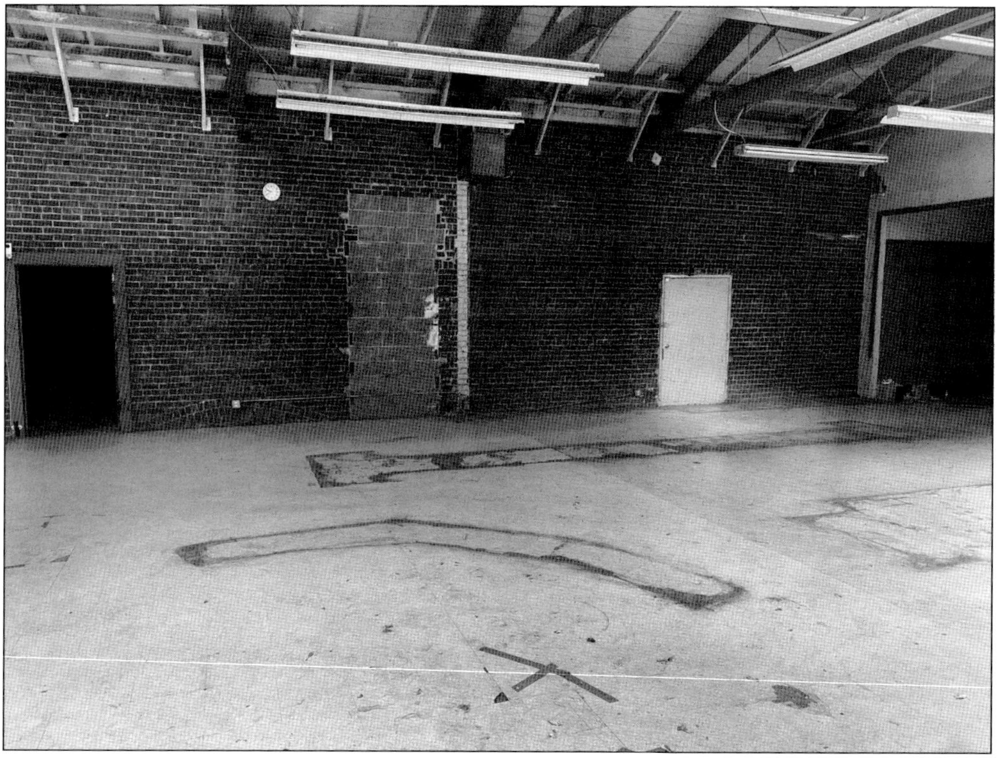

Another building on West San Carlos Street formerly owned by John Locurto stands unoccupied today and is at risk of being torn down for future development. Previously known as Sam's Downtown Feed and Pet Supply, it recently closed its doors for good after a generation of serving the community. Hopefully, the building will be purchased for restoration rather than being demolished for redevelopment. These photographs depict the worn exterior and interior condition of the building; hopefully it will be restored to its former golden age. (Both, courtesy of Ted Ramos.)

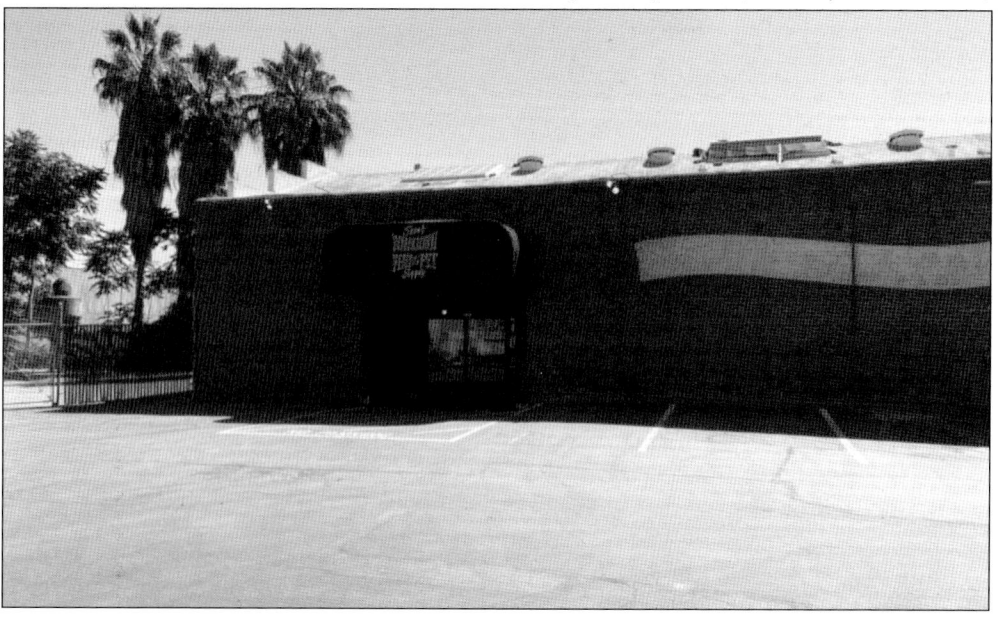

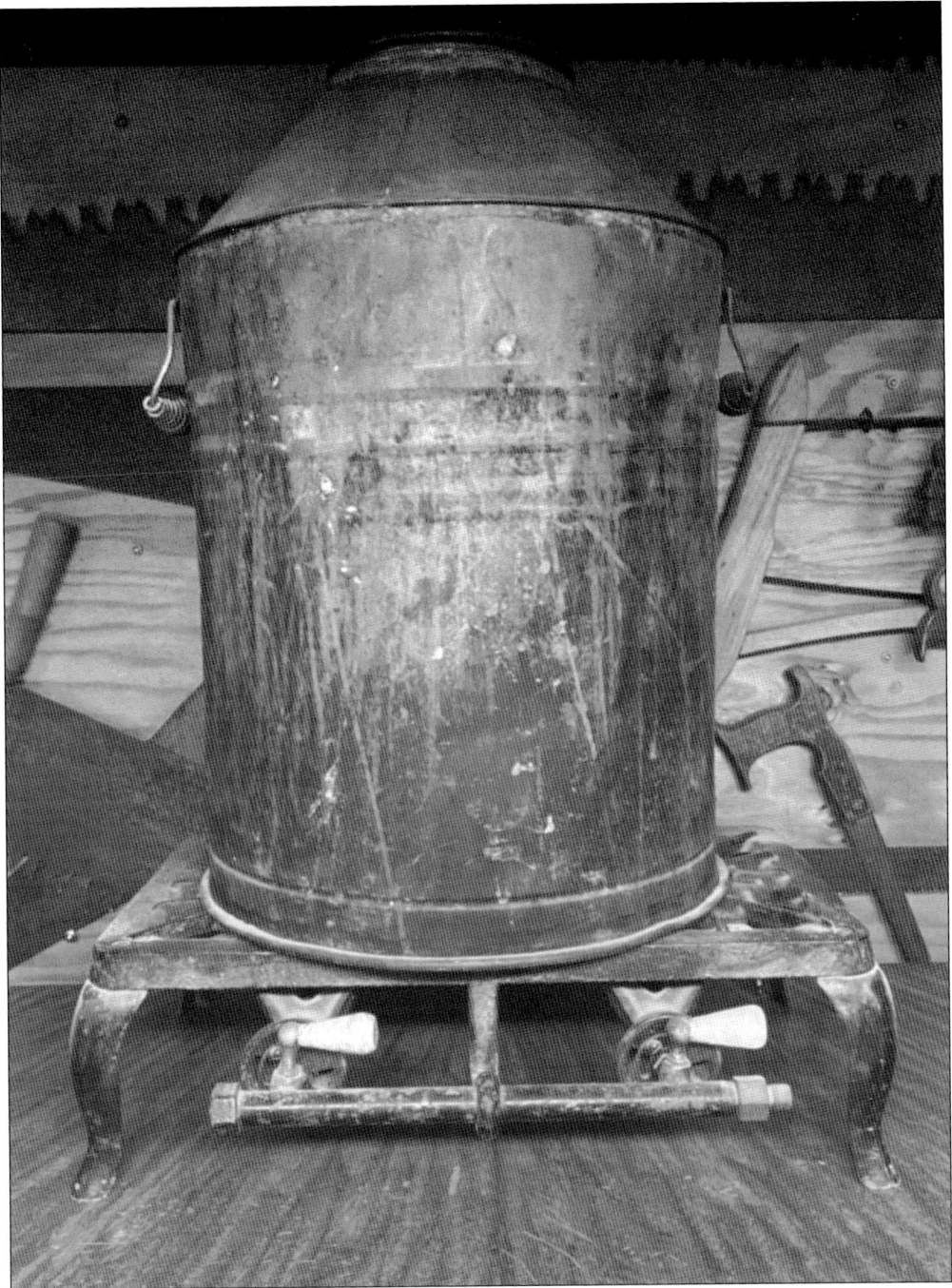

San Jose's Prohibition history is evident not just in its buildings but also in the artifacts that have survived the years. This still, discovered in a barn at a farmhouse in the hills south of San Jose, is a prime example. It was likely used for personal consumption and perhaps for a bit of extra income by producing a few additional bottles to sell. Today, this still belongs to a private collector whom the author was fortunate enough to meet and who remains a good friend. (Courtesy of Mark Cozzalio.)

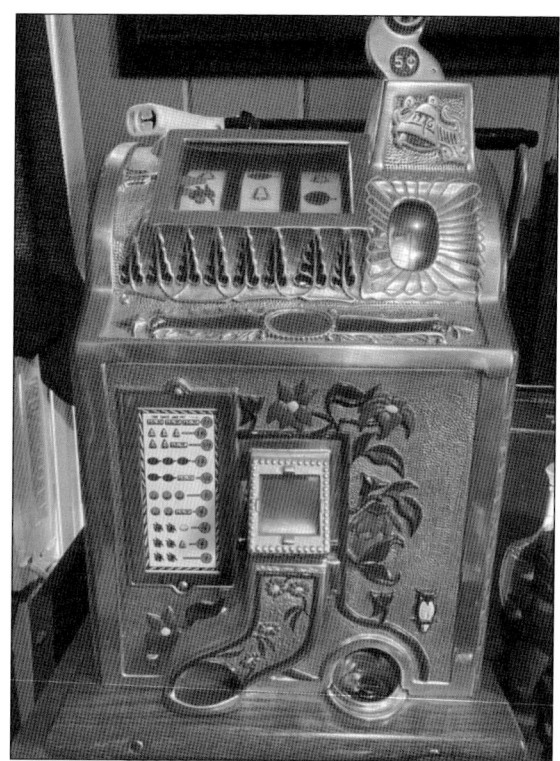

Another artifact from San Jose's Prohibition era is this slot machine belonging to the Locurto family. This slot machine originated from John Locurto's Almaden resort, Locurto's Gardens. In addition to selling illegal alcohol, Locurto also operated a full casino in the back room featuring table games and slot machines. This artifact is a reminder of the illicit activities that took place during Prohibition in San Jose. (Courtesy of Craig Locurto.)

This slot machine originated from the 410 Club, which was owned and operated by Frank Gairnese. While the 410 Club was not primarily known for gambling, it did have a couple of slot machines inside, which occasionally caused trouble along with the liquor raids. This slot machine remains in the possession of the Gairnese family, serving as a tangible reminder of the club's colorful past. (Courtesy of Tony Gairnese.)

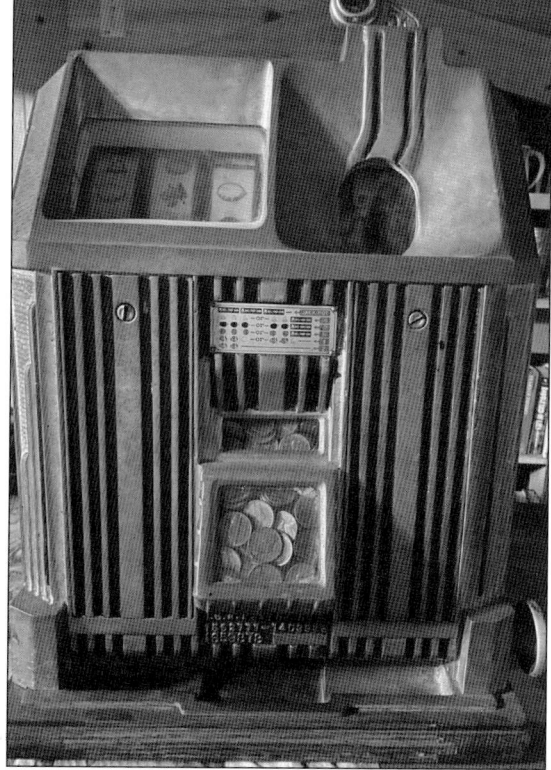

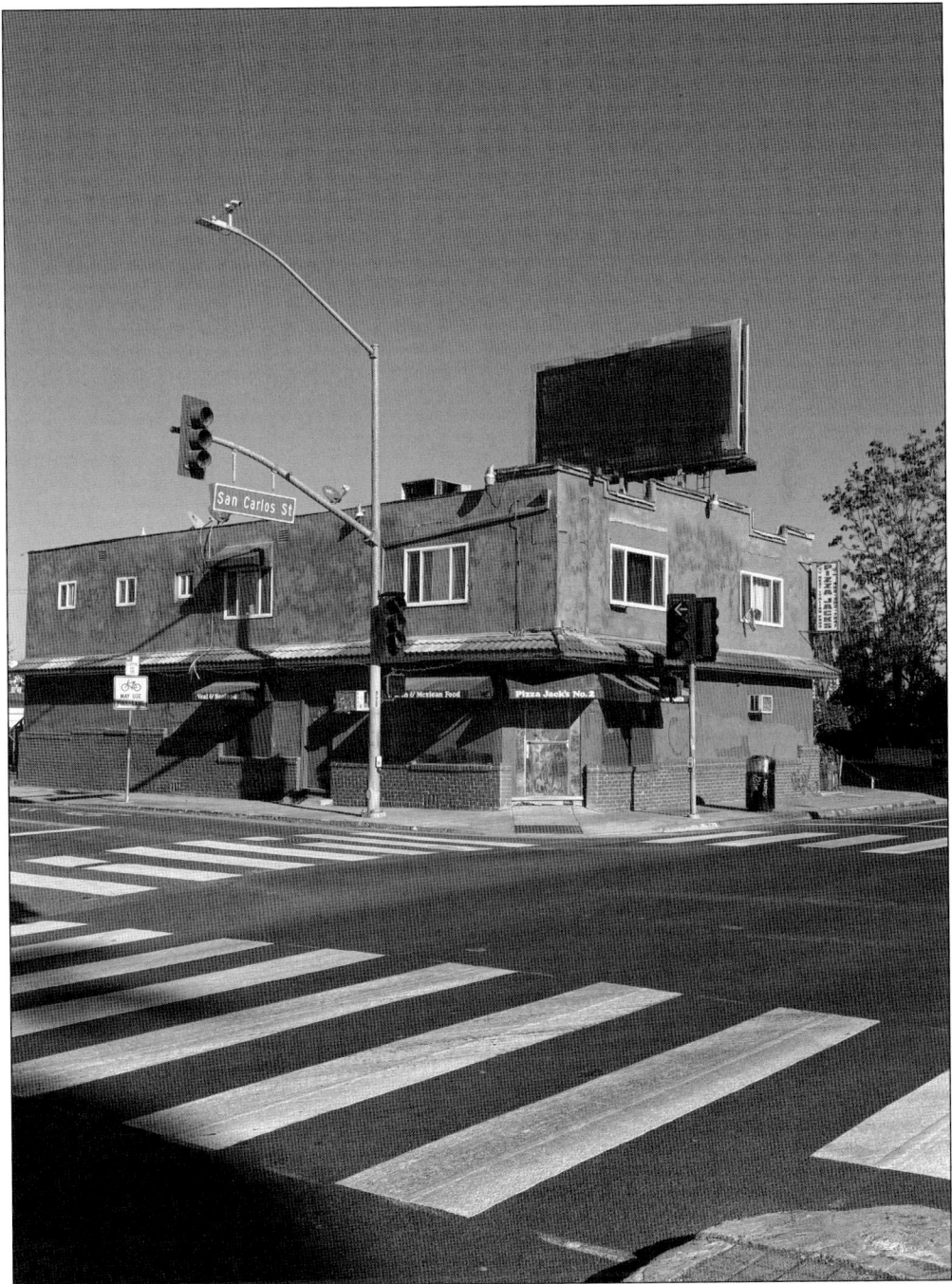

This building, which still stands on the corner of West San Carlos and Sunol Streets, was once Sam Loproto's grocery store, later transformed into Sam's Cavern. Sadly, the building now appears to be in poor condition and is at risk of demolition, much like many other buildings on the block. It stands as one of the few remaining structures from Little Tijuana. The colorful building as it appears today is a reminder of the area's colorful past. (Courtesy of Ted Ramos.)

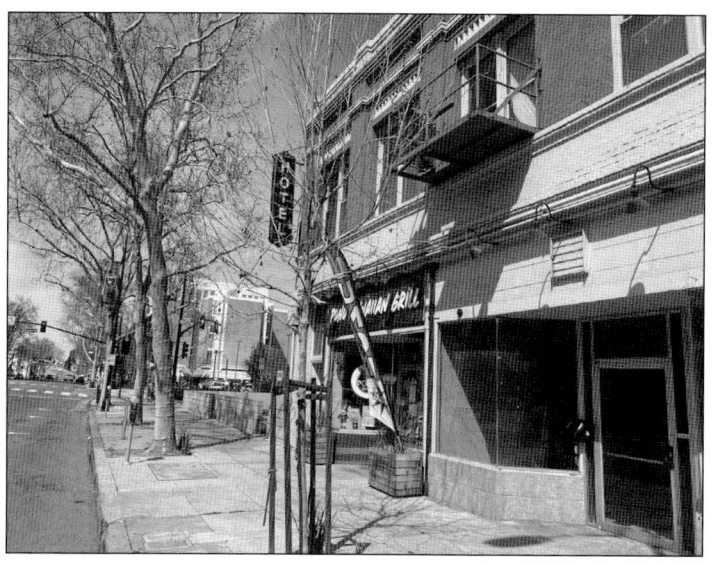

The building that housed the Argonaut Hotel at 86 North Market Street stands as the sole original structure left on North Market Street between Santa Clara and St. John Streets. While the second story of the building appears to have been unoccupied for some time, the first floor remains in operation as a restaurant. The old neon hotel sign that adorns its exterior adds to the charm. (Courtesy of Ted Ramos.)

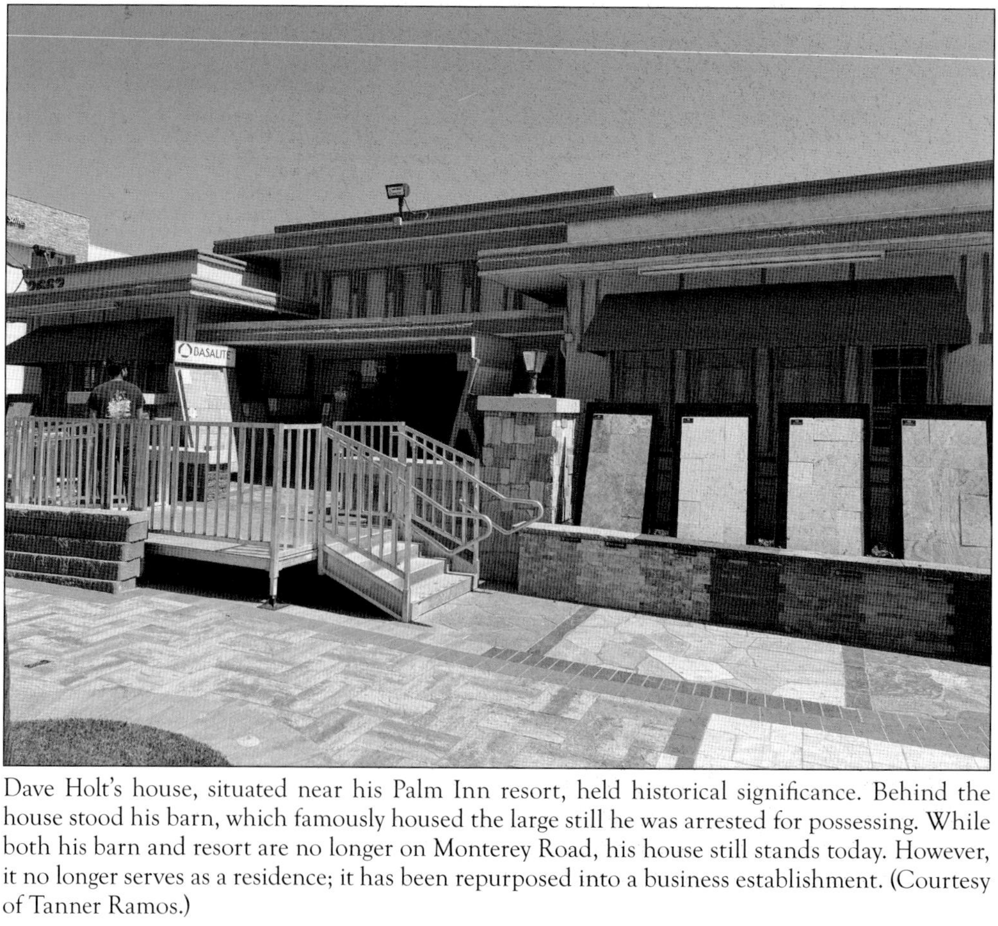

Dave Holt's house, situated near his Palm Inn resort, held historical significance. Behind the house stood his barn, which famously housed the large still he was arrested for possessing. While both his barn and resort are no longer on Monterey Road, his house still stands today. However, it no longer serves as a residence; it has been repurposed into a business establishment. (Courtesy of Tanner Ramos.)

The historic Knox building, located on South First Street, stands today much as it did in the past. Restored to its former glory, it now serves as office space. Furthermore, it has been recognized and registered as a historic building, ensuring its preservation for future generations to appreciate. (Courtesy of Tanner Ramos.)

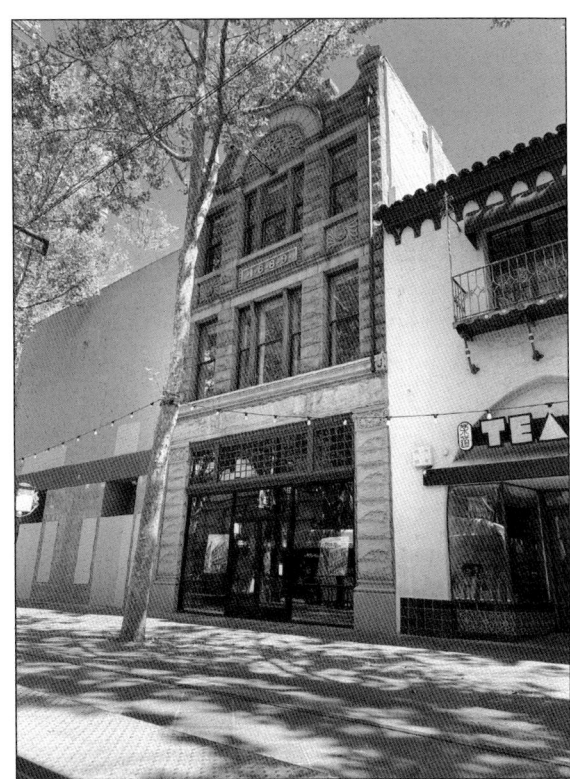

The structure of the Alviso Hotel still stands today, though it bears little resemblance to its days of selling illegal booze. Currently unoccupied, the building last functioned as a bar. Despite its current state, locals still refer to it as the Alviso Hotel. Hopefully, efforts will be made to restore this historic building to its former glory. (Courtesy of Tyler Ramos.)

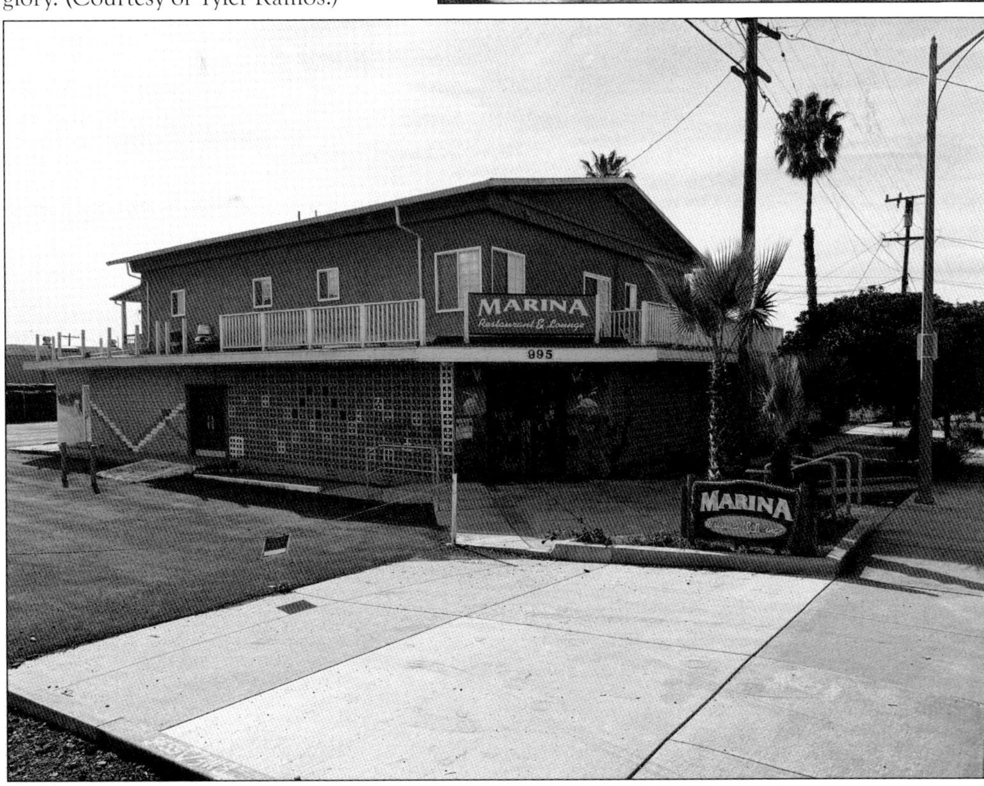

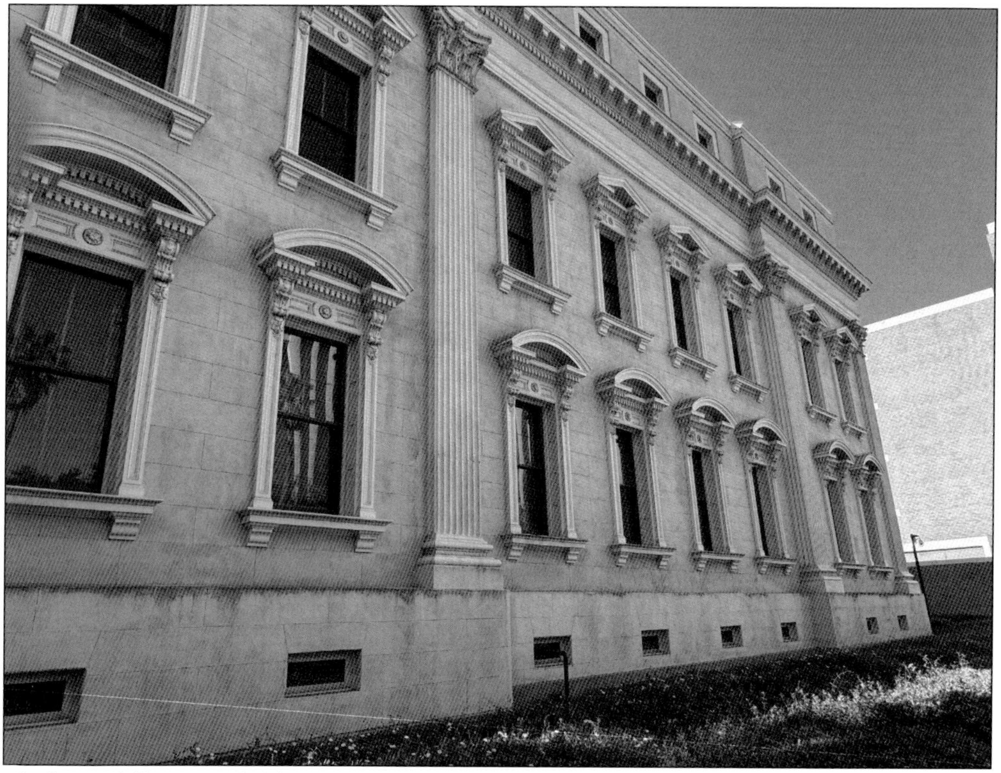

The beautifully restored old Santa Clara County Courthouse on North First Street remains in use today as a courthouse, maintaining its historical significance. This courthouse played a pivotal role in adjudicating all the San Jose Prohibition cases. It also served as the backdrop when Sheriff Lyle displayed and publicly destroyed all the confiscated stills from his deputies' raids. In the photograph below, an unidentified Prohibition agent stands in front of one of the confiscated stills in front of the same courthouse, highlighting its connection to the Prohibition era. (Above, courtesy of Ted Ramos; below, courtesy of History San Jose.)

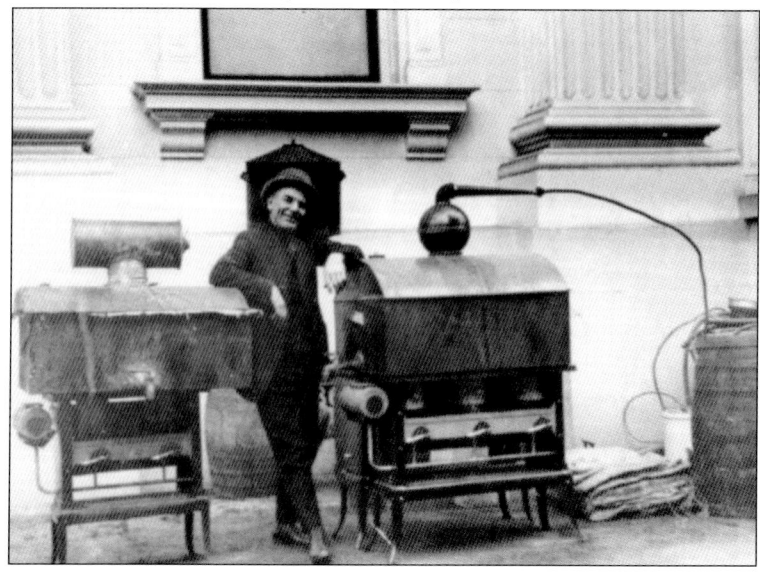

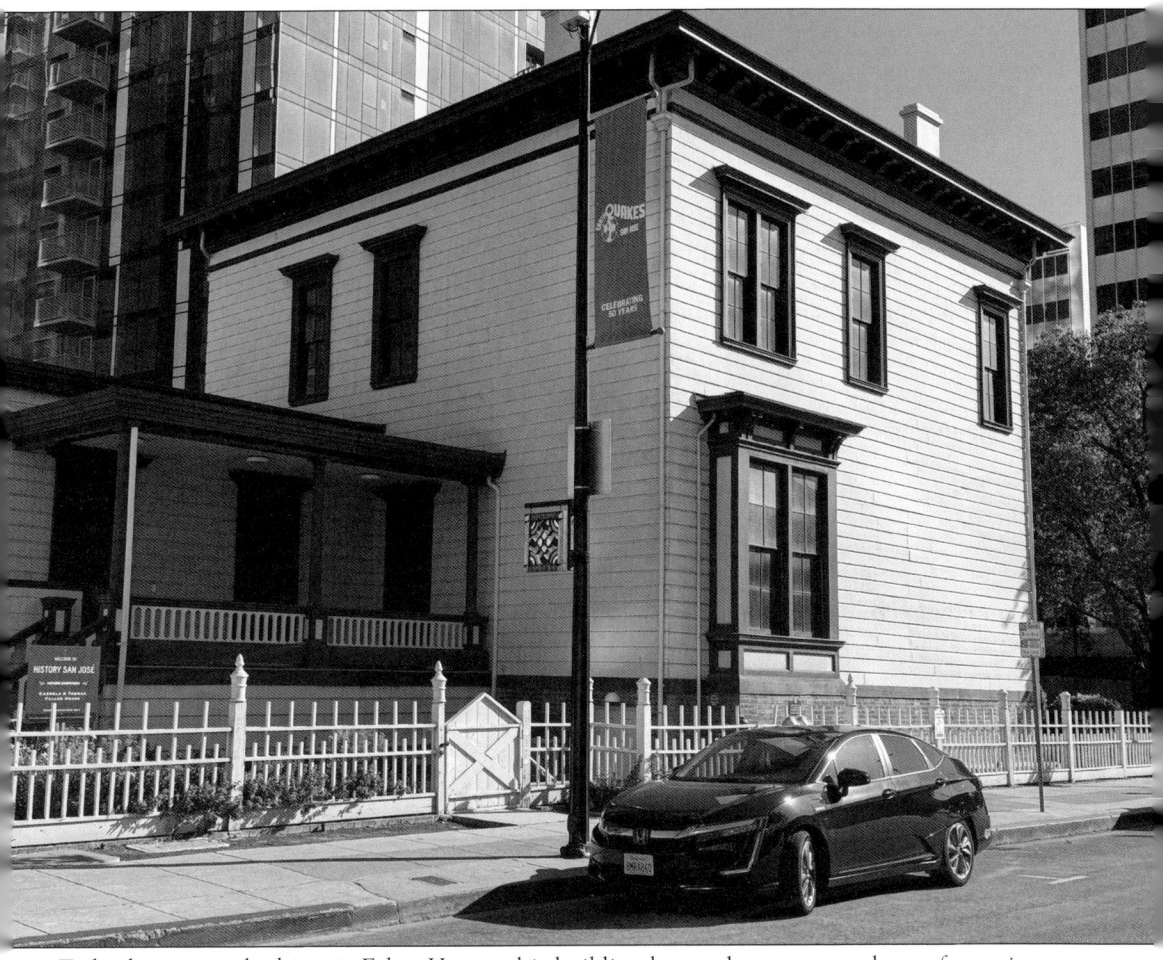

Today known as the historic Falon House, this building has undergone several transformations over the years. In the past, it was the Italian Hotel and later Manny's Cellar. Restored to its former glory, this house still stands in the middle of downtown and now serves as an educational institution, offering insights into San Jose's rich historical past. (Courtesy of Ted Ramos.)

Discover Thousands of Local History Books
Featuring Millions of Vintage Images

Arcadia Publishing, the leading local history publisher in the United States, is committed to making history accessible and meaningful through publishing books that celebrate and preserve the heritage of America's people and places.

Find more books like this at
www.arcadiapublishing.com

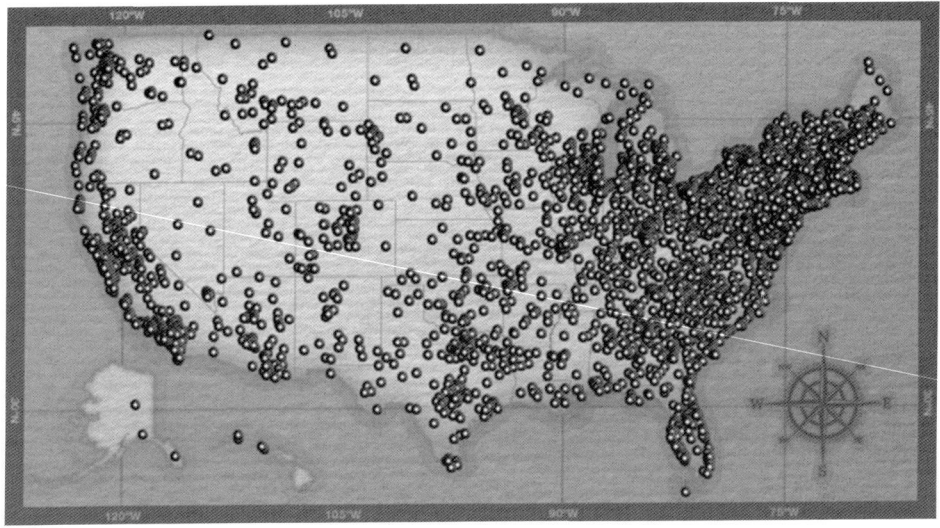

Search for your hometown history, your old stomping grounds, and even your favorite sports team.

Consistent with our mission to preserve history on a local level, this book was printed in South Carolina on American-made paper and manufactured entirely in the United States. Products carrying the accredited Forest Stewardship Council (FSC) label are printed on 100 percent FSC-certified paper.

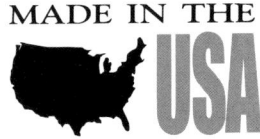